Enigmatic Tibet

Col. M N Gulati

Manas Publications
New Delhi - 110 002 (India)

MANAS PUBLICATIONS
(Publishers, Distributors, Importers & Exporters)
4858, Prahlad Street,
24, Ansari Road, Darya Ganj,
New Delhi - 110 002 (INDIA)
Ph.: 23260783, 23265523 (O); 27131660
Fax: 011-23272766
E-mail: manaspublications@vsnl.com

First Published, 2005

ISBN 81-7049-235-1
Rs 495/-

Typeset at
Manas Publications

Printed in India at
Nice Printing Press
and Published by Mrs Suman Lata for
Manas Publications, 4858, Prahlad Street,
24, Ansari Road, Darya Ganj,
New Delhi - 110 002 (INDIA)

Enigmatic Tibet

His Holiness The Dalai Lama

om ma ni pa dme him

"Hail! The Jewel [Grand Lama] in the lotus-flower!"

This book is dedicated to the

People of Tibet

who have sacrificed their all for the love of their Religion, Liberty and Spiritual way of life.

om ma ni pa dme him

"Hail! The Jewel [Grand Lama] in the lotus-flower!"

Preface

During the last three or four centuries, hundreds and hundreds of books, articles, research papers have been brought out by publishers from various nooks and corners of the world stretching from Varanasi to Vancouver, from Kathmandu to Kansas. You look into any bookshop in any major town in the world you would find a number of titles on Tibet, its people and culture, its religion and rituals, its mysteries and magic, besides its art and demons. Till lately, the authors were mostly travelers, adventurers, traders, and above all, the missionaries, all mostly Europeans with a sprinkling of Asians amongst whom Indians had been in preponderance. However, since the Tibetan Diaspora, the Tibetans themselves having got educated in the western style, they have come out with a number of authentic publications to educate the world at large about true identity of Tibet, its religion, geography and political status, the duality in governance with a built-in system of checks and balances. However, a major hurdle for the neo-western-educated Tibetans has been finding the correct English equivalent for Tibetan concepts and terminology. Of necessity, this has to be accepted till the English become proficient in Tibetan and vice versa. Only then English language would acquire the capacity to produce truly authentic translations of Tibetan works.

Nonetheless, with the few Tibetan authors already active in the western publishing world, a number of ill-conceived misconceptions about their religious rites, gods, demons and spirits, the so-called magical practices, have been set right, while in some cases a scientific basis has also been established for the so-called mysteries and magic. Western parapsychologists and internationally renowned psychiatrists have validated what, till lately, used to be classified as old women's tales. In the process, Tibetan system of medicine and diagnostic techniques has also received recognition. So has the near-death, death and after-death experiences of *Atma* to a Hindu, *Ruh* to a Muslim and Soul to a Christian has been given due credence. Needless to say that some of these neo-writers have been rather subjective about their own country and people, for obvious reasons of course. But that could be accepted as part of the evolving process of finding roots in strange new lands.

So why yet another book on Tibet?

If the reader would care to glance through the last five chapters he would find the raison de etre for this new Book on an otherwise hackneyed subject. In the earlier fourth chapter titled 'Reincarnation', new ground on the Theory and Practice of Reincarnation as a comparative study from amongst various Faiths has been briefly covered. It highlights the Tibetan religious tolerance to a degree unprecedented otherwise, and their deliberate non-prostelyzing attitude towards adherents of other Faiths. Muslim mosque and Christian church in Lhasa! A Roman Catholic missionary admitted in a Buddhist Gelug-pa monastery, provided with exclusive facilities and education on Tibetan Buddhism; an Englishman marrying the sister of Panchen Lama while residing in Shigatse and learning about Buddhism in the Monastery of Tashilhunpo; a Caucasian lady spent almost a decade in studying and practising Tibetan Buddhism and became the only white person to be honoured with the title of Lama (not a monk, but a true Lama); brief compilation of some political prophecies come true; the Tibetan Oracles of whose unsolved enigma Lord Curzon spoke of; the 'Death Horoscope' of which most of us have never even heard of; the Nechung Oracle almost dictating the lines on which vital matters of State be tackled, albeit the government or the Gyalwa Rinpoché were not bound to accept the Oracle's advice in toto; the phenomenon of 'birth marks'; the 'Fantastic Tree', one of its own kind that modern science cannot possibly replicate nor explain the phenomenon in 'rational' terms; introduction of Psychic Astrology; Crystal gazing into the past as well as the future; intuitive ability; establishing contact and communication with the spirit world; Telepathy — the list may go on and on, each one requiring at lease one volume by itself.

During the late 1960's the Author was personally involved in giving a helping hand to a few thousand Tibetan refugees. He witnessed their physical and mental agony in having been driven out of their homes and hearths. Their plight reminded him of the suffering his own people had experienced in the aftermath of Partition of Indian in 1947. The Book has therefore been dedicated to the People of Tibet. It covers, very briefly, some of the aforesaid voids, and ends with a prayer for restoration of Tibet as an independent sovereign State. Miracles do happen. Didn't they in Eastern Europe?

Col. M N Gulati

Gratitude

I have not been to Tibet, not even as a POW in 1962 when the Air Force Station Commander turned down my fervent entreaties to permit me to go for extremely urgent military duty. He put his foot down and did not allow what would have been the very last sortie to Ziminthaung helipad. Of course there was a little of that usual Army-Air brawl, but he was much too senior to me, and absolutely adamant. So I missed Tibet by inches! And since the PsOW were kept miles away from Lhasa, I felt a sort of sense of unhappy relief over the outcome of that episode. However, before the decade of 60's came to an end, I had plenty of interaction with Tibetan people — the refugees who came in their thousands over the Shipki-la and we put them up in ramshackle shacks, made by them only, to work as road-gangs on the Hindustan-Tibet Road whose construction I had the privilege of superintending.

They were filthy, sick and wounded, weighed under a heavy load of emotional trauma. They had very little clothing or any other possessions for that matter. But of course they had some brick-tea, a little tsampa and their very personal bowl for tea-tsampa drinking-eating. Their condition was indeed deplorable. I felt a sort of personal guilt, a part of collective guilt, since they were the victims of betrayal by our top political leadership whose empty rhetoric delivered from a high moral pedestal did not do any good to man or beast, except to the leader himself who was portrayed as a world statesman by his cronies. I felt a sense of deep anguish for these highly spiritual peaceful people who were being made to suffer for no personal fault of theirs. So the orders trickled down from my headquarters: audit or no audit; present for work or absent due to sickness — all those enrolled on the road-gang must be paid full wages, besides being rendered all possible medical-material help within the limited resources of a Task Force Commander.

I am profoundly grateful to the leaders of the Tibetan roadside camps for organizing their men and maintaining discipline and high morale, for observing various festivals and putting up cultural shows from time to time, showing off their special costumes and make-up, for inviting me and my staff to give us a glimpse of Tibetan culture and dances before their deities. They had their problems, but faced them with courage and fortitude, uncomplaining and smiling. I for one learnt from them the value of spiritual strength. They inspired me to study about their country, religion and culture. I am thankful for those rustic Tibetan contacts that have ultimately got me a Doctorate, and motivated me to write this book — belated of course; but better late than never.

A work of this nature by an author who has never been to that country and had only limited personal contacts with the people has, of necessity, to be based on historical records compiled by various writers over a period of few centuries. This work is not the history of Tibet and its people; it is not an exposition of Buddhist teachings and philosophy nor does it explain their tantric traditions and practices; it is not a compilation of their mysteries, magical practices and miracles nor of feats of human endurance borne out of yoga; it is not a dissertation of doctrines of karma, birth and incarnation nor is it an explanatory note on the famous "Tibetan Book of the Dead", and near-death experiences, dreams and psychic phenomena; and it is not meant to justify the institution of oracles and their trances although it does portray them in fair light. This work is a conglomeration of all that it is not supposed to be, as aforesaid. It covers a wide panorama of Tibetan life, customs, traditions, beliefs, practices, food and religion. In short, it covers Tibetan way of life in one small volume where each of these topics might require a number of volumes. It gives a bird's eye view of wide spectrum of kaleidoscope that indeed Tibet was before the Chinese communists totally brutalized the country and its people. However, this work does categorically say, in the words of His Holiness, that:

* Buddhism is not a religion; it is a way life;
* Buddhism does not give any place to a divine Creator;
* Mind and matter can affect one another, but one cannot become the substance of the other.

I have liberally quoted from the works of various saints, intellectuals, religious and political leaders going back over decades and centuries. It is virtually impossible to contact those authors and their publishers at this point of time. I have therefore made every effort to acknowledge their contribution. I am deeply indebted to each and every one of them personally. Credits have been liberally given. If some have been inadvertently missed out, my apologies to them, please. However, the comments — good, bad or indifferent — are entirely mine; so are the errors that might have crept in, I alone am responsible for the same.

I am personally indebted to Mrs. Vijay Suda for taking great pains to carefully review the entire text and correct the numerous mistakes. I am profoundly grateful to Wing Commander S.K. Sharma who made some valuable comments and suggestions towards improvement of the last five critical chapters.

Last, but not the least, I am extremely grateful to the personal staff of His Holiness The Dalai Lama for sending an autographed photo of the Dalai Lama, and to their Home Department for some beautiful pictures which they promptly provided to embellish this Work.

Glossary

Amban	A high Manchu or Mongol official representative of Emperor of China stationed at Lhasa from 1728 to 1912.
Amdo	Tibetan name for northeastern portion of ethnic Tibet; was incorporated as Ch'ing-hai province of China in 1928.
Bardo Thodol	The Tibetan Book of the Dead
Chenrezi	Buddha of Compassion, Patron Saint of Tibet: the Deity whom each Dalai Lama manifests in human form
Chhang	A common name for local beer amongst the hill tribes; brewed from barley in Tibet, and from rice in some other areas.
Chikyap Khenpo	Chief of the monastic branch of Tibetan Government. Equivalent of Lord Chamberlain in English
Chöd	A rite of magical self-sacrifice
Chörten	Stupa shaped masonry structure which often contains religious relics or the ashes of deceased lamas or monks who were great teachers
Chu	River

Chushi Gangdrug	Tibetan Guerrilla organization founded by Gompo Tashi Andrugtsang in 1958
Dob-dobs	Warrior monks
Dapon	General of the army
Do-kham	Eastern and northeastern portion of ethnic Tibet comprising Kham and Amdo
Dorje	Spiritual thunderbolt and scepter of the gods
Dotsed	A monetary unit representing 50 sang-gang, equivalent to ten Indian rupees at price levels as in 1950.
Dri	Female of the species bos grunniens called yak in English. In Tibetan, only the male is called yak.
Dzong	A fortress; headquarters of an administrative unit
Dzongpon	Title of Administrator of a dzong
Gelong	Title of a fully ordained Buddhist monk
Ge-lug-pa	Name of the reformed Yellow Hat sect whose head is the Dalai Lama
Gomchen	Great Hermit
Gompa	A generic term denoting a monastery, nunnery or temple
Hum	Tibetan symbol for divine life force
Kalon	Minister in the Government
Karma-pa	Name of a sub-sect of Buddhism
Kashag	Tibetan Governing Council of Ministers, comprised of four officials, three from nobility and one monastic
Khal	Unit of weight equal to about 32 lbs.

Kham	Name of the eastern province of Tibet
Khatag	A ceremonial scarf made of white silk or cotton
La	A mountain-pass
Losar	Tibetan New Year Festival
Monlam Chenmo	Great Prayer Festival of Tibet
Naljorpa	Tibetan magician
Ngari Korsum:	Name of the western province of Tibet
Nying-ma-pa:	Name of the unreformed Buddhist sect which follows the teachings of the 8th century Indian preacher, Padma Sambhava
Phurba	Magic dagger
Pön (Bon)	Ancient shamanistic religion of Tibet
Ragyapa	Special community of beggars to whom was assigned the task of disposal of the dead
Ridro	A small monastery or hermitage
Rinpoche	Mystic title = 'Precious One': The highest titular honour in Tibet, conferred on persons believed to be reincarnations of famous religious teachers
Sa-kya-pa	A semi-reformed sect which was politically dominant in the time of Mongol Emperors of China
Sang	A generic term for a bank note: 5, 10, 25, or 100; in 1950 five sang was equal to one Indian rupee.
Shab-pe	Title of a minister in the governing council (Kashag)
Silon	Title of the Prime Minister

Tamka	A unit of Tibetan currency based on the Nepalese pattern
Thonka	Ritualistic Tibetan Buddhist banner painting mounted on silk brocade
Three Jewels	Buddha, Dharma (his teachings), and Sangha (the monkhood)
Trungyik Chemo:	Council comprised of four monk officials
Tsampa	Roasted barley flour; the staple food of all Tibet.
Tsang	The two central provinces of Tibet are known as Ü-Tsang. The western one of these two is known as Tsang and its chief city is Shigatse.
Tsekhang	Finance Department
Tsepon	Finance Minister
Tsi-pa	An astrologer
Tso	Lake
Tsongdu	The National Assembly of Tibet composed of high secular and monastic officials and representatives of large monasteries.
Tulku	Tibetan incarnation
Tulpa	Thought form entity
Tumo	A form of yoga which generates extra body heat
Ü	The eastern of the two central provinces of Tibet together called Ü-Tsang, in which the capital city of Lhasa is located.
Yidam	Tutelary Deity

Contents

List of Illustrations

Dalai Lamas of Tibet

1	Gedün Truppa (Title accorded posthumously)	1391-1475
2	Gedun Gyatso (Title accorded posthumously)	1475-1542
3	Sonam Gyatso (Title given by Altan Khan in 1548; strictly speaking, he was the 1st)	1543-1588
4	Yönten Gyatso (Great grandson of Altan Khan)	1589-1617
5	Ngawang Lobzang Gyatso	1617-1682
6	Tsang-yang Gyatso	1683-1706
7	Kezang Gyatso	1708-1757
8	Jampel Gyatso	1758-1804
9	Luntok Gyatso	1806-1815
10	Tshultrim Gyatso	1816-1837
11	Khedrup Gyantso	1838-1856
12	Tringle Gyastso	1876-1933
13	Thubten Gyatso	1876-1933
14	Tenzin Gyatso	1935-date

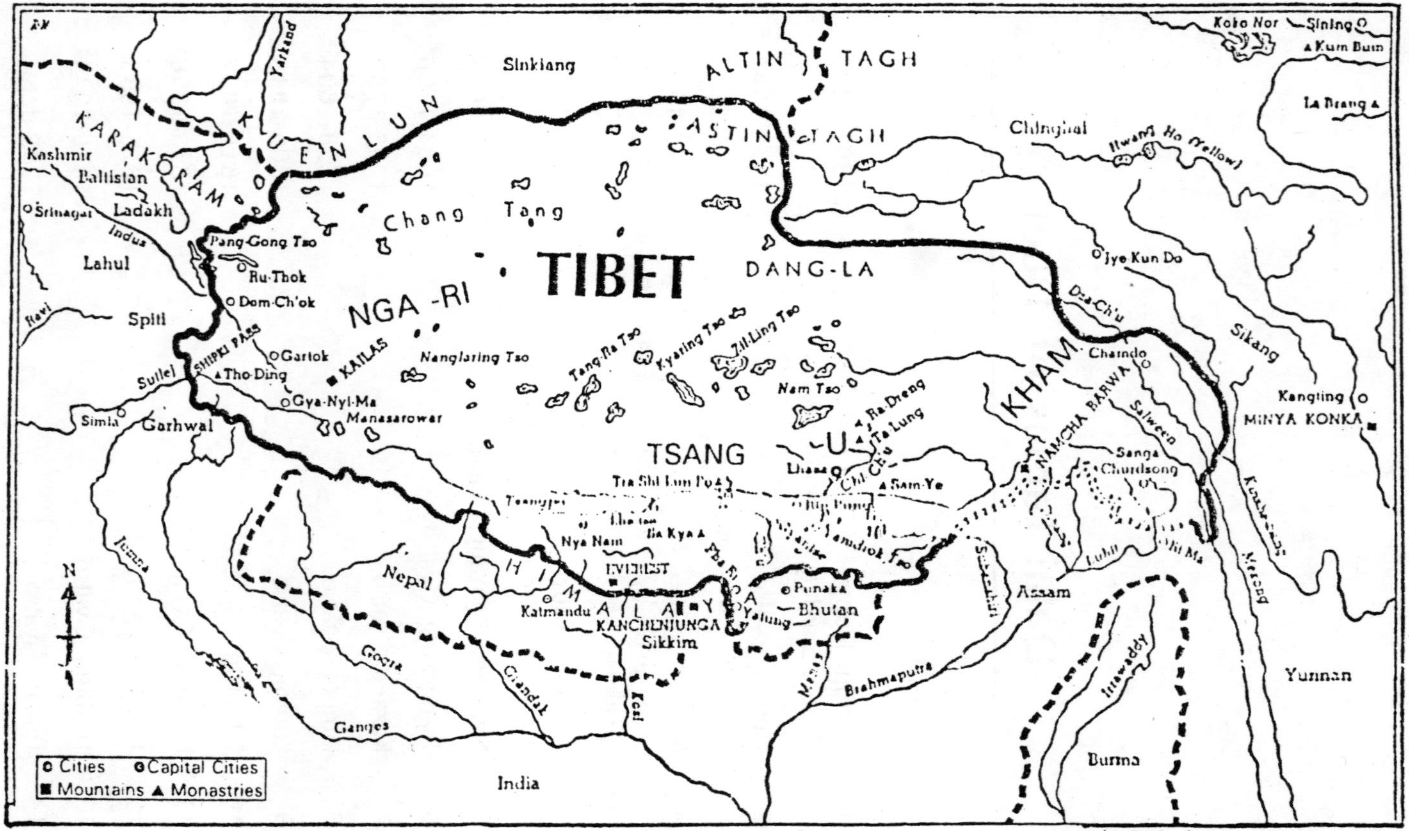

TIBET (Based on Tsung-Lien Shen Map)

Not To Scale
Boundaries Unauthenticated

1

Prologue

Anger cannot be vanquished by anger, and past history has disappeared into the past. What is more relevant is that in the future there actually be real peace and happiness through developing a friendly, meaningful relationship between China and Tibet. For this to be realized, it is important for both sides to work hard, to have tolerant understanding and be open-minded. — 'Fruit grows on the tree of patience'.

His Holiness The Dalai Lama

The Sanskrit name for Tibet is 'Bhota'. Along the Indo-Tibetan borders the Tibetans are therefore known as 'Bhotias'. To the outside world the country is known as Tibet, the name derived from Mongolian 'Thubet', or Thai word 'Thibet', and the Arabic 'Tubbat'. However, to the Chinese it has been 'Tufan' — indeed in the ancient past Tibet was a "toofan" (storm) against China in the Hindi sense of the word; Tibet did play havoc with the Chinese in the distant past! No wonder therefore the country was an enigma to the Imperial Power of Chinese Empire, even though the tables are now turned in a big way against the Tibetans who don't call their country as

'Tibet'. For them it is 'Bod' or 'Poyul', the 'land of snows',[1] predominantly a plateau averaging 12,000 feet above sea-level. It is a great mass of snow-covered high mountains and peaks, glaciers and green forests, grasslands and numerous salt-water lakes with habitations spread over 4,000 to 17,000 ft AMSL. They are used to their high altitude living environment of rarefied air, of high and dry winds, intense cold with little precipitation. It is indeed a vast country. The 'ethnographic Tibet' used to be spread over an area of 1.5 million square miles, about half the size of the United States, while the 'political Tibet' is reduced to a mere 470,000 square miles of sparsely populated territory.[2] An iron bridge at Tachienlu in the east used to separate Ethnic Tibet from China while a white stupa known as Chorten Karpo marks the limit of Ethnic Tibet's northeastern frontier at Karchu.[3] The central region of the country is the province of Ü, having the capital city of Lhasa.

---

1. Snow blindness on account of severe glare caused by the afternoon sun is a serious problem for the traveler. Heavy-duty sunglasses are a must. Since most Tibetans cannot afford to get the same, they improvise by applying lampblack on the eyelids and around the eyes to partially deflect the glare. Improvised spectacles using black yak hair—'sun-nets' of yak hair—are commonly used by the poor.
2. The total population of Tibet has been a controversial figure for decades, estimates varying between one million and thiryt-three millions! While the Chinese have been underplaying the number of Tibetans, the Dalai Lama has generally placed the estimate at six million. From the available data, in 1950, there were around 2.5 million Tibetans, about half of them in ethnic Tibet and the other half in multi-ethnic border regions. The present estimate of world wide Tibetan population is about 2.5 million in the so-called 'ART' (Autonomous Region of Tibet), 2.9 million in the old Tibetan territories now absorbed by the Chinese in their provinces, and about 1, 20,000 living in exile, making a total of 5½ million, which figure is close to what the Dalai Lama has been claiming all along. In fact, if we take into consideration the number of Tibetans died as a result of Chinese occupation, about 1.2 million, the Tibetan population adds up to nearly seven million—*Tibet: The Facts,* Dharmsala, 1990 and *Tibet, Tibet* by Patrick French, Harpers Collins, 2003, p. 288.
3. Shakabpa W.D. Tsepon: *Tibet: A Political History,* 1967, p.2.

Shigatse, the seat of Panchen Lama, is the second biggest town in the province of Tsang, lying to the south-west of Ü. The region just north of Ü and Tsang provinces is a vast endless high-altitude plateau of deserts and grasslands known as Chang Tang, the infamous 'Aksai Chin' to the Indians. Eastern Tibet was known as Kham while to the north of Kham[4] lies what the Tibetans knew as Amdo, but to the Chinese as Qinghai. The region to the far west is called Ngari.

Tibet is bounded by Chinese Turkestan and China proper to the north and east; Kashmir in the west; and western India, Nepal, Sikkim, Bhutan, Assam and Burma towards the south. The land falls from west to east and from north to south. The country is enclosed by mountain ranges on three sides: Kuen Lun and Tang La ranges to the north; the great massif of Karakoram and Ladakh mountains on the west; and the majestic sweep of the Himalayas for about 1,500 miles to the south. These natural barriers lead to division of Tibet into three main regions known as Chol-kha-sum:

- Ü-Tsang: the central region between Ngari Korsum in the west to Sokla Kyao;
- Dotod (Kham): From Sokla Kyao to the upper bend in the Yellow River;
- Amdo: From the above Machu bend to Chorten Karpo.[5]

Tibet was, and perhaps still is, a country of wonders. One may keep on wondering till the end of wonders but still not find the right explanation, or any explanation at all for that matter, for miracles and magic, clairvoyance, telepathic communications, et al. Can a person really become invisible? Walk hundreds of miles in a day? Send messages over the wind? Generate extra

4. Much of Kham has now been absorbed in Chinese provinces of Kansu, Szechuan and Yunan, while Amdo region has been separated from the rest of Tibet and renamed as Chinghai.

5. According to a Tibetan saying, the best religion comes from Ü-Tsang, the best men from Kham, and the best horses from Amdo.

body heat to survive in icy weather without any clothing?[6] Survive on water and fresh air for weeks? — These are some of the interesting topics that made Tibet a true enigma to the outside world.

In The "Beginning"

Those who called Tibetans as uncivilized backward illiterates seem to forget that it was not Darwin, but the Tibetans who postulated the hypothesis that Homo-sapiens, the 'thinking animal', is evolutionary end product of simians. The legend has it that the human race evolved from an ogress named Dras-rin-mo and the male counterpart was Hilamanju, the ancient monkey-god, Hanuman, of Hindu mythology. Eons passed. Hilamanju crossed the Himalayas and there married a she-devil of the mountains. The Compassionate Spirit of the Mountains gave some magical grain to the young progeny of apes, which they ate. The results were wonderful. Their tails and hair grew shorter day by day, and finally disappeared completely. Generations later, the progeny of the two simians evolved into human form when Tibetan God, Chenrezi — Avaloketisvara in Hindu mythology — provided the simians with seeds of grains — wheat, rice and barley — and told them to cultivate the same in the soil. If the western civilization and scientific community could accord such high status to the Theory of Evolution-cum-Survival of the Fittest-concept, why deny the same prestigious status to the Tibetan concepts which came to identical conclusions much before Darwin and his concept. However, most ancient Tibetan scriptures claim that human life did not evolve on planet earth. A race of men known as Lha came from a distant galaxy to what is now known as Tibet and colonized the earth. They created matter, food and artifacts through the power of their minds. 'Their bodies glowed with an inner radiance'. In course of eons they lost their knowledge of space-faring technology, and became isolated from their original moorings. Thus the Lha who came from Sirius,

6. The author has personally witnessed a few 'yogis' in deep Himalayas in icy cold weather without any clothes on, while the onlookers were in heavy woollens. Their abode? Almost bare caves.

a binary star in the constellation Canis Major, some 8.6 light years away from earth, are the real ancestors of Tibetans, and not the Darwin's monkeys. Some credence began to be given to this hypothesis when in 1938 Chinese archeologists discovered 'little human bones with disproportionately large skulls' in the caves around Baian-Kara-Ula Mountains.[7] All said and done, the legend remains a legend, a fairytale at best.

A similar legend is prevalent in Tibet about the formation of the planet earth. In the beginning there was a complete void, all dark and empty. Strong winds blew for countless years creating Dorje Gyatram, 'a great double thunderbolt in the form of a cross'. Huge drops of rain fell from the thunderbolt. The great rain that fell for countless years created the primeval ocean. A gentle and smooth wind blew over the placid waters of the ocean, churning it back and forth, giving rise to light foam that soon brought a cream like substance to the surface. As cream turns into butter, so did this foam into planet earth. The legend is carried a step further to explain the creation of our universe of four worlds and eight islands, and so on it goes.

Advent of Buddhism

Buddhism made its entry into Tibet between the 7th and 11th Centuries A.D. It came from India via Kashmir and Nepal. Prior to that, Tibetans were nature-worshippers and their religion was called Bön. The combination of the two gave birth to a powerful national faith which admirably suited the Tibetan psyche. Transmigration of soul is the cardinal principle of Buddhism, as it is of Hinduism — the well known "Wheel of Life" as often depicted in Tibetan tradition — "The Cycle of Transmigratory Existence" to be more precise. It is an "intellectual rather than an emotional religion"[8] and Karma, the doctrine of retribution, is the fundamental binding factor of the Faith. Its Four Noble Truths:

---

7. Brennan J.H.: *Magical Techniques of Tibet;* USA, 2002, p. 2.
8. Dalai Lama: *My Land & My People:* p. 47, 241-42

- "True Suffering" means Samsara — the entire round of existence, of birth, death and rebirth;
- "True Cause" means Karma and delusion, which are the causes of suffering;
- "True Cessation" means the complete disappearance of the preceding two truths;
- The "True Path" is the method by which true cessation is obtained;

and the Eightfold Path are fundamental to Buddhism. If we bear in mind the fundamentals of Four Noble Truths, the Eightfold Noble Path, and the concepts of Samsara, karma, arhat, Buddha and nirvana, we come to the realization that Buddhism was not, and is still not, a religion in the traditional sense of the word. It was, and continues to be, a philosophy rather than a religion. This is particularly true of the ancient, sometimes also referred to as the primitive unreformed sect of Buddhism. The doctrine and its constituents have been lucidly dealt with by the Dalai Lama in his Autobiography.

According to Buddhist philosophy (read Indian civilization) the history of the Universe is said to be divided into five great ages (kalpas). These were conceived in the mind of the Dhyani Buddha — Amitabha in Sanskrit, and Incarnated in the Panchen Lama — created by Dhyani Bodhisattva, that is to say Avaloketisvara and incarnated in the Dalai Lama, and finally blessed by Manushi Buddha — Sakya-Muni, The Prince Siddhartha of history, the ascetic Gautama. Christianity finds this doctrine of Reincarnation a particularly knotty problem to rebut. However, many Christian theologists subscribe to this doctrine and believe that it is a true phenomenon. The Doctrine of Reincarnation is founded on the Doctrine of Karma, the latter in essence implies paying off ones debt in a future life, or paying debts of past life in this life. Similarly, the Doctrine of Regression is an established principle so much so that memories of experiences within the womb have been brought to life. And when the subjects were regressed beyond the womb, recollection of past lives also came alive. Recollection of memories of past lives is not merely Tibetan or Asiatic experience; it is a universal phenomenon. To most Westerners these ideas sound ridiculous. Be that as it may, it is part of the Eastern cultural milieu. Western para-psychologists have done fair amount of research on this subject. Thousands of case studies have been investigated and found true; but all that is not within the scope of this work. Suffice it would be to add that there is considerable commonality between the Christian and Lamaist ethics: three sins of the body — murder, lust and theft; four sins of the tongue — lying, grumbling and reviling; three ins of the heart — coveting the goods of others, desiring to do evil to others and secret dissent — form the maxims of their faith; and so on and so forth regarding capital sins and virtues. Notwithstanding many commonalities between the two faiths, one outstanding difference was, and still is, concept of one Supreme Creator, one God who is the prime mover of this Universe. Absolute denial of the existence of God was, and still is, the major point of variation and disagreement.

The Tibetans have contrived a marvelous mechanism of repeating their prayer millions of times — *Om mani padme hum* — through a system of prayer wheels powered by gushing water. The prayer is printed hundreds of times on a drum, in golden letters, or on paper in ordinary ink. The hand held prayer wheel (*'mani chuskor'* in Tibetan) consists of a hollow cylindrical copper box, which revolves around a spindle, one end of which forms the handle. The cylinder is turned by means of a piece of copper attached to the string. A slight twist of the hand makes the cylinder revolve, and each revolution represents one repetition of the prayer, *'Om mani padme hum'*, which is written on a scroll inside the miniature cylinder. It is continuously rotated so that God's grace continues to accrue to the Tibetans, if not the mankind. This is certainly not a laughing matter, nor a strange phenomenon as it may sound. In fact, in our own religion, the 'pandit' or the 'granthi' keeps reading the scriptures, or reciting the mantras, while the rest of the family is busy in their day to day mundane activities.

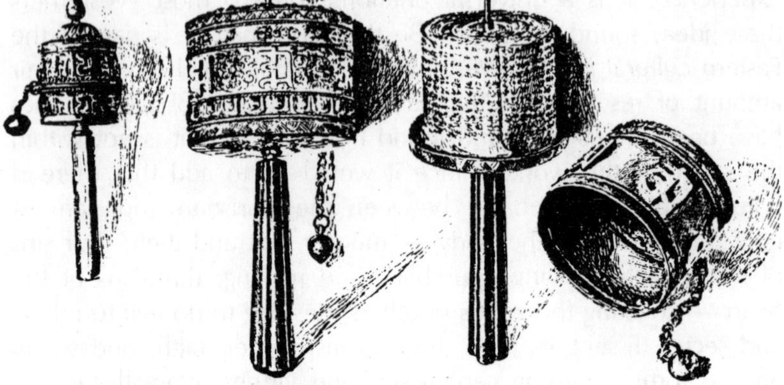

Copper and Silver Prayer-Wheels

Wind Prayer-Wheels

Miniature Prayer Wheels

The creed of total nonviolence led to complete forsaking of martial arts and training amongst the Tibetans. The mountain-top d'zongs (forts) gave way to gompas (monasteries). The living incarnation of Tibet's patron saint, Chenrezi, His Holiness the Dalai Lama (Gyalwa Rinpoché in Tibetan) came to occupy the supreme position in the holy land. Feudalism and aristocracy flourished, so much so that the splendid silk robes the nobles wore had their sleeves about a foot longer, below the hands, denoting leisure and complete absence of physical labour. Consequentially, the British successfully carried out a military expedition to Lhasa all the way from the plains of Bengal-Assam over almost insurmountable terrain. Was it that the Tibetan prophetic Almanac for the Wood-Dragon Year (1904 A.D.), forecast centuries ago, had to be fulfilled as a matter of destiny?[9] More about this in a later chapter.

Mongol Suzerainty

In 1207, Ching-gis Khan, the great Mongol world-conqueror marched his armies towards Tibet but the invasion was forestalled by various Tibetan chieftains joining together to pay a handsome annual tribute to the great Mongol. About thirty-two years later when the Tibetans failed to make the annual payment, Godan Khan, the grandson of the Great Mongol invaded and occupied the country, burnt down the Reting Monastery north of Lhasa and slaughtered five hundred monks and laymen. However, the day to day administration remained in the hands of the Tibetans — Sakya Pandita, the Abbot of Sakya Monastery was the Viceroy of Tibet on behalf of the Mongols, followed by Sakya Lama, Phagpa, in 1253, and so on and on for nearly five centuries till the Dzungar Mongols invaded Tibet in 1717 and seized Lhasa. In short, the period of Mongol suzerainty over Tibet may be said to have lasted till about the end of the seventeenth century during which period Tibet was autonomous, if not more or less independent, particularly after the death of Gusri Khan. Having wrought such havoc on the peaceful populace, the Mongol Prince took a 'U' turn in the 'Ü' Province and sought religious instruction from Sakya Pandit, head

9. Avedon: op.cit. p. 14-16.

of one of the four principal Buddhist sects in Tibet. Thus, the Mongols, having successfully overcome so many nations ultimately failed to penetrate the immense mountainous-spiritual barriers of Tibet. Instead, they were subdued by Tibetan spiritualism. Concurrently, in 1253 King Louis IX of France deputed Friar William on what turned out to be the most important Christian Mission to the Mongols. It was like a two-pronged spiritual attack on Mongolia. However, Buddhism continued to prosper amongst the Mongols, and in course of time Mongolia claimed a measure of suzerainty over Tibet by virtue of a (Mongolian) Lama Phagpa being declared by Kublai Khan in 1260 as head of the Buddhist church with the title of "Great Precious Prince of the Faith".[10] Meanwhile, Buddhist creed of total nonviolence also transformed the martial Tibetan race into a docile people.

The initial wave of Buddhism that swept Tibet was dominated by the old unreformed Karma-pa sect. The King of Tsang supported by the religious hierarchy ruled the country. But in 1642 Gusri Khan, a Mongol Prince of Qosot tribe supported by his followers and other Mongol tribesmen of the Gelug-pa sect invaded Tibet. They defeated the King of Tibet who was killed in battle. Thus the Karma-pa Lamas were removed and the Dalai Lama of the day, Lobzang Gyatso, the "Great Fifth" of the Gelug-pa sect was established as the religious head of the country, while Gusri Khan himself exercised the secular powers as the King of Tibet. The relationship between the two was "an example of the purely Central Asian concept of Patron and Priest in which the temporal support of the lay power is given in return for the spiritual support of the religious power."[11] This elastic and flexible concept of shared power was the basis of relationship between the Mongol Emperors of China and their Lama Vice-regents for Tibet. This idea cannot be translated into modern political cut and dry terminology as has been interpreted by the Chinese Communists, the Indian Prime Minister Jawaharlal Nehru as well as the Government of Great Britain in terms of Chinese suzerainty over Tibet. In the confusion

10. MacGregor John: *Tibet: A Chronicle of Exploration;* p. 14.

11. Richardson H.E.: *Tibet And Its History;* pp. 40-41.

of interpretation of terminology they lost sight of the basic fact that Tibetans are not Chinese, nor were they ever part of the Chinese State; Tibet was an independent State in its own right and the relationship between the Chinese Emperors and the Dalai Lama was based on the concept of Patron and Priest.

The 1911-Revolution in China resulted in the end of Manchu dynasty and establishment of a Peoples' Republic with Yuan Shihkau as the President. He issued a decree on April 12, 1912, declaring Tibet as a province of China. Concurrently, in order to enforce the decree, the new Republic launched an attack on Tibet to which the British Government took serious exception and retaliated by refusing to recognize the new Republic itself. The Chinese attack was halted. There were frustratingly repetitious discussions on the definition of 'suzerainty'. Gyalwa Rinpoché was looking forward to some such opportune moment to assert Tibetan independence. He returned to Lhasa, rejected the Chinese claim to suzerainty and declared Tibet as a completely independent country. The Chine troops in Lhasa were disarmed. On 6th January 1913 the Chinese commander, Chung-yin, and the remnants of his garrison were ignominiously marched off southward to return to China via India. Tibet was now a completely independent country, in fact and in law.[12]

Gedun Truppa was a leading missionary of the Gelug-pa sect of Buddhism. He founded the great monastery of Tashilhunpo at Shigatse and was its Abbot till his death in 1475. A few years after his death, it was discovered that he had incarnated in a young child, Sonam Gyatso, who was recognized as the third incarnation of Gedun Truppa. He was a brilliant scholar and a dedicated missionary of exceptional zeal. Sonam Gyatso visited Mongolia in 1578 and prevailed on the powerful young Mongol Prince Altan Khan of Tumed to fall in line with the Gelug-pa school of Buddhism. The Khan was greatly impressed by Sonam's knowledge and spiritualism. In recognition and gratitude, Altan Khan honoured Sonam with the title of "Dalai Lama Vajradhara" — Talé (Dalai in Tibetan meaning 'ocean'), Lama is priest, and Vajradhara is a Sanskrit word meaning 'Holder of the Thunderbolt'. Later, this

12. The subsequent Simla Conference and British shenaningans are not within the scope of this work.

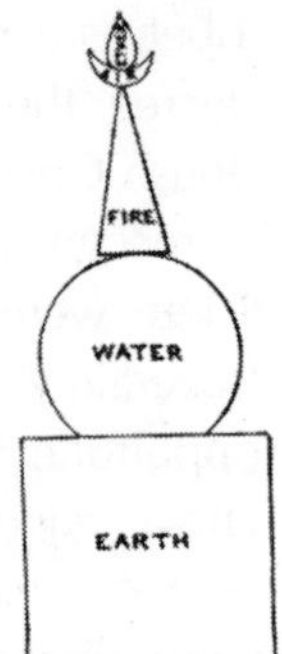

CHORTEN, SYMBOLISING THE ELEMENTS.

Chorten: Symbolizing the Elements

title was retrospectively applied to his two predecessors, Gedun Gyatso and Gedun Truppa as a posthumous honour; thus Sonam Gyatso went down in history as the Third Dalai Lama.[13]

It was during the reign of the 'Great Fifth' that the institution of Panchen Lama came into being when the Great Fifth ordained his beloved tutor, Ch'ösgyi Gyaltän, as "Panchen Rinpoché", the High Priest of Tashilhunpo Monastery, second only to the Dalai Lama in the hierarchy of Tibet's Incarnate Lamas. The Panchen was declared as an incarnation of Amitabha, whose spiritual son is Avolokita, the Tibetan God incarnate in Gyalwa Rinpoché, the Dalai Lama. The designation 'Dalai Lama' is used the world over as a spill-over from Central Asia; but in Tibet he is referred to as Gyalwa Rinpoché.

Symbolism: Prayers by Proxy

Prayer flags and chörtens are like hand and glove. These are tombs of the dead, and lamas gone by. *Chörtens* are walled towers. Their height varies from six to fifty feet. The entrance and exit to a habitation are invariably marked by a *Chorten*. It is a symbolic structure. Tibetans are careful to pass a chörten always on their left. The word Chörten literally means a 'receptacle for offerings'. It is believed that chörten is the Sanskrit equivalent of *dhatugarbha* which over a period of time got corrupted to *dagaba.*[14] The word pagoda is derived from *dagaba*. Every Tibetan spiritual motif has its origin in Indian civilization. Although cremation of the dead was the normal practice in India, it was customary to bury the bodies of specially venerated persons in stone mausoleums called stupas. One can see a number of them dotting the Indian countryside. These are essentially commemorative monuments. Sacred relics of Buddha after his parinirvane (death) were also similarly preserved in stupas. The Indian stupas, Buddhist to be more precise, have a hemispherical form with a circular base at the bottom supporting a massive solid dome. In course of time the Tibetan stupas underwent a process of evolution; from more or less round or hexagonal base they became elongated structures. Their purpose also underwent

---

13. Ibid. p. 42.

14. Maraini Fosco: *Secret Tibet*; p. 60.

transformation in as much as a stupa became a cenotaph rather than remained a mere tomb; it became a sort of memorial for the person or cause that it commemorated, a 'representation in miniature of lamaist cosmology' depicting the five elements of nature — earth as the base of the tower, water, fire, air in between, and ether at the top.

The human body is made of these elements, and disintegrates into the same elements after its essence, the soul, has left. In other words, the chörtens symbolize the elements.

In Tibetan Buddhism it has taken the form of prayer wheels mounted on spindles fixed in sockets of walls, houses, chörtens, etc. Then there are table-wheels turned by fingers; portable wheels turned by hand; tiny wheels turned by wind; large wheels turned by man/animal power; and above all else, is the largest wheel turned by hydraulic power.

All these wheels are imprinted with the usual prayers hundreds and thousands of times, perpetually in motion, as if prayers are being recited on behalf of whosoever has provided the energy for rotation of the wheel. The survey-spies deputed by the British from the Survey of India carried their instruments in their prayer-wheel-boxes when they went out in disguise to carry out geo-physical survey of the unknown lands in the eighteenth and nineteenth centuries, as if they were continuously chanting the mantra: *Om Mani Padme Hum* (Hail to thee, the Jewel in the Lotus).

A further evolutionary process in this direction took the pilgrim to the desired sacred spot, not by walking on his two feet — Nay, he went prostrating the entire distance. He would lie down completely flat in the required direction, mark the point where the body ended by a stone, get up, and repeat the process from that stone-mark onwards. This process of prostration would be repeated for hundreds of miles. A modification of this devotion was to prostrate width-wise. The most popular route for such circumambulation was the Lingkhor — a circular road around Lhasa, about eight km long. It could take a pilgrim three days of prostrations length-wise, and five days width-wise. Such was the depth of religiosity in the heart of Tibetan Buddhists. The

Lingkhor enclosed the valley's two sacred hills on one of which stood the Potala, while the other had the honour of Chokpori, the chief medical college run by the government.

There appears to be a tendency amongst western travelers to, and writers on Tibet to exaggerate the negative aspects of traditional Tibetan medical practices. Since the sanitary conditions and health care facilities were rather primitive, it was but natural that infectious diseases, small pox, gastro-intestinal, leprosy, venereal diseases, et al, would be prevalent on a large scale. Indeed they were. But that does not grant a license to modern medicine to describe the traditional Asian systems in pejorative terms. Tibetan medical system was quite advanced in its own way and their diagnostic techniques proved to be more accurate and to the point without the aid of modern technology and instrumentation. However, this aspect is much beyond the scope of this work; suffice to say that while pills rolled out of excreta of venerable high Incarnations and their urine are merely superstitions and certainly not part of the Tibetan system of medicine, their drugs formulated out of medicinal herbs have proved their worth. After all, what are Aloe Vera and all the rest of products developed and being marketed in the United States and Mexico, and from there to all over the world? Some odd instances of a piece of paper with a prayer written on it being ingested; touch of a monk to cure a headache; wearing blessed rosary made out of human skulls; et al, should not be generalized to represent Tibetan medicinal system. There is no denying that the doctors of Tibet were monks, but most of them were well qualified professionals who had undergone serious studies and training for more than a decade before they could practice medicine.

Another mistaken notion: it was the tip of the tongue, and not the tongue, that was anointed. It is wrongly believed that Tibetans greet with their tongue thrust out of their wide open mouth. The actual process is: While greeting, or presenting a gift, the person opens his mouth wide, draws his breath in deep sigh, showing the tip of his tongue. That is the Tibetan traditional way of expressing loyalty and devotion.

2

Monastic Governance

The more you study Tibet, the more enigmatic you find the country, its religion and culture. No wonder therefore that the first Dalai Lama came to be so designated only after his death. He was born in 1391 at Shabtod in the central Tibetan province of Tsaṇg. Name: Gedun Truppa. He took his initial vows as a monk at Narthong Monastery in 1405 and subsequently became follower of the reformed orthodox Yellow Hat sect known as Gelug-pa. Monks in both the sects took exactly the same number of vows: two hundred and fifty three. Yet another astonishing contradiction[1] is that the Monastery of Tashilhunpo at Shigatse was established in 1447 by a leading light of Yellow Hats — none other than Gedun Truppa who became its Abbot and came to be known as the Panchen Gedun Truppa, later Panchen Lama for short. He died at Tashilhunpo in 1475 at age eighty-four. Next on the list came Gedun Gyatso born in Tsang. He took his initial vows in 1486, studied at Tashilhunpo and Drepung, and came to be known as the reincarnation of Panchen Gedun Druppa. He established the monastery of Chokhorgyal, about 90 miles southeast of Lhasa. The waters of a nearby lake were considered sacred. The reflections from this Lake were reputed

1. It is a contradiction in that Panchen Gedun Truppa was posthumously accorded the status of the First Dalai Lama.

to prophesy future events. During this period Tibet was going through an unfortunate phase of religious war-like situation when Gedun Gyatso, the Abbot of Drepung, died at Drepung in 1542 at the age of sixty-five.

Title of Dalai Lama

After about a year Sonam Gyatso came on the scene, born at Tohlung near Lhasa. He was soon recognized as the reincarnation of Gedun Gyatso and studied at Drepung monastery. A brilliant scholar, excellent teacher, a popular personality with a knack of resolving difficult situations, he succeeded in putting an end to sectarian violence. His position as Abbot of Drepung certainly proved useful in this role. However, sometime in 1560 fighting broke out in Lhasa between followers of Gelug-pa and Ka-gyu-pa. The local lamas were powerless in controlling the internecine conflict. Sonam Gyatso was requested to intervene, and he managed to bring the fighting to an end. Later in the summer of 1562 when Kyichu River broke its stone dykes and flooded Lhasa, Sonam succeeded in saving many lives and rendered great humanitarian service to the people. At this point of time, there were lamas aplenty, but there was no Dalai Lama as such. As luck would have it, Altan Khan of the Tümät Mongols sent a large delegation with camels, horses and provisions to Tibet inviting Sonam Gyatso to Mongolia. The journey through the wilderness of snow-desert lasted one hundred and seventy days. The Tibetan party reached the Mongol capital[2] in the summer of 1578.

The Khan treated the visiting Lama with great reverence. Sonam Gyatso undertook a programme of religious instructions for the Mongols. The Khan was so impressed by the teachings of Lord Buddha, as well as sermons and wisdom of Sonam Gyatso, that he became a convert to Buddhism. The Ten Principles of Lord Buddha were adopted by the Khan with an injunction that all his people would abide by the same. In return

2. The Tibetan name for the Mongol capital is Khar Ngonpo, meaning blue fort. Here the Khan promised the visiting Lama that he would raise a golden statue of Lord Buddha.

for his teachings, the Khan gave a number of presents and mementos to Sonam Gyatso. But the most precious gift that Sonam received from the Khan was the title of Dalai Lama — 'Dalai' in Mongolian is "ocean", meaning thereby that the Lama's spiritual knowledge was as broad and as deep as an ocean. Sonam was also given a seal inscribed with the Title: "Dorje Chang" = "Holder of the Thunderbolt". In return, Sonam conferred on Altan Khan the title of "Religious King, Brahma of the Gods". The site where these ceremonial exchanges took place acquired a certain degree of sanctity and Sonam Gyatso, hereafter the Dalai Lama, proposed establishing a monastery there, while Altan Khan agreed to finance the Project. The monastery was named Thegchen Chonkhor.

For the Tibetans, the Dalai Lama is Gyalwa Rinpoché, but he is Dalai Lama for the outside world. Similarly the terms 'Red Hats' and 'Yellow Hats' may convey an impression of sectarian rivalry in as much as one sect indulges in diabolical practices while the other is pure and lofty; but that is not so. The essential difference between the two is that the Red Hats follow the old translations of doctrinal scriptures while the Yellow Hats follow the later translations from which non-Buddhist influences have been expunged. All the same, both are Buddhists, like amongst the Hindus the Sanatan Dharmis follow the old school and Arya Samajists follow the reformed texts, but both are Hindus all the same. Thus it would perhaps be more appropriate to refer to them as the 'Old Translation School' and the 'New Translation School'. One may not agree with this old and new school business for the simple reason that the colour code has its own significance. In Tibet the yellow colour is associated with the notion of purity and growth; red is associated with physical strength and power; black is connected with force and warfare while white denotes peace and tranquility. Be that as it may, one visibly pronounced difference between the two sects is the drawing of 'Swastika'. It is a very ancient symbol of Hinduism which rapidly escalated to become like the 'coat-of-arms' of Nazi Germany. The Germans borrowed the symbol from the east. In China, Japan and Tibet the Swastika is associated with Buddhism. The Yellow Hats, the

Gelug-pa sect, uses the Swastika as pointing to the right while the unreformed sect, the Bön, generally use Swastika pointing to the left.

Since the title of Dalai Lama was conferred on Sonam Gyatso by Altan Khan for the first time during the former's visit to Mongolia, how come Sonam came to be recognized as the Third, and not the First, Dalai Lama? This too is an enigma! Of course Sonam Gyatso was properly the First Dalai Lama; but the Tibetan religious hierarchy retrospectively conferred the title on the earlier two incarnations of Chenrezi: Gedün Truppa as the First Dalai Lama (1391-1475) and Gedün Gyatso as the Second Dalai Lama (1475-1542). Thus Sonam Gyatso became the Third Dalai Lama, the Gyalwa Rinpoché for the Tibetans.

While returning from his visit to China, the Gyalwa Rinpoché, the 'Great Fifth', visited a number of places en-route, delivered many more sermons, converted large chunks of population to Buddhism, and ultimately left for home in 1588. On the way he fell ill and died. His body was cremated and the ashes taken to Lhasa where the same were preserved in Drepung monastery. Next year a son was born to a Chokhur tribal chief in Mongolia. The boy happened to be the great-grand son of Altan Khan, and was reported to be an exceptional child very different from other children of his age. Tibetan monks went all the way to Mongolia to investigate the reports and were convinced that the boy was the reincarnation of Sonam Gyatso, the Dalai Lama. A number of other senior monks from Tibet made the journey to confirm the truth. All agreed that the boy was indeed the reincarnation of Sonam Gyatso. However, the parents of the boy refused to part with the child until he was older. The boy was therefore put through his religious education and training in Mongolia itself under the supervision of Tibetan senior monks. In 1601 when the child, now named Yonten Gyatso, was twelve years old, the religious hierarchy of Tibet arranged for him to be brought to Tibet and installed as the Fourth Dalai Lama. Consequentially, close spiritual relationship developed between Tibet and Mongolia as a result of which the Ge-lug-pa ("the

Virtuous") sect, the 'Yellow Hats', emerged as the stronger sect. Lozang Chosgyan, a poor humble scholar from Tashilhunpo was appointed as Yönten's spiritual teacher. He was the first Panchen Lama which means "Great Scholar". Since then the reincarnations of Lobzang Chosgyan[3] have been known as the Panchen Lama. It was also around this time that a religious aristocracy known as Trülku came into being. They lived in their 'sumptuous' mansions in the monastery but, as a matter of rule, they did not take any direct part in the affairs of the monastery. They remained aloof even though they occupied a prominent place in the hierarchy of Lamaism. Under the communist regime it is very doubtful if any aristocrats like Trülku would have been allowed to survive.

Governance of Tibet (As it was, and still is while in Exile)

The politico-religious philosophy of Tibet has been aptly described as "A Government of the God, by the God, and for the God". It used to be a sort of 'reincarnatory monarchy'. When it is said: 'For the God', it must not be misconstrued as 'For the God-King, the Dalai Lama'. Religion was the all pervading spiritual force in every Tibetan's life, and so it was in the organization and functioning of the government. But it is totally erroneous to say that the Government of Tibet was run by the monks. Contrary to general belief, the Tibetan Government was, and still is while in exile, half monk and half laymen. Monasteries provided the basic socio-politico-religious nucleus that inspired the polity in all matters of life and death. However, that did not ignore the laity; on the contrary it was a system of duality, of checks and balances that ruled the State unified at the top in the person of the Dalai Lama. The nerve centre of the entire fabric of not only Tibet proper but also of large parts of Central Asia was the capital city — Lhasa, "Land of the God", which was notorious for its filth, dirt and stinking smells so much so that the nobility often carried small scented handkerchiefs for their noses

---

3. According to Hugh E. Richardson, Chokyi Gyaltsen, 1570-1662, was the First Panchen Lama. Also Shakabpa Tsepon W.D.: *Tibet: A Political History*, p. 67.

— and that is where the God-King lived and ruled from. But he did not rule the country in the traditional sense of the word 'rule'. This function was entrusted to a hierarchy which had a monk and a lay person at every level down the chain. The monks were generally 'Incarnates' drawn from the 'Three Pillars of State' — the monasteries of Drepung, Sera and Ganden which together held nearly 22,000 monks, a veritable army of 'state guests'. The total number of monks in Tibet was estimated at between quarter and a half million since every family contributed at least one member to the religious order. Women were also admitted to the monasteries but the number of nuns was very small. The term 'Lama' is often loosely used by western writers. That is not correct. The title 'Lama' means 'exalted' or 'superior' one. Hence every monk or novice who lives in a monastery cannot be called a lama. The monk officials mostly belonged to the dominant Gelug-pa ('Yellow Hat') sect. The lay counter part of the administrative set-up came from the nobility. The latter were generally more strict. The Tibetan proverb applies to them most aptly:

If the fox be made the king,
He will above all be hard on foxes.

The Dalai Lama is the spiritual and temporal leader of Tibet. In theory, the power of the Dalai Lama was absolute, but in practice he did not exercise his authority without consultation with his ministers and high officials concerned. Although the 'Great Fifth' could have kept secular authority firmly in his own hands, he did not do so. Instead, he preferred to delegate the secular powers to the office of the Regent, a sort of Prime Minister; and this practice has been followed by nearly all his successors. However, his religious functions always took precedence over his secular duties. In order to assist him in governing the country, he used to delegate his secular powers to a hierarchy known as De-Pa-Zhung — Government of the Chief. This was the official Cabinet known as the Kashag, comprised of four ministers headed by a clerical while the other three ministers were, and still are, lay personnel drawn from nobility. The

Secretariat and the Finance office worked under the Cabinet and performed the day to day functions of the government. The Cabinet and these two offices constituted the pivot of the government. Duality was built in the system by appointing monks and lay officials to the same post. Thus there were two Prime Ministers (Silon) — one lay and the other a monk — and the administration was divided into civil and religious branches. This duality was itself a novelty and an enigma, but all the same it did work satisfactorily. Both worked in harmony. However, possibility of conflict could not be ruled out in such a system of 'checks and balances'. Thus the government represented equally both the religious and secular communities. Nonetheless, the religious counterpart generally took precedence over the lay official, more so since the secular community existed for the religious community, and not vice versa. Like in a democracy, civil is supreme; so it was in Tibet that Religion was supreme. By the same token, after the Dalai Lama exited from his current human body and till his reincarnation[4] was discovered, as well as during the long period of his minority, a Regent (Gyaltsab) was elected from amongst the highest incarnate lamas and invested with full powers to run the government of the country. The election was conducted by the members the National Assembly (Tsongdu) specially summoned for the purpose. The candidates for the post of Regent had to be from the highest class of incarnate lamas, the Tsho-Ch'en incarnations of one of the "Three Pillars of State" — the monasteries of Drepung, Sera and Ganden. They are known as the "regal Incarnations" and there used to be 'about half a dozen such qualified incarnations in the whole of Tibet'.[5] During the period of Regency which could be anything from ten to eighteen yeas, the Regent used to be the head of both the spiritual and temporal administration.

4. Lama Karmapa Pakshi who recently made some headlines belonged to the Kar-ma-pa sect of Buddhism. He was a contemporary of Kublai Khan in his Court. Future incarnations of the Karmapa Lama took place after his dealth. "It is interesting to note that these were the first incarnations recorded in Tibet".—Ibid; p. 65.

5. Shen Tsungi-Lien and Shen Chi Liu: *Tibet and Tibetans*, 1953, p. 102.

There was absolutely no question of a lay official ever occupying the exalted chair of a Regent. He used to maintain a small court and a liaison office of his own.

The Regent was not an absolute authority by himself. It was the Council, the Kashag comprised of three lay and one monk official, which was the chief executive body that attended to all private and national issues. And that was so even when the Dalai Lama was in full control. The Kashag was required to study and express their views on all matters referred to the Dalai Lama through the office of the Prime Minister for final decision. Thus the Kashag exercised authority, rather a privileged-control over a wide range of governmental activities including executive appointments — governors, executive officers, district officers, etc. The next in administrative hierarchy used to be an administrative body divided into various functional departments: Financial, Political, Military, Economic, Judicial, Foreign, and Educational. While the Finance Department (Tsethang) was composed of four lay officials, all other departments had an element of duality: they were headed by one lay and one monk official. In so far as the religious affairs were concerned, these were under the Lord Chamberlain, the Chikyap Khenpo, who headed a council of four monks known as *Trungyik Chemo* who presented its views to the Dalai Lama through the office of the Prime Minister. The four *Trungyik Chemo* and the four Tsepon frequently met in joint session to discuss matters of political importance and such other important issues. This joint body discussed the issues in the National Assembly whose decisions, usually without alteration, were forwarded to the Dalai Lama through the Kashag and the office of the Prime Minister.

The Private Treasury of the Dalai Lama and the Forest Department of the country were the sole prerogatives of the Lord Chamberlain.

It would be seen from the foregoing that the western ideas about the so-called feudal aristocracy and dictatorship of the Dalai Lama were largely misplaced. In fact, Tibet had its own exclusive brand of democracy admirably suited to meet its requirements of cultural, religious and literacy levels of development. The Manchus went out of their way in encouraging disparaging concepts of governance of Tibet for their own ulterior motives. And the Chinese Communists went the whole hog to obliterate the sacred precious position of the Dalai Lama to merge an independent country as one of their provinces.

The monks and the monasteries were restricted to their monastic functions only; the sole exception was during the Lhasa *Mönlam*, the Great Prayer, when thousands of pilgrims congregated in the Capital City for New Year celebrations. It was only during that three weeks period that the entire city was placed under control of the monks of Drepung Monastery to maintain discipline, law and order. Crowd control was their main function. This was essential since there used to be no police force in the whole of Tibet — the people were so law abiding indeed. This handing over of power to Drepung also acted as a check on the local administration.

Stratification of Tibetan Society

Tibet was a feudal theocracy with the Dalai Lama at the apex of social and political structure. Each Dalai Lama is the reincarnation of his predecessor. Thus, in other words, it is one and the same 'Soul' who has been ruling Tibet ever since the institution of Dalai Lama came into being in 1578 A.D., with retrospective effect from 1391, as Gedün Truppa was posthumously considered as the First Dalai Lama, the God-King who was an incarnation of Chenrezi, the Buddha of Mercy, who made a vow to protect all living beings. The 'First' ruled till 1475. After he 'retired to the heavenly fields', Gedun Gyatso was also posthumously recognized as the Second Dalai Lama. This concept of the same person, rather the same Soul, the same 'Incarnation of the Mind', ruling as Priest-King is so alien to modern western thought that it is nothing but a major enigma in itself. Then come the ger-ba, the aristocratic lords numbering about 150 to 300 families in all. They formed a hierarchy in themselves, in distinct order of precedence, stratified as follows:

- De-bon: the families descended from the ancient kings of Tibet, prior to the advent of the Dalai Lama;
- Yab-shi: the families descended from the previous Dalai Lamas.
- Mi-dra: the families whose one or the other member had performed act(s) of exceptional service to the country leading to their ennoblement.
- Gyu-ma: While the above three groups constituted barely about thirty families — the exclusive wealthy elite from whose ranks came the senior officials of the Government — the large majority of nobility fell in the last group, the 'common' lot. Most of this category had one small estate. But even these small estates were extremely lucrative. A typical small estate could comprise of a few thousand sheep, a thousand yaks, about two hundred agricultural serfs and any number of nomads. The annual output of a small estate could be about 36,000 kg of grain, 1,800 kg of wool, and about 500 kg of butter, besides the various perks that accrued by virtue of holding an official position in the government, more so since 'very few nobles had a reputation for integrity'.

The vast majority of the rest of the population was serfs, locally known as mi-ser (Literally 'yellow person'), a few slaves and some outcasts.[6] They were the equivalent of Indian society's scheduled castes and untouchables. The serfs were tied down to their masters and were classified as under:

- Tre ba: They were indentured to both monastic and lay nobility. They were the wealthier group and were tax-payers. They held title to hereditary lands but were obliged to provide transport corvee — a severe form of tax under which the family had to have ready, at any time, animals, fodder, accommodation, provisions and guides for the officials, of officially sponsored personnel moving through their areas. The village headmen were generally chosen out of this lot of wealthy serfs.

6. Grunfeld: op.cit (p.8)

- The other group of serfs apparently belonged to the poorer class, known as du-jung ('small smoke' i.e. small households). They did not have any hereditary lands but certainly enjoyed the status of hereditary serfs.
- While both the above categories of serfs belonged to either the monasteries or nobility, the third category belonged only to the government.

Notwithstanding the above, the elder brother of the Fourteenth Dalai Lama, Thubten Jigme Norbu, has listed five 'ways of life' in Tibet: valley farmers; mountain nomads; traders; monks; nobility and lay members of the government. Strictly speaking, the nobility is not a hereditary class and a Tibetan noble is accorded respect not because of his birth, but by virtue of the responsibilities he shoulders. The monasteries worked for the good of public in the neighborhood by providing them land and money when required, supplying grain in times of need, perform religious duties on as required basis, provide medical treatment. A monastery was a sort of a sanctuary for the public at large, a second home so to say.

Officially speaking, slavery was non-existent in Tibet. But the practice of slavery was very much in existence, albeit on a very small scale. This has been confirmed by Sir Charles Bell who served many long years in Tibet as the official representative of Government of British India. This was particularly so in Chumbi Valley whereas across the border in Bhutan, the number of slaves was much larger. Sometimes the children were stolen from their parents when they were very young, and brought up as slaves by the master. Or when the parents were too poor and sold off the child to some man who paid what was known as sho-ring — 'price of mother's milk', a paltry sum indeed.[7]

Another oddity prevalent in Chumbi valley was the continued existence of the ancient Bön faith amongst the people of Upper Tromo. It was reported that an Oracle from Lhasa had come down to Chumbi valley and had established himself in one of the monastery. Through his divinations and prophecies, he was

7. Bell Charles, Sir: *Tibet: Past & Present:* Oxford, 1924; p. 78

responsible for perverting the followers of Bön faith and converting them to Buddhism. In the process, about eighty families of Bön faith had been enticed away by the Oracle. The local people also claimed that through his magical practices some leading men of the area including four headmen had already died. This Oracle was said to be possessed by some supernatural power, a demon indeed.

The nomadic tribes formed a large component of Tibetan society of yore. Their main contribution to the economy was their cultivation of the yak (gyag in Tibetan) — a large humped sturdy bovine mammal having long silky hair on the sides and on the tail. It is an all-purpose animal, uniquely adapted to the terrain and climate of Tibet. Yak is the basic beast of burden for the Tibetan, found wild or domesticated, and is most useful, dead or alive. There is hardly any part of this animal which is not used in one form or the other — the hair to make tents; hair of tails for religious ceremonies; hide for boots, belts, bags, case covers, etc.; meat as a valuable source of protein; butter from yaks' milk for tea, food, lamps, cosmetics, religious ceremonies, etc. Above all, its dung is a major source of fuel in Tibet. Outsiders mistakenly use 'yak' as a common noun for both genders; the female of the species is actually known as dri. Yak to a Tibetan is like a camel to a nomadic Arab.

It is noteworthy that the Dalai Lama always came from the poor or middle class segment, and never from the rich powerful nobility — barring an odd exception of course. His poor parents and siblings became rich overnight and joined the ranks of nobility. He is the incarnation of Chenrezig,[8] the Buddha of Mercy — known in Indian Buddhism as Avaloketisvara, 'the Compassionate' one, who descended to Tibet to deliver all 'mind-possessors' from the vicious cycle of birth and death. According to Buddhists' belief, an individual is caught in this cycle till he has earned enough merit to free himself from this cycle and propel his soul

---

8. Chenrezig is the Tibetan name of Buddha of Compassion, of Mercy. *Chen* is the eye, *re* is the corner of the eye, and *zig* means "see". In other words, Chenrezig is Compassion personified who takes care of the needs of all beings.

to a state of heavenly bliss called *nirvana*. This cannot be accomplished in a few births since the scope of work is vast. Therefore, the Incarnation of Chenrezig cannot die till His mission is completed. Consequentially, he merely leaves one body and, in Tibetan terminology, he 'retires to the heavenly fields' from where he returns to earth again and again to complete his mission. His soul thus transmigrates to another human body, the intervening critical period between his 'death' and rebirth being a maximum of 49 days. He has already achieved the stage of near-nirvana and is a bodhisattva, but instead of seeking full nirvana, he has elected to return to earth unselfishly in order to help others to achieve that state.

Although the Dalai Lama is loosely referred to as the 'God-King', it must be clearly understood that the Dalai Lama is not God even though he is venerated as God. Nor is he a representative of a supreme deity; he is a manifestation of the divine deity in earthly form. To cap it all, the Dalai is not a Tibetan term; it is a Mongolian word meaning "ocean of wisdom"; thus Dalai Lama is a "Lama with oceans of wisdom". In Tibet this term is unknown; there he is referred to as Gyalwa Rinpoché (the "Victorious One") or Kyabngon Rinpoché (the "Precious Protector"). He is the highest incarnate Changchub Sempa, but certainly not the only one. Almost every monastery in Tibet had such an incarnate lama. These incarnations, or Trulku are divided into four grades. The Regents are chosen from the highest grade of Trulkus. The succession to the position of Gyalwa Rinpoché is essentially a spiritual matter; it is political only to the extent that the Gyalwa Rinpoché is also the secular head of the country.

Ceremonial[9]

A special audience is granted to highly placed visitors to Lhasa. It is held in the great hall of the Dalai Lama during the daily Drungja ceremony which is attended by all the monk-officials. A special guide, Letsenpa, explains the procedural formalities to the

9. This portion is deliberately written in the present tense for lucidity of text: the Author.

visitor concerned. He is required to wear court clothing — a brown silken coat and a short yellow jacket. The Letsenpa accompanies the visitor to the plinth of the temple before the Kesang Potrang, where a large number of pilgrims, sometimes as many as 500-1,000 may be waiting to be let into the audience hall to receive the blessings of the Dalai Lama. The pilgrims are not merely Tibetans only; a large number come from Central Asia too. Soon thereafter, Drönyer Chemo, the High Chamberlain and Master of Ceremonies invites the Rinpoché, i.e., the highly placed visitor into the Small Palace. As soon as the last of the visitors is in, the Dalai Lama himself enters the hall. Every one present rises, and bows low. Every one takes his seat after the Dalai Lama has seated on the throne. On one of these occasions the Dalai Lama's father and eldest brother were the chief visitors. So this was a very special audience. They both slowly walked up towards the throne. The emotionally poignant moment came when they prostrated three times before the Dalai Lama, like every body else. The ceremony of Mendel Tensum followed. A statuette of God of Long Life, a small religious book, and a Chörten symbolizing the body, word and spirit of Buddha were pressed against the foreheads of the Father and the Brother. They were then blessed by the Dalai Lama. "Respectfully I handed a costly scarf to the High Chamberlain whose duty it was to accept all gifts for the Dalai Lama. Then I went up close to the throne to receive my brother's blessings. ... He did so with quiet dignity by laying his hands on me". Only high dignitaries and monks were honoured by being blessed with the laying-on of the hands; the others were blessed by being touched with a tassel by the Dalai Lama. A similar ceremony used to be repeated for the high dignitaries before the Regent. Ceremonial drinking of strong buttered tea and eating of rice followed after which, once again, the visitors prostrated three times in the regular fashion. The Dalai Lama arose immediately and left the room with the Regent and other dignitaries of his Court, while the rest of the congregation stood by reverently, bowing low.[10]

---

10. The Regent and the Dalai Lama salute each other by touching forehead to forehead.

Thubten Jigme Norbu and his mother Dekyi Tsering

His Holiness The Fourteenth Dalai Lama with his mother

New Year Sermon

The author has witnessed the Pontifical benediction at Rome. The Pope blesses the large multitude in a single gesture. But the Tibetans are more demanding; they want individual blessing through personal contact. However, the manner of personal blessing varies with the social rank and position of the pilgrim. The Dalai Lama blesses by placing both hands on the head of the people he respects the most; for instance his father, close blood relations, heads of states, etc. while in other cases only one hand, or two fingers, or just one finger only. The last category is the multitude which used to come to Lhaṣa all the way as mere visitors or pilgrims. They were blessed by touching the head with coloured ribbons attached to a short stick. The point to note is that in every single case there was personal contact, between the God-King and his subjects, directly or indirectly.

Tibetans perform prostration before deities, gods and High Lamas, own guru, sacred scriptures, etc., in the usual Chinese style of *kowtow*[11] with the slight difference in that before kneeling, one lifts the arms above the head, joins the palms, and then brings the folded hands successively in front of the forehead, the mouth and the head. That is how it appears when performed in slow motion; otherwise the three postures overlap. The process is generally repeated three times. The other style of prostration is the usual Indian style. It is called kyang chag in which the person lies flat on the ground. This is reserved for some very special occasions only. Some extraordinarily devoted persons perform this type of prostration, say one hundred thousand times, touching their forehead to the floor each time so much so that a sort of bump. develops on their forehead.

The eldest brother of the Fourteenth Gyalwa Rinpoché being an incarnate Lama was admitted to the Kumbum Monastery for his education and training. By age fourteen, Jigme had acquired a fairly wide knowledge of teachings of Padmasambhava and was therefore a fit candidate for admission in the Tsogchen, a great

11. This used to be obligatory while in audience before the Emperor.

college of more than three thousand highly intellectual monks who devoted themselves to the scholastic life. Tsogchen had various Tratsangs or faculties — Menpa Tratsang for medicine; Gyüpa Tratsang for meditation; Dükhor Tratsang for mysticism and Shadpling Tratsang which taught logic and debate. Each Tratsang had its own Dukhang, or great hall. Jigme appeared before the Khenpo, the Abbot Superior who tested him for his suitability to enter the Shadpling Tratsang. He had a number of books kept beside him. Picking up one of them casually, he opened a page at random and loudly read a passage which Jigme had to recite and complete. Jigme did not fail even once. The second part of the first great test was held by the Shengo, the superior magistrate of the Monastery of Kumbum, a sort of Proctor. Jigme prostrated three times before him also, as was the custom. The Shengo tested Jigme from three books only, and declared him 'passed' in all of them after which Jigme could take part in the assembly of his fellow monks as a full fledged monk. He could now onwards carry his traditional hat of yellow wool in his hand and a few years thereafter, on his left shoulder.[12]

After his family had moved to Lhasa, Rinpoché Thubten Jigme Norbu had left Kumbum monastery without completing his prescribed course of studies. After he settled down with the family in Lhasa, it was high time for him to resume his academic career. Since Drepung was the superior monastery over Kumbum, obviously, Jigme had to continue his academics in Drepung. It is the biggest monastery in Tibet. It had nearly ten thousand monks on its rolls. While suitable quarters were being made ready for Jigme, the financial implications of entering Drepung were analyzed. As part of initial round of visits Jigme as the newcomer would have to seek prayers from each monk, and make a present in cash to each monk. In other words, he had to pay for their prayers! It was called kugye. About eight thousand monks were entitled to receive a present on Jigme's kugye. After negotiations handled by Jigme's father, it was agreed that each monk would receive a present of one gormo. Beside this kugye, there would be cost of katas, butter-

---

12. Norbu Thubten Jigme: *Tibet is My Country,* pp. 79 and 115.

lamps and the reception Jigme would have to host on his installation in Drepung.[13] By now the reader would have concluded that butter is universal in Tibet; at least it used to be since the Chinese may not have left any behind. So are bones. Bones of animals are not buried or hidden; they are left following the principle of 'as is where is'. All sorts of bones are scattered all over the place. The children play with them, throw them here and there. May be, they loved to see bones.

As usual, it was the court-astrologers who decided Jigme's date of entry into Drepung. On the appointed day he, accompanied by his parents, friends and a retinue of servants, set off for Drepung. He was received by the Chief Abbots, the Drepung Lachi, and representatives of Gomang Tratsang and the Samlo Khangtsen, with all the honours due to a Rimpoché of his rank. Fortunately for Jigme, music of trumpets and oboes was prohibited in Drepung. While it was a common practice at Kumbum, the strict rules of Drepung forbade music and trumpets. So it was a quiet dignified reception. Jigme's 'household' in Drepung comprised of his cook, another servant, a monk named Tseten appointed by the Monastery to be his mentor during the first period of stay, and a Mongolian scholar, Ngawang Nyimala, who was to be his teacher in Drepung. Tseten informed Jigme, with a touch of pride, that Drepung had six Abbots and four Tratsangs while Sera and Ganden had nearly half that number. The four Tratsangs of Drepung were: Loseling, Deyang, Ngagpa and Gomang. Each of these was divided into about twenty khangtsens. The monks were allocated to various institutions according to what part of the country they came from. Jigme had to pass the entrance examination for the sixth class of Gomang Tratsang as the very first step. This class had about one hundred students taught by two monks. The entire day, from four in the morning to about nine at night was a continuous period of intense study and prayers.

New Year Festival (Mönlam Chenmo)

The New Year festivities called Mönlam Chenmo provided a welcome break. The numerous performances, mostly cham or

---

13. Norbu Thubten Jigme: *Tibet: Its History, Religion & People*, p. 180.

dances of one type or the other, each lasting for hours accompanied by music made by trumpets, drums, oboes, and cymbals, were the main source of entertainment along with plenty of food and drinks. However, the "Black- Hat" dancers with their long chains of human bones were a class by themselves, more so because the dancers represented demons.[14]

The end of the Festival was symbolic in as much as it signified dissolution of all the evil of the Old Year into nothing. This was done by the Chief Magi getting hold of the paper image of evil, screwing it up and throwing it into a fire burning under a cauldron of oil, followed by a bowl shaped out of a human skull filled with raw spirit which raised the flames leaping up higher than the huge masks of demon-dancers themselves.[15] And that was also the end of three weeks of New Year holidays! During this period of festivities, crowd-control and maintenance of law and order got special attention. As long as the Dalai Lama and other high dignitaries were in the City, the people behaved in a disciplined manner. The soldiers were around all the time making sure that all went well. However, as soon as the high dignitaries had gone back to Potala and the soldiers withdrawn, the monk-police had their hands full, using their thick staves at random.

The beginning of the New Year called for another twelve days of celebrations which were on a much smaller scale, but more dignified. Theological disputations became the order of the day. Flags of various sizes and colours decorated the streets. Powerful monks carried their temple and monastery flags in an endless procession which finally reached the Potala. An enormous two-hundred-foot wide colourful banner, known as Ghöku, with its costly golden brocade kept in a special house, used to be lowered from the windows of the Potala in full view of the public. Its protective covering would be peeled off, to loud admiration and applause of the masses below. Here was the culmination of weeks of celebrations.

---

14. Ibid; p. 181-86.

15. Ibid; p. 187.

3

The Potala

The Potala is the Paradise of Buddhas,
Palace of Chenrezig.
To east, west, south and north,
There is a Potala on this earth;
From the Land of Snows to the Lho Potala,
Potala of the Southern Seas.

Tibetan saying[1]

The 'Potala' is the official residence of the Dalai Lama, and also the working headquarters of the Government of Tibet. It is the seat of authority in Tibet. The act of identification and recognition of the reincarnation was complete only after the Gyalwa Rinpoche had entered the Potala; and it was there only that the God-King used to receive the seals of his office. The name 'Potala' is not of Tibetan origin. Tibetan scholars believe that it is the corruption of the word 'Potaraka', the hill-top abode of Avaloketisvara which, according to Hindu mythology was, and still is, the southern most tip of the Indian peninsula, Cape Comorin. It is not merely a huge red and white building; it is more like a

1. Quoted by Thubtèn Jigme Norbu in *Tibet: Its History, Religion, and People,* England, 1969, p. 247.

fortress, whose gilded roofs glitter beautifully in Lhasa's clean air and bright sun. Perhaps it is one of the largest buildings in the world and covers the top of the entire hill; it is more of a city in itself, being the centre of religious life of Tibet.

The construction-completion of Potala, the Winter Palace of Gyalwa Rinpoché (the Dalai Lama), is the most characteristic example of Tibetan enigmatic behaviour. Its construction was commenced by an ancient King of Tibet about 1,300 years ago as a pavilion for meditation. The main audience hall itself is an enormous square structure, totally enclosed, lighted from a central well supported on huge painted wooden pillars. The eight lucky signs are hung on these pillars, repeatedly. The Potala was greatly enlarged by the Fifth Dalai Lama, the "Great Fifth", during the seventeenth century. The central part of the present building is thirteen storeys high. It was built on his orders but he died when the structure had gone up to merely two storeys height only. When the Gyalwa Rinpoché knew that he was dying, he told his Prime Minister (Desi), Sangye Gyatso, to keep his death a secret because he was afraid that if it was known that he was dead, the construction work would come to a stop. The people would naturally refuse to work for free when they would come to know that the Gyalwa Rinpoché was no longer alive to extract work out of them.

A 'Fake' Dalai Lama

The Desi was a clever man, and devoted too. He found a monk who resembled the Dalai Lama and worked out a plan to keep the death of the Fifth a secret for fifteen long years that it took to complete the work. And he succeeded in hoodwinking the entire country and many foreign visitors in believing that the Gyalwa Rinpoché was very much on the throne, alive and working! How could he possibly ignore His Holiness's order: The Gorkhas have a characteristic proverb to illustrate this:

There is no answer to an order;
There is no medicine for death.

However, the Desi secretly got a stone carved with a prayer for a reincarnation and got it embedded into the walls. This stone can still be seen in the second storey of the Potala.[2] It was a well kept secret; only the personal attendants of the Dalai Lama, a monk of the Namgyal Dratsang monastery, and of course the Desi knew of the Dalai Lama's death. The Desi announced that the Dalai Lama had gone into meditation for an indefinite period and was therefore not to be disturbed under any circumstances. However, any one wishing to see the Dalai Lama on a matter of extreme urgency could do so alone in the private room of the Lama. The public at large accepted the Desi's announcement at its face value without a doubt. Meals were taken into the room as usual and everything was done to make it appear normal, as if the Great Lama was alive and well. Persons standing outside the Lama's private quarters could hear the continuous sound of hand-drum and bell used in rituals signifying that the Lama was in deep meditation. The Lama's ceremonial gown was placed on his throne in the audience hall to mark his presence on State functions. The people accepted that and acted as if the Gyalwa Rinpoché himself was present. However, when high dignitaries from Mongolia came for an audience, the Desi arranged for them to call on the Lama in his private chambers where the monk from Namgyal Dratsang monastery dressed in ceremonial robes of the Dalai Lama acted the role. The deception continued to work. The fiction of the Fifth being in prolonged meditation remained alive. The fake Dalai Lama went through the usual polite rituals with the guests. In fact, this went a long way in perpetuating the myth since the visitors spread the word that they had an audience with the Dalai Lama. Similarly, titles were given in the audience hall before the Lama's ceremonial robes and his seal was affixed on all official orders. The poor 'fake Dalai Lama' must have felt totally lost in that vast space; indeed he had a hard time for fifteen long years! Unbelievable, but there it is! Sometimes he was beaten into obedience, and sometimes bribed; but the dramatic performance continued till the building was finally completed after fifteen years in 1695. Considering the intention behind the whole show, the persons concerned could surely be forgiven for the 'deception'.

---

2. Dalai Lama: *My Land & My People:* op.cit. p. 53.

The north wall of the audience hall is yet another 'deception, but it is more of an architectural effect rather than an attempt to deceive any body. What appears to be the north wall is in fact a screen, advanced several feet from the actual wall. The screen is covered with silk needle work, appliqué, depicting various religious scenes. The seven-foot-high throne of Gyalwa Rinpoché is set against this screen. The other walls of the great hall are covered with oil paintings.

Potala Completed

Indeed, it is not a mere building; it is more of a huge complex of chapels and ceremonial halls perched atop a harsh rocky mound as if it was built by nature as part of the rocky outcrop, a stark red and white fortress with its roofs of pure gold gleaming in the sun. The two wings of the Potala were painted, neat and clean white. These buildings were used for housing and offices of lay members of the staff, and for various other non-religious functions. The central part of the complex used to be the headquarters of religious life in the Potala, and was therefore painted rich dark red. It is slightly higher than the White Palace. The main building is nearly one thousand feet long, thirteen storeys high. One may easily get lost in the maze of corridors and stairs. The pilgrims' main entrance begins in the chamber so dark that on entering it from bright sun light outside, one may see nothing for a moment. Here lies the great prayer wheel, about twenty feet high and eight feet in diameter. A stick is jutting out from the wheel. As the great wheel moves, it activates a sharp clink on the bell. Every pilgrim must turn the wheel. From this entrance chamber the visitors keep climbing along dark corridors lit by butter lamps, or small slits of open sky-lights. The great halls for ceremonial occasions, about thirty-five chapels, richly carved and painted, four cells for meditation, and the mausoleums of seven Dalai Lamas — each about thirty feet high and covered in solid gold and precious stones — were located in the central complex. The tomb of Ngawang Lobzang Gyatso, the 'Great Fifth' Dalai Lama (1617-1682), which reaches up about sixty feet through three storeys bursting out into a golden canopy on the roof, is particularly revered. The relics are all buried inside and Thubten Jigme Norbu confirms that there are no mummified bodies as some people believe. Only one of the temples in the entire complex is really dark — the Temple dedicated to Chenrezig himself. Here the image is really very small, barely eighteen inches high, placed on a long altar where there are many other images. A golden butter lamp kept in front is always lighted.[3]

The western part of the complex had housing facilities for about two hundred monks while the eastern portion housed government offices, meeting halls for the National assembly, school for monk-officials, a special prison for VIP prisoners, and accommodation for some lay officials. As for the Gyalwa Rinpoché himself, his apartment was on the top storey, about 400-feet above the rest of the town. He had just four rooms and the one he used most was barely 25 feet square! Its walls were covered with historical paintings so detailed that no individual portraits were more than an inch high. Like all important buildings in Tibet, it faced south. The four corners had defensive turrets where the Tibetan army used to keep watch. Besides all these odds and ends, the Potala was a cavernous store house for thousands of scrolls, precious gifts, enormous libraries full of records of centuries of Tibetan history and culture, strong rooms containing riches beyond estimation and accounting. The most interesting collection was "two thousand illuminated volumes of scriptures written in inks made of powdered gold, silver, iron, copper, conch shell, turquoise and coral, each line in a different ink."[4] Indeed, the Potala was the center of Tibet, 'the abode on earth of the earthly incarnation of Chenrezig, Lord of Mercy, Protector of our country'. Eight to ten feet long monastic trumpets were often blown from the rooftops. At noon every day two conch-shells, one having a higher note than the other, were blown. The combination made a peculiar sound locally known as 'Ee-Uu'.[5]

---

3. The Potala was heavily bombed during the mass uprising. How much of this description is in the present tense and how much should be in the past—well, the Author is not in a position to say categorically. And the POWs of 1962 were not taken to Lhasa!

4. Dalai Lama: *My land & My People;* pp. 53-54.

5. Taring Dohna Rinchen: *Daughter of Tibet;* London, 1970, p. 143.

The Potala Palace

Natural Setting

Decorated for Festivities

The Fourteenth Dalai Lama on his Throne

Now, any doubts about the fabulous riches of Tibet, and why the Chinese and the British were hankering after that land-locked isolated country? (Just before the Second World War, there were only six Europeans in the entire country) In the words of the Dalai Lama, "the best-known quality of Tibet in the recent past was its deliberate isolation."[6] Nonetheless, there is an inherent contradiction in their attitude towards isolationism. They apply the most strict rules and regulations to keep foreigners, particularly Europeans, out of their country. But when a white man manages to arrive in their midst, they do not put him behind bars or expel him; instead, they go out of their way to welcome him and make a fuss about him. Xenophobic enigmaticism of the most strange kind! Indeed, they are fascinated by the white man and his accoutrements. For what to the rest of the world are products of ordinary day to day scientific advancements and inventions, are to them miracles of magic.

The hill on which the Potala is built is known as Marpori. There is a small lake, barely three hundred yards long, just behind the Potala at the foot of the hill. It is fed by a tiny stream. Lö Khang, the 'House of Serpent', is located in the middle of this lake. The image of Potala is reflected in the placid waters of the Lake. About fifty coracles made of yak skin were brought to this lake every year on the fifteenth day of the Fourth month, Lord Buddha's birthday, when people used to gather in large numbers dressed in festive costumes and rowed around the island enjoying the picnic parties. The fifteenth day of the next month — the fifth month: June-July — it was once again festival time when the whole of Tibet went out on picnics. "This was called the World Prayer, as everybody prayed then for the happiness of all living beings all over the world."[7]

The College of Medicine is built on the next hill known as Chogpori. For the Tibetans, the Potala is the centre of spiritual and political life. It is a symbol of spiritual rather than temporal greatness of the fifth Gyalwa Rinpoché, the 'Great Fifth'. While in

6. Dalai Lama: op.cit.. p. 59.

7. Taring Dolma: op.cit. p. 151.

Lhasa, the Tibetans refer to the Potala as Phobrang, meaning the 'Palace of earthly Incarnation of Chenrezig'. According to Thubten Jigme Norbu the winter Palace of Gyalwa Rinpoché in Lhasa is not the only Potala; there are other Potalas too. One is supposed to be near Shanghai, the Lho Potala of the Southern Seas. The eastern home of Chenrezig is said to be in Shengshi province. It is known as Rio Tsen ga, or the 'Palace of Five Mountain Peaks'. The western Potala seems to be an imaginary creation in Urgyen which the Tibetans believe may include Kashmir also. The northern Potala is thought to be in Shambhala which could be in Tibet itself, or even in Moscow! In short, besides the Lhasa Potala, all other Potalas are a product of the mind. However, Shambhala is the subject of an interesting travel-book written by the great Lama, Stag tsang ras chen whom Sengge namgyal[8] (about 1590-1620), the King of Ladakh, had invited to his Kingdom.

The Second Panchen Lama has recorded in his autobiography that "on the fourth day of the sixth month of the Fire-Ox year (1697), he received a letter from the Desi, saying, 'Up till now, I have concealed the death of the Dalai Lama. His reincarnation has been brought to Nankartse, and I request you to proceed there and perform on him his religious rites.' ..."[9] The Panchen Lama confirmed that he was an eyewitness to a declaration made before a large gathering at Nyethang by the Desi that the Fifth Dalai Lama actually died in 1682, and giving out the reasons for his concealment of the event for fifteen long years.

Lhasa

Lhasa was, and for all practical purposes it still is, a sacred city, the capital city of Tibet, well known as "The Forbidden City". Before the Chinese occupation in 1959, its population was estimated at around 30,000; and if the neighbouring monasteries were included, it could be taken as around fifty thousand souls. The City is situated in the Kyiv Chu valley at an

---

8. Although his mother was Mohammedan, the King himself was staunch Buddhist—A *History of Ladakh* by A.H. Francke, Delhi, 1904, p. 27
9. As quoted by Shakabpa: op.cit 125, note 3.

altitude of about 12,000 feet AMSL. The climate is comfortably temperate with the maximum going up to about 80° F in summer and rarely falling below 5° F in winter.

Lhasa was the spiritual and temporal seat of His Holiness, Gyalwa Rinpoché, the God incarnate. Above all, the most sacred image of Tibetan religion that of Jowo Rinpoché,[10] the precious Lord, and a statute of Lord Buddha believed to have been blessed by Him, were enshrined in the Tsuglakhang, Lhasa's Central Cathedral. It was the magnet that attracted pilgrims from all over Tibet and beyond much of Central Asia. The capital city used to be just about two miles long and barely half a mile wide from north to south. It has been considerably expanded after the Chinese occupation to meet their domestic needs. There are a number of historic monuments in the city. The old temple, Tsuglakhang, is situated in the heart of the city. Legend has it that below this temple there used to be an underground lake in which visions of the future could be seen.

Tibet used to be one country in the world that was literally bathed in religion. In fact, religion was the best aspect of Tibet symbolized by a large number of monasteries all over the country. One wonders if the Tibetans themselves knew how many monasteries they had! The most outstanding feature of Tibetan religion is the system of reincarnating Lamas topped by Gyalwa Rinpoché, the Dalai Lama, as the God-King. This system has been operative in Tibet from about the twelfth century onwards. The country is known more for the reincarnations, ritual dances often denigrated as 'devil dances', oracles, magicians, trances, ascetics, et al. This is rather unfortunate since the very large number of devout priests who spend a life time in daily religious observances,

---

10. Tibetans have an interesting story about Ben of Kongpo, his dirty boots and deep trust in Jowo Rinpoché. Since the statue of Lord Buddha in the Central Cathedral in Lhasa acceded to Ben's request to visit his village in response to Ben's immense faith in the intrinsic goodness of the Lord, a river and a rock in the vicinity of Ben's house in Kongpo became famous pilgrimage centres—People claim that they can perceive the shape of Lord Buddha on the surface-waters of Jowo River, and the Lord's form on the face of Jowo Rock—Sogyal Rinpoché: op.cit. pp. 242-243.

meditation, study, religious discourses and training of novices, management of monasteries and keeping discipline amongst the thousands of monks, conducting religious ceremonies for the families and lay public — all such virtuous attributes of Tibetan religious life are generally lost sight of and relegated to routine matters. Complete solitude, prayer and meditation, piety and tolerance, nonviolence in body and mind — these are the essence of a Tibetan priest's life. Above all, fanaticism has no place in Tibetan religious dogma. And these aspects should naturally occupy the pride of place while dealing with Tibetan religious life, rather than ritual dances, superstitions and magical formulae. Incidentally, outsiders are prone to refer to all Tibetan monks as lamas. That is not at all correct. All lamas are monks, but all monks are not lamas. Only Incarnate monks are accorded this honouric title of Lama, and a few others like Alexandria David-Neel who distinguish themselves by 'their ascetic lives or miracles' performed. More about her in a later chapter. That is why "all Lamas have the right to give their blessings and are revered as saints."[11]

Lhasa's three circular roads were also sacred in their own right — the Nangkhor by which the pilgrims entered the Tsuglakhang; Barkhor, the second circular road or market place; and the third outermost road, the four-mile Lingkhor, or the Holy Walk. The Barkhor runs in a circle round the Central Cathedral. During the New Year festivities the City is crowded with people from all over. Although Lhasa used to have hordes of visitors, surprisingly, there were no hotels, restaurants or eateries in the city, nor in the countryside. While absence of such facilities in the countryside is understandable, how could a city like Lhasa cope up with crowds of pilgrims, traders and other visitors. Well, that is how it was. Open house hospitality was the norm. Or a large group would make camp outside the city. Most Tibetans used to consider it an honour to welcome a visitor to their household, a custom that was rarely abused. However, during the period from end of First World War to 1950 when Tibet enjoyed complete independence, a number of hotels and restaurants had come up.[12]

---

11. Heinrich Harrer: *Seven Years in Tibet*, p. 125.

Lhasa's life is mostly concentrated on this road, the Barkhor. Besides being Lhasa's central business district, all religious and military processions start and end here. During the New Year festivities, the fifteenth of the first Tibetan month is particularly auspicious. On this day, the Dalai Lama used to do his solemn circuit of the Barkhor. The beautiful artistically made figurine of butter in different hues lined the street with their master artists keeping vigil. The God-King used to stop every now and then to appreciate the butter figures. He was followed by the entire hierarchy strictly in order of their official precedence. The nobles carried a smouldering stick of incense in their hands. On public holidays many of the faithful swarmed the street. Some walked, others successively prostrated most of the distance; but all kept mumbling their prayers. However, the religious were just one part of the whole. There were pretty women too, showing off their fashions and jewelery, new frocks and frolics, flirting a little with the young nobility. And as usual in any city worth its name, there were women of easy virtue too. Men were not far behind in showing off their dresses and fashions. Civil officials of the fourth rank and above wore glossy yellow silk robes. Their hats were particularly attractive — large in size, plate-shaped with brims of blue-fox furs. The furs were imported from Hamburg! Their cultured pearls came from Japan, turquoises from Iran via Bombay, corals from Italy and amber from Berlin. Asiatic refinery among the nobility managed to overcome the constraints of geography and complications of international trade. After all, Tibetans were not that dumb as the rest of the world often believed! In short, Barkhor was, and perhaps still is, 'a centre of business, sociability and frivolity'.

The Lingkhor enclosed the valley's two sacred hills on one of which stood the Potala, while the other had the honour of Chokpori, the chief medical college run by the government. Beyond the Lingkhor stood Norbulingka — His Holiness's Summer Palace. The

---

12. After the Chinese brutalization of Tibet, out of 12,227 shops and restaurants in Lhasa in 1992, only 300 were owned by the Tibetans while the rest were all Chinese property—*Tibet: Proving Truth from Facts;* Dharmsala, 1994; p. 94.

grounds around the Norbulingka were so fertile that 'radish grown there weighed twenty pounds and the cabbages so large you could not put your arms around them'.[13] Fruit trees[14] like peaches, apples, pears, cherries and walnuts were grown, in backyard gardens or in estates of the rich. Fresh apples were a special attraction. Those having a rich crop used to preserve some quantity by burying them in sand, about three feet underground, so that they had fresh apples for the New Year celebrations. Flowering plants, willows and junipers were galore. In short, all Tibet is neither all rock nor stone, nor is it all a high altitude sand-desert. Another misconception about Tibet and its land-tenure system has been that all peasants were tenants. 'All land belonged to the State' was a mere concept. A peasant owned his land. It was heritable property. He could lease or mortgage it, and he could not be dispossessed of his land in settlement of other claims. The misleading notions about the land system in Tibet were spread by vested interests for their own ideological-cum-political reasons.

Jokhang and the Ramoche are the largest and most famous of all the temples in Lhasa. Incidentally, no house in Lhasa was allowed to be more than two storeys high since it was considered blasphemous to compete with the height of the Central Cathedral.[15] However, the Winter Palace is practically nineteen stories high, built more than three hundred years ago. Since there were no skyscrapers in Europe or America at that time, its architecture and construction technology is a reflection on the high standard of Tibetan's technical expertise. Notwithstanding the enormous size and height of the Winter Palace, the living quarters of the Dalai Lama in the Potala are quite spartan, besides being small and modestly furnished. The living room has a magnificent view of Lhasa and surrounding mountains. A small bedroom, a study, a house-chapel and a kitchen — that's all that constitute the abode of Gyalwa Rinpoché of the Tibetans, the Dalai Lama to the rest of the world, and the God-King revered by all.

---

13. Dalai Lama: op.cit. p. 56.
14. Mango-trees grew wild. The fruit was small and hard, but still quite tasty.
15. Norbu Thubten Jigme: *Tibet is my Country*, p. 177.

4

Reincarnation

The Concept and Practice of Incarnation

In olden times the ancient religions believed that the deceased continued to exist as a whole being. There was certainly good rustic sense in that belief, except that the concept of 'whole being' was out of place. That is why the dead person was buried with food and other necessities of life to be able to continue life in reasonable comfort, as evidenced by archeological findings in Egypt and Mesopotamia. The ancient Aryans too believed in the preservation of personal identity after death. The origin of custom of 'sati' may, perhaps, be traced to the same belief and principle. This ritual was followed in India amongst some sections of the Hindus till as late as the twentieth century until it was legally banned. We may reasonably conclude that the concept that after death man continued to exist as a whole being continued to prevail till the Vedic philosophy developed the concept of "impersonal fusion" with the source of all existence in the universe. In turn, this led to formulation of concept of immortality of the essence of 'life-breath' which, pari passu, gave rise to the idea of *samsara* — immortality of the *Atma* thereby giving rise to the concept of reincarnation. In other words, for all practical purposes samsara, the round of existence means Reincarnation which, according to Hindu or Vedic philosophy, implied 'Divine Justice' being delivered by the gods Yama, Soma and Indra. By implication, it means that thousands of Buddhas will come to planet earth for emancipation of all those who continue to be entangled in the web of birth-death-rebirth. This process takes aeons (kalpas) and carries on ad-infinitum. In his attempt at salvation of the world Lord Buddha preached on *Sutras* (doctrinal treatises) as well as *Tantras* (instructions in spiritual method) with Four Noble Truths as basics: True Suffering; True Cause; True Cessation; and the True Path. According to his teachings, Samsara may be divided into six divisions. In descending order, these are: GODS; Demi-Gods or Titans; Human Beings; Yi-dag or Pretas; Animals; Hells. The 'beings' take birth in any of these realms following the laws of Karma. The Meritorious Karma takes the being to the realms of gods, demi-gods, and men. Demeritorious Karma leads to rebirth in the lower realms of animals, pretas and hell. The consequences of one's Karma may be experienced in this present life, or in the next life, or in subsequent lives. Whichever way it goes, the Karmic debt has to be settled and that forms the basis of reincarnation.

On the face of it, this idea of 'divine justice' went contrary to the law of karma, a fundamental principle of Hindu thought and philosophy. But that contradiction is merely superficial. As you sow, so shall you reap. One's actions and behavior in the present life dictate the type of person one would be in the next birth. Thus, reincarnation is the practical way in which one is rewarded or punished for the quality of actions during the current life time, in whatever form it might be. It therefore becomes mandatory for the Atma to reincarnate, that is, to enter a new material existence, and go through the cycle of life and death till the karmic debt is fully repaid.

Human body has form and colour. It can be perceived. But the mind is formless, so its source or cause must also be formless. Both mind and body come into existence as the conception takes place. Obviously, the source of the body is the parents. But are the parents the source of the mind also? That cannot be so, since mind is formless and therefore cannot be generated by or through a formed being, the body or the brain. "The essential

1. Dalai Lama: *Autobiography*, p. 238

mind is naturally pure".[1] Since matter cannot produce mind, mind cannot produce matter either. It therefore stands to reason that the source of the mind would be a mind that pre-existed the conception. To take this reasoning one more step forward: the mind which pre-existed the conception must be a continuation of a previous mind. The fact that a lot of children and adults can recall incidents from their previous lives is a well known phenomenon. In short, any and every one of us had a previous life(s) and after exiting the current human frame, future life will also exist. Samsara is bondage and Nirvana is liberation from this bondage. All beings are reborn, again and again, till they reach perfection of Buddhahood — Nirvana and Mahaparinirvana, the stage of supreme Enlightenment, which dawns only at death. No wonder therefore that Tibetans generally do not celebrate birthdays of masters; "we celebrate their death, their moment of final illumination."[2]

Liberation from bondage in cycles of births and rebirths require the mind to be 'focused on external objects of contemplation' for which the images of deities are found to be most useful.

Over a period of centuries, it has come to be accepted that Reincarnation is essentially a Buddhist doctrine. Its concept and practice is Buddhist in principle. That is not correct. Since Buddhist thought and philosophy has its roots in Hindu Dharma, so does its concept and practice of Reincarnation, the difference being in the extent and universality of the belief and its practice in daily life. Reincarnation is accepted as the natural process of life in the Bhagvad Gita, the Song Celestial. This process has to be followed by every mortal being. A person is born in this world with talent and abilities that have accrued to him from other lifetimes. However, eventually they all reach a level plane. Again, it would be totally incorrect to assume that belief in rebirth or reincarnation is an exclusive eastern prerogative. Far from it. A number of western intellectuals had as much faith in the dogma of rebirth as any one of us. Henry Ford, for

---

2. Sogyal Rinpoché: op. cit. p. 110.

instance, started believing in the theory of reincarnation at an early age of twenty-six.[3]

Certain Shalokas of Bhagavad Gita beautifully explain the philosophy on which the concept of immortality of soul is based. Translation of Sanskrit version of Shalokas #13, 22 and 23 from Bhagavad Gita:

As the dweller in the body experienceth in the body
childhood, youth, old age,
so passeth he on to another body;
the steadfast one grieveth not thereat.

As a man, casting off worn-out garments,
taketh new ones,
so the dweller in the body,
casting off worn-out bodies,
entereth into others that are new.

Weapons cleave him not,
Nor fire burneth him,
Nor waters wet him,
Nor wind drieth him away.

In other words, the soul is immortal. It never dies or extinguishes; hence man is an immortal being. The essential life-breath remains the same; it is only the outer form that keeps changing.

Reincarnation in Tibetan-Buddhist System

According to Hindu Dharma conscious memory cannot be transmitted from one life to the next, while in the Buddhist system it is accepted as a matter of routine that what belongs to the present psycho-mental life does pass from one life to another,

3. Other prominent westerners who believed in the principle of Reincarnation include: General Patton, Kipling, Arthur Conan Doyle, Gauguin, Swedenborg, Goethe, Schiller, Tolstoy, Mahler, David Lloyd George, Sibelius, et al. The list goes on and on and they belong to various regions of the Planet Earth.

albeit it is a different matter altogether as to how much of conscious memory of present life shall pass on to the next, and how could that be retrieved, if at all. Since the karmic debt of present life is carried to the next, it stands to reason that the psycho-mental reservoir of conscious memory could also be carried over. In the case of high incarnations of Tibet, it certainly does although one cannot say the same categorically in the case of those lower on the scale. Herein lies a major deviation in the Hindu and Buddhist practice of the doctrine of Reincarnation. In fact, the very basis of the process of recognition of the Dalai Lama involves manifestation of past life, certainly in singular if not in the plural sense. And this is not mere fairy tale business: psycho-therapists of international repute, psycho-astrologers, and psychiatrists have proved through scientifically monitored experiments-cum-treatment of psychic patients that memories of not only the immediate past life, but of many lives beyond, can be recalled through hypnotic regression. In this connection one may cite the experiences and writings of Dr. Brian Weiss,[4] Dr. Elisabeth Kübler-Ross, and Dr. Raymond Moody, amongst many others.

Dr. Brian Weiss is not the only psycho-therapist to have had first hand experience of past lives of his patients. A large number of many others, both in the East and the West have had similar experiences — A young man approached Psychologist Leo Sprinkle of University of Wyoming in Laramie to cure him of his paralyzing fear of dogs. When hypnotism failed, he asked the patient to go back in time to his first terrifying encounter with dogs. The patient described the time of his life as a woodman in medieval times when he was attacked by wolves. This 'recalled memory' simply cured the young man; he was no longer afraid of dogs. In exactly the same manner of treatment, a woman

4. *Many Lives, Many Masters* in which Dr. Weiss recounts the true story of his treatment of a psychic patient is an international bestseller. The patient could recall eighty-six past lives, some from the stone ages, and was ultimately fully cured. His other books covering similar ground are: *Only Love is Real; Through Time into Healing; Messages from the Masters.*

was cured of her fears of drowning. After a couple of more similar experimental treatments, Psychologist Sprinkle was himself transformed, and contrary to his Christian Faith he became a strong believer in the Eastern religious dogma of Reincarnation.

Reincarnation: Kamaljit Kour in Punjab

Hundreds of fascinating instances, not mere stories, of remembering past lives, particularly by children, have been recorded, investigated and corroborated by independent observers. Dr. Ian Stevenson[5] of University of Virginia has recorded a number of such cases. However, one most reliably corroborated and interesting instance of rebirth-reincarnation comes from Punjab in India. When it came to the notice of His Holiness the Dalai Lama, he deputed a team of Tibetan scholars to investigate the case. It has been recorded by Kalsang Yeshi under the title of "Kamaljit Kour: Remembering a Past Life" and published in a New Delhi journal in June 1984.

Kamaljit Kour was born in a Sikh family in a village in Punjab, India. Her father was a school teacher. During a visit to a neighbouring village, she asked her father to take her to another nearby village. When she persisted in her strange request, and the Father wanted to know the reason why, she told him:

> This is not my home. One day my school friend and I were riding on our bicycles when we were hit by a bus. My friend died on the spot. I was taken to local hospital and later shifted to Ambala. On her insistence her Father took her to the village she wanted to go to. On the way, she instantly recognized the place where she was hit by the bus. On reaching a cluster of houses, she recognized the house where she claimed she had lived. The neighbours and the householders all confirmed Kamaljit's story and told her astonished Father that Rishma, a sixteen years old girl, had been killed in the accident. Kamaljit insisted on visiting her old home where she asked for her old school

5. *Twenty Cases Suggestive of Reincarnation* by Dr. Ian Stevenson, University of Virginia Press. Charlottesville, 1974; also: *Children Who Remember Previous Lives,* ibid. 1975-83

photo which she looked at with great delight. When Rishma's grandfather and uncle arrived, Kamaljit promptly recognized them and named them without hesitation, or making any mistake. She showed her Father the other rooms of the house, and asked for her old school books, ribbons, two silver bangles, and the maroon coloured suit. Her aunt explained that Rishma owned all these things. Then Kamaljit led the group to her uncle's house where she identified many other things. Next day she met many other relatives of her past life. The next day she refused to go back with her Father who somehow managed to convince her to go back home.

Kamaljit's old and new family started to put the whole story together. Kamaljit was born ten months after Rishma had died. Maroon was Rishma's favourite shade for the suit; so it was for Kamaljit. Rishma's family had no knowledge of reincarnation and such spiritual matters; but they and every one else around was convinced that Kamaljit was indeed their Rishma, born again.

While Dr. Brian Weiss's subject was a patient under hypnotic regression, Kamaljit recalled her past life under totally natural conditions. Yet another and equally fascinating instance of recalling memory of past life under completely natural conditions, amongst numerous others, is of an elderly man Arthur Flowerdew[6] from Norfolk, England. Right from the age of twelve this elderly person used to experience mental pictures of some great ancient city in the midst of a desert. As he grew in years, the mental pictures became clearer and more vivid. But he did not attach much importance to the subject until, by sheer chance, he happened to watch a BBC documentary on an ancient Jordanian city of Petra in Jordan. His story of the past experiences spread. The Government of Jordan invited him to Jordan along with the BBC producer of the Documentary to record his reactions to various scenes of Petra. Flowerdew had never seen or read any book on

---

6. Sogyal Rinpoché: *The Tibetan Book of Living and Dying*, Rider, London, pp. 89-90.

Petra, nor did he have any knowledge of archeology. However, his knowledge and understanding of most intricate details of Petra were most astonishingly accurate and knowledgeable as if he was an expert archeologist on the subject. Flowerdew also explained the purpose of one of the structures: it was a guard room where Flowerdew had been on guard duty and was killed in the 1st Century B.C. He explained a number of more intricate details which even the expert archeologists were not, and could not have been, aware of. After some more investigations by the experts, there remained no doubt that Flowerdew was the reincarnation of that soldier in the guard room. The incident further proved that rebirth need not necessarily be in the same region or country, nor in the same religious realm.

Whether one's religion accepts or not, the world at large has come to accept that there is life after death. Tibetan beliefs were not merely 'cock and bull' stories; they were based on hard evidence derived from years of *tapasya*, meditation and renunciation. A startling number of those who have survived this near-death experience have been left with a conviction that life continues after death. "What happened to me at that time is the most unusual experience I have ever had. It has made me realize that there is life after death."[7]

In the words of His Holiness the Dalai Lama: "The basis on which Buddhists accept the concept of rebirth is principally the continuity of consciousness ... there is a constant cycle, in which the universe evolves and disintegrates, and then comes back again into being ..."

Attributes of Consciousness

Human life on planet earth is transitory; it lacks a sense of reality and permanency. It is totally illusory. The aggregates that generate human existence are subject to the laws of cause and effect, and hence undergo constant transformation. There is no permanency in their actions or existence. They are *anitya*, impermanent, devoid of 'self' and do not have an abiding principle. These are —

---

7. Grey Margot: *Return from Death: An Exploration of the Near-Death Experience*; London, 1985, p. 105.

- *Rupa*: the body, having the senses and the material form;
- *Vedana*: the feelings generated by the senses imparting exclusive personal experience;
- *Sanna*: the cognition, the ability to distinguish and classify experiences;
- *Sankhara*: the mental states that ignite and initiate the process for action and consequent experience;
- *Vijnana*: the consciousness, it is the vital element that provides a sense of awareness of sensory impulses and experiences.

Since it is assumed that there is no permanent 'self' or 'consciousness', it is one's karma, past or present, that dictate the course of existence and level of rebirth. It is not the 'self' but the karma that accompanies the Atma from one life to another, irrespective of the level of existence. It is not at all necessary that the rebirth shall take place only in the human realm. In fact that rarely happens; nor is it necessary that a male entity shall be reborn as a male. Far from it. There is no permanency of sex or format. In so far as Tibetan Buddhism is concerned, religion, race, region are not the attributes of the 'consciousness' that takes rebirth. These are all subject to change, guided by the laws of karma. What matters is the 'deeds' in the present existence, or left over debts of deeds from previous existence(s). The 'karma-yogi', the doer of deeds has no independent existence as such. However, it is incorrect to say that "there can be no psycho-mental element transmitted from one life to another" as mentioned in the '*World Religions: Comparative Analysis*'. Recent studies and experiments in the field of parapsychology to unravel the mysteries of the mind, the soul, life after death, influence of our past lives experiences on our present behaviour pattern, et al, have proved beyond any doubt that traces of one life are carried forward to the next: to what extent by which subjects? — that is a moot point since it is subjective in its essentials. Be that as it may, reincarnation in a human frame is a distinct possibility although this privilege may not be extended to all.[8]

---

8. One computer analysis has placed the odds in a time span of years at one against five followed by sixteen zeros. And this equals five million times the age of the universe.

Thubten Gyatso, the Thirteenth Dalai Lama on Throne

Norbulingka: The Summer Palace of Thirteenth Dalai Lama

Mind and body go hand in hand; however, according to Buddhist philosophy in some regions of existence 'beings' may have only minds, and no bodies. While mind is formless, both body and mind must have immediate source and they begin as soon as conception takes place. But mind cannot be a byproduct of the conception since matter cannot produce a formless entity; conversely, mind cannot produce matter. According to Buddhist beliefs, mind must be the byproduct of another mind that existed before conception took place. In other words, "mind must have continuity from a previous mind".[9] Hence there must be "successive rebirths that allow the continuum of mind to be there ... So there is no place given to a divine creator, nor to beings who are self-created; rather everything arises as a consequence of causes and conditions. In the case of mind and body, although one can affect the other, one cannot become the substance of the other". This in turn proves the existence of a past life. To carry the idea to its logical conclusion, there must also a future life. This thought process is the basis of Hindu and Buddhist belief in existence of life after death. On this basis one could even say that there is no death at all. It is merely a change of form of the being, as pointed out earlier in the shaloka from Gita.

Search for the Fourteenth Gyalwa Rinpoché

Thupten Gyatso, the Thirteenth Gyalwa Rinpoché, left for the heavenly fields on December 17, 1933. Like most others of his ilk, he knew in advance that his 'time' was approaching. Accordingly, he left his instructions and the testament for his people. Since he was aware of the impending disasters for his people, he wanted to be of help to them even after he had gone. Naturally, the first problem his people would face would be to locate his rebirth, his reincarnation — the direction, the compass point, in which to look for the location of his rebirth. He specifically indicated that rebirth would be in the East. All orthodox incarnate lamas sleep and die in a sitting posture,

9. Dalai Lama: *Autobiography*; p 236; and as quoted by Sogyal Rinpoché; p. 94.

facing southwards. But when his corpse was checked by monk-attendants, they were flabbergasted to observe that the head was no longer facing south; it had turned towards the north-east. They set the corpse right and resealed the mortal remains of the Divine. During another check some time later, a similar situation was encountered. During his lifetime, the Thirteenth had often expressed a desire to visit China. Coupled with the head turning east, it was a strong indication that rebirth would be in the eastern region. So it happened.

Soon a few more similar indications occurred. The Oracles of the "Three Pillars of State" also turned eastward and presented the traditional scarves. But the oracles are not the only institution of divining the future. Another coincidence was the growth of a huge star-shaped fungus on the east face of the pillar of the shrine in the Potala where the jewel-inlaid tomb for the departed god-king was under construction. In order to obtain a positively confirmed 'recognition', the entire force of Tibetan prognostic science is mobilized under the lama divinities. It encompasses forecasts by oracles, mathematical divination, dreams-interpretation, reading of visions, et al. All the prophecies may not tally, more so because the plurality of sources is bound to produce some contradictions. More weightage is therefore accorded to the prophecies made by the State Oracle of Nechung (Nai-Ch'ung) Monastery.[10]

Visionary Waters

Above all, there are a number of lakes in Tibet where, after appropriate prayers are offered, one can read one's future, read the visions predicting future events. However, sacred waters of the Lhamo Lhatso (Lha-Mo Nam-Tso) — an oval-shaped lake less than a mile in circumference situated about ninety miles southeast of Lhasa at an altitude of 17,000 feet — was believed to be Tibet's foremost visionary body of water in which the future could be seen. This sacred lake is specially noted as the favourite haunt of Pan-Dan Lha-Mo, the patron goddess of Gyalwa Rinpoché.

10. There was only one Lady State Oracle in Tibet. She lived with her husband, Senangse, at Tema in Drepung Monastery.

The image of this deity is installed in a temple on the shore of this Lake. It is believed that the best time to visit the Lake is the fourth month of the Tibetan year (roughly May), and the most auspicious day is the fifteenth of the month. Here intensive prayers are conducted before resorting to perceive the vision(s). Any 'Tarun, Deepak and Hari' (Indian version of Tom, Dick and Harry!) cannot see the visions; only the person(s) entitled to receive the visionary forecasts would get to see them; in this case it was the newly appointed Regent, Reting Rinpoché. Sometimes the visions may appear as letters of alphabet, and sometimes as pictures of places or future events. Sir Charles Bell was given the following description of the vision to be seen in the sacred waters of the Lake called Chö-kor-gye situated in Southern Tibet in which it is said to be possible to foresee future events:

> "The water of the lake is blue. You watch it from the hillside. A wind arises, and turns the blue water into white. A hole then forms in this white water, the hole is blue-black. Clouds form above this hole; and below the clouds you see images showing future events."[11]

The Regent went to the sacred Lake at Chokhorgyal in 1935, the Tibetan Wood Hog Year. After praying to the goddess for divine guidance and making sacrifices to appease the demon spirits, he squats, Buddha-style, alone on the banks of the holy water which lies in perfect tranquility.[12] Reting Rinpoché contemplated the serene surface of the water for the vision to appear. Soon he discerned three letters of Tibetan alphabet float into view: Ah, Ka and Ma besides an image of a great three-storied monastery, capped by gold and jade green rooftops from which a track led to a farmer's house with turquoise tiles.[13] The Regent's dream of the same farm house confirmed his vision. Incidentally, the Thirteenth had at one time stayed in this monastery and while passing by this house he had paused and remarked

---

11. Bell Charles, Sir: *Portrait of the Dalai Lama*; Collins, 1946, p. 41.
12. Shen Tsung-Lien: *Tibet and the Tibetans*; p. 91.
13. Dalai Lama: *My Land & My People*; p. 22.

how pretty the house was[14] — a contributory factor towards confirming the 'recognition'. This was a lucky day for the Regent. If the first attempt had failed, the entire procedure had to be repeated all over again. Tsepon W.D. Shakabpa, author of "*Tibet: A Political History*" was also a member of the same delegation. He has recorded: "I confess that I did not see any vision; ... Many people have told me that they have seen visions of their future in the sacred lake; others, like myself, have seen nothing at all ...."

The vision the Regent saw was letters of Tibetan alphabet; it might as well have been letters of Sanskrit alphabet, a religious symbol, a human figure, a scene, or whatever. A scribe was deputed to sit next to the Regent who dictated whatever he saw. That was the standard practice. And it was Top-Secret, according to military security classification. After the trance was over, he retired to his private quarters where, amidst constant invocations for divine guidance, he contemplated over the day's events carefully analyzing his perception of the vision, comparing it with previous prophecies and known relevant facts thereby weaving the entire data into a coherent whole. A mental picture of the country and its surroundings where the reincarnation was to be found was thus formed to enable further search and investigations.[15]

The Regent made his report to the National Assembly, which deputed three search-cum-reconnaissance parties across Eastern Tibet — one southeast to Dakpo, another to Chamdo, capital of the eastern province of Kham and the third to the northeastern region of Amdo. Each search party was headed by an incarnate lama and a high-ranking lay official representing the religious and secular communities of the country. The two heads of the search parties were thoroughly briefed about the habits, life style, physical marks on the body, etc., of the previous incarnation. Thus briefed and furnished, the search parties set out on this 'singular adventure of god-quest' the Tibetans call 'making the recognition'. "According to Buddhist theory, every being possesses three outlets of expression, namely, body, speech and mind. Each of these may

14. Grunfeld: op. cit. p.11.

15. Shen Tsung-Lien: op. cit. pp. 91-92.

take a separate incarnation." The birth of Gautama Buddha himself is shrouded in prophecy. His mother, Queen Maya saw in a dream that a white elephant was descending from heaven. When she gave birth to Sakya-Muni, she was picking up an olive branch. Legend has it that the new born baby immediately rose to his feet and walked seven paces towards each point of compass, exclaiming: "This is my last reincarnation". The baby was named Siddhartha. Again, legend has it that it was prophesied to Siddhartha's father that his new born son was destined for great things — a conqueror of empires, or to become a Buddha?

Thus there were three main incarnations of Gautama Buddha — Incarnation of the 'Body', Incarnation of the 'Speech' and Incarnation of the 'Mind'. The last named is the most important and that is what, Cha-ne Dorje of the mind, the Dalai Lama is said to be incarnated from; Jam-pe-yang of the speech is supposed to be found in the Chinese emperor but that is considered most doubtful.[16] The Cha-na Dorje incarnation is usually held to be in the Panchen Lama.[17]

It is the 'incarnation of the mind' that is the true reincarnation, and that is what the search parties are really looking for. They have therefore to be extremely careful in making their selection. The final confirmation of the true incarnation comes from the distinguishing marks on the body of the young boy that would distinguish the incarnation of the four handed Chenrezi from ordinary mortals. Some or all these signs could be:

- Large ears.
- Two pieces of flesh, like moles on his torso under his arms, near the shoulder-blades indicating the place where his previous arms are supposed to have been — Chenrezi is depicted as having large ears and four arms, the moles replacing the second pair of arms.

---

16. There is a certain contradiction in this regard. While generally the Dalai Lama is accepted as Incarnation of the Mind of the Buddha, Sir Charles Bell says on page 131 of his book, *Tibet: Past & Present,* "The Dalai Lama is the Incarnation of the Body."

17. Bell Charles, Sir: op. cit. p. 132.

- An imprint like a conch-shell on one of the palms of his hands.
- Marks as of a tiger-skin on his legs.
- Eyes and eyebrows that curve upwards on the outside and are rather long.

It is not necessary that every Reincarnation must bear all the above signs. For instance, the Thirteenth Dalai Lama had the first three signs on his body before he was recognized as the Reincarnation. Further, when he used to bless the pilgrims, people around him used to find it difficult to look him in the face since an unearthly light used to emanate from his countenance.

Once again, this business of birth-marks is no fairy-tale. Thousands of cases of children having birth-marks at the site of previous mortal wounds; children speaking foreign languages to which they had no exposure at all in their new incarnation; some same children knowing where treasured objects were hidden or buried some thousands of miles away, decades or centuries earlier — such case-studies have been scientifically investigated and recorded. Therefore, there is no reason to doubt the Tibetan version of such instances. In fact, we have proof of this phenomenon right from Dalai Lama himself — His baby brother died when he was only two years old. It is customary amongst the Tibetans to consult the lamas and astrologers before a funeral. Some times even oracles are also consulted. In the present case his parents were advised that the baby's body should not be buried or cremated; it should be preserved so that he may reborn in the same house. "As proof, a small mark was to be made on the body with a smear of butter. This was done, and in due course my mother had another baby boy — her last child. And when he was born, the pale mark was seen on the spot of his body where the butter had been smeared. He was the same being, born again in a new body ..." Unbelievable; an enigma indeed! But it must be true, for the simple reason that His Holiness the Dalai Lama himself has vouched for the incident.[18]

---

18. Dalai Lama: *Autobiography,* pp. 52-53.

The Village and House of the High Incarnation

After six months of strenuous efforts, Kewtsang Rimpoché, the high Lama of Sera monastery saw in Kumbum a replica of the monastery of Reting's vision. The party examined a number of potential candidates and finally hit upon a boy in a small farming village of Taktser, two days east of Kumbum. Taktser is in Dokham district: Do means the lower part of a valley and Kham is the eastern region of Tibet inhabited by a distinctive race of Tibetans called Khampas. The high mountain to the south of village was considered abode of the guardian deity of the place whose natural beauty, a feast to the eyes, provided the backdrop for the monastery of Karma Shar Tsong Ridro, a famous place in the religious history of Tibet. It was founded by Karma Rolpai Dorje, the fourth reincarnation of Karma-pa, the very first incarnation recognized in Tibet. The great reformer Tsongkhapa was initiated as a monk in this small beautiful monastery. Lower down was the still smaller, but perhaps more magnificent monastery of Amdo Jhakera with its emblem of Dharma Chakra (Wheel of Religion) supported by deer of copper and gold on either side. Prayer flags fluttered all over the houses and the two monasteries. The present Dalai Lama, the Fourteenth in the Line, came from these surroundings. May He live long to see emancipation of Tibet from the Chinese yoke!

Meanwhile, the Seventh Panchen Lama gave a helping hand in the matter. It may be recalled that the Fifth Dalai Lama had bestowed the monastery of Trashilhünpo on his learned teacher, the Panchen Lama, as a living and declared him an incarnation of Ö-pa-me. Unfortunately, this gesture of gratitude on the part of the Fifth led to constant struggle for power between the two highest incarnations, which the Chinese have exploited to the hilt. However, a detailed discussion of this problem, or the forays of Gusri Khan and the devastation caused by his forces right up to Shigatse, are beyond the scope of this work. Suffice is to say that in 1642 the Fifth was led in State to Shigatse and enthroned in the audience hall of the palace while Gusri Khan and Sonam Chospel sat on thrones a little lower than the Dalai

Lama. The Khan then offered Mendel Tensum consisting of a gold image of Buddha, a book of scriptures, and a small Chörten (stupa) representing the body, the speech and the mind of the Buddha respectively. The Khan then declared the Dalai Lama as the Supreme authority over all of Tibet from Tachienlu (Kanting) in the east to the Ladakh border in the west. In other words, Gusri Khan conquered Tibet with his own forces but gave it as a gift to the Fifth Dalai Lama. Hereafter, it was his responsibility to militarily defend Tibet and to protect the person and authority of His Holiness. Thus his position was equivalent to that of "Defender of the Faith".[19]

The direct teachings of Buddha are enshrined in the *Kagyur.* This is a collection of some eighty-four thousand discourses on ethics, philosophy, morality, discipline and administration. This was the law for the Buddhist Church and instructions for the lay to be imbibed by the people according to their capacity and level of intellect. The *Kagyur* also embodies some explanatory expositions given by the chosen disciples of Lord Buddha. It includes the Four Great Tantras — the Tantra of Activity, the Tantra of Application, the Tantra of Perfection and the Tantra of Perfection Supreme.[20] While the *Kagyur* is the basic canonical scripture, a number of intellectuals-philosophers, both Indian and Tibetans, have written voluminous commentaries to elaborate on the basic teachings. These are embodied in the *Tangyur,* which is next in importance and sanctity to the *Kagyur.* There are two hundred and twentyfive volumes that comprise the *Tangyur,* which were compiled over a period of decades, if not centuries. Every monk had to master these basic scriptures before he could undertake the study of Tantras. The extent of study and mental effort involved in the process is in itself sufficient indication of the intellectual advancement of a monk to rise to the level of a Lama.

The digression aside: meanwhile the Panchen Lama had been making his own enquiries and, while on his death-bed, he

19. Petech L.: *China and Tibet in the Early 18th Century;* Leiden, 1950, pp. 219-221.

20. Norbu Jigme Thubten: op.cit. p. 310

had drawn the attention of the leader of the official Delegation to the small boy from Lönpa whose mother had brought the child to be blessed by the Panchen Lama. The child had got hold of the tassel with which the Panchen used to bless the people, and would not let it go. He too therefore suggested to investigate the boy from Tengster, a pasture land for the bigger neighbouring village of Balangsta besides two others boys. In Tibet of yore, even infants were imbued with the spirit of religion. They enjoyed playing in the area where emblems of the Three Jewels were installed — Buddha, Dharma and Sanga.

The search for the Fourteenth Dalai Lama was a very delicate matter of great national significance. It required a high degree of integrity, conscientiousness and discretion. The Government Delegation comprised of about forty members under the joint leadership of a high ecclesiastical and a high lay official, Kyetsang Rimpoché and Künsangtse Dzasa, respectively. This Delegation operated from Kumbum for nearly two years in its search for the true incarnation of Chenrezi. Absolute secrecy was of the utmost importance. Therefore, a small investigating team comprising of Kyetsang Rinpoché and three others disguised themselves as merchants on a business trip. On the pretext of brewing some tea, they gained entry into the kitchen.[21] One thing led to another. Then they asked for permission to stay overnight in the house, which was readily granted. It was a single-storey square building with a courtyard in the middle. The lower part of the house was built in stone and the upper part of earth. The edges of the flat roof were lined with turquoise tiles. The main gate faced south and its top was decorated in traditional manner with spears and flags. A tall pole in the middle of the courtyard had a large prayer flag fluttering in the air. A Tibetan mastiff guarded the front gate. Horses, mules and cattle were kept in a yard at the back of the house. The cattle were eight cows and seven dzomos, a cross between a yak and a cow.[22] The house had no windows or openings on the outside

21. The servants generally sleep in the kitchen

22. Yak means a male animal, like the bull; the female of the species is called dri.

walls. However, there were two chimneys and three air-holes in the roof. The bizarre shape of wooden-gutter pipes from the roof was the subject of special attention since the Regent had also perceived similar gutters in his vision on the sacred waters of Lake Lhamo-Lhatso.

It was a simple happy rural family, contented and in peace.

They played with the little Boy for a long time, and indirectly interrogated him in detail in his home. Lama Kewtsang Rinpoché of Sera Monastery was dressed in poor clothes disguised as a servant. The person who was disguised as the master was conducted to the main house while others were shown the servants' quarters. The Lama was wearing a rosary that belonged to the Thirteenth Gyalwa Rinpoché. The little boy seemed to recognize the rosary and wanted to have it. The Lama promised to give it to him if he could guess who he was. The boy promptly replied that he was Sera-aga, "a lama of Sera". The Lama asked who the master was, and the boy gave the name of Losang. He also knew the name of who the real servant was: Amdo Kasang. And next morning when the party was getting ready to go, the Boy insisted on going with them. Since an Incarnate Lama of Kumbum monastery had recently died, the villagers assumed that the visitors were looking for his incarnation; nobody at all suspected that they had the Supreme Incarnation in their midst.[23]

> "It is common for small children who are reincarnations to remember objects and people from their previous lives. Some can also recite the scriptures although they have not yet been taught them.[24] ... The visitors were convinced that the reincarnation had been found .... They believed that the first letter, Ah, stood for Amdo, which was the name of our district. Ka could have stood for Kumbum, which was one of the largest monasteries

23. Dalai Lama: *Autobiography;* pp. 22-23.
24. Dr. Ian Stevenson, M.D., Professor of Psychiatry at the University of Virginia has collected numberous case-studies of children who exhibited xenoglossy, the ability to speak a foreign language to which they were never exposed.

> in the neighborhood, and the one which the Regent had seen in the vision; or the two letters Ka and Ma might have signified the monastery of Karma Rolpai Dorje on the mountain above the village."[25]

All the details were reported to Lhasa by telegram. There was only one telegraph line in Tibet, from Lhasa to India. Therefore, the message had to be sent in code from Sining through China and India; and by the same route an order came back to bring the Boy at once to the Holy City.

'Final Recognition': Tenzin Gyatso

The technique of identifying the reincarnation of Dalai Lama is so well documented and, perhaps equally well known too, that the details regarding the child-to-be—The Dalai making a correct choice between the original and exact duplicate personal possessions of the departed Dalai, etc. — like the rosary, walking stick, silver pencil, damru,[26] spectacles, eating bowls, speaking in the Lhasa dialect, addressing the disguised Lama that he was a Lama from Lhasa, et al — need not be gone into here. Suffice would be to say that Lhamo Döndrub easily managed to convince Kyetsang Rinpoché, and other members of the Delegation that he was the true incarnation, after which the boy from Lönpa was no longer on the short list. Early next morning the Rinpoché quietly left the house without even thanking and taking leave of the hosts for their hospitality. Secrecy had to be maintained at all costs, but the cat was out of the bag soon thereafter with rumours of all sorts spreading around the countryside. Since the area where the family of the Fourteenth Gyalwa Rinpoché lived was then under Chinese control, the Moslem Governor of the area, Mapufang, had to be consulted. He twice summoned all the three boys who were short-listed and decided to make a test of his own. He offered a box of sweets to all three. One took a handful while another was scared to take any, but Döndrub took only one and ate it discreetly. The Governor knew who the right boy was. He

25. Dalai Lama: *Autobiography;* pp. 23-24

26. A damru is crafted from two half skulls.

presented a roll of cloth to the parents of other boys and sent them home while Döndrub was ordered to be placed in Kumbum Monastery which was in Chinese territory. The responsibility for looking after the Reincarnation now fell on the shoulders of the elder brother Norbu who was a monastic student there.[27]

There is a widespread superstition in Tibet that before a high incarnate lama is reborn, the district where he is born will undergo suffering and hardship. The crops in Taktser failed for four years before Döndrub was born. The Family itself went through hard times. Many cattle and horses died. His father also fell seriously ill before the child was born. However, as soon the Dalai Lama-to-be was born, his father suddenly became perfectly alright.[28]

The Chinese Governor Mapufang demanded his pound of flesh before he would let Döndrub leave for Lhasa. His appetite grew manifold after he received the initial ransom of one hundred thousand Chinese dollars. He demanded a further sum of three hundred thousand Chinese dollars. The problem had to be referred to Lhasa and it could be done only by sending message by courier. It took months to get an answer from Lhasa. But that large sum of money could not be raised locally. The delegation from Lhasa had to borrow the money from some Moslem merchants going to Lhasa to settle with the Governor. Before letting the Boy be taken to Lhasa, Mapufang demanded that a senior official be left behind as hostage for a set of scriptures written in gold, and a complete set of Thirteenth Dalai Lama's clothes be sent to Kumbum Monastery. All this was also agreed. At last, the Incarnate Dalai Lama, born into a poor farming family at dawn on 5th Day of the 5th month of the Wood-Hog Year corresponding to 6th July 1935 as the third male child, left for the Sacred City a week after his fourth birthday.[29] The caravan included Döndrub's family including his elder brothers Gyelo Thondup who was nine and Losang Samten who was six, the search party and the Moslem pilgrims on their long and perilous journey to Mecca for Haj. There were neither

27. Dalai Lama: *Autobiography*, p. 25.

28. Ibid; p.26.

29. Sixth month of the Earth Hare Year corresponding to 1939.

roads nor carriages in Tibet at that time. So the youngsters rode in a palanquin called a treljam which is attached to two poles and is carried on two mules. The journey took three months and thirteen days. Meanwhile the National Assembly had issued a Proclamation declaring Döndrub's as the Fourteenth Dalai Lama. The caravan consisting of about fifty people and 350 horses and mules was ceremoniously brought to Lhasa in 1939 and Döndrub installed as the Fourteenth Dalai Lama with great pomp and show.[30] The main functions and the events preceding it came as an unbelievable surprise to his parents. The Tibetan band played the British anthem learnt from their British instructors: "God Save the King"! Thus a poor farmer-family child, Lhamo Döndrub, became the God-King. Regent Reting shaved the child's head before the image of Lord Buddha in the Jokhang temple and renamed the boy Jetsun Jamphel Ngawang Lobsang Yeshi Tenzin Gyatso — Holy Lord, Gentle Glory, Eloquent, Compassionate, Learned Defender of the Faith, Ocean of Wisdom — in short, Tenzin Gyatso. Meanwhile, the hostage taken by Mapufang also managed to escape his clutches.

Reting Conspiracy

As advised by the State astrologers, the Regent in consultation with the National Assembly had fixed the date for the ceremony of Sitringasol, enthronement of the Gyalwa Rinpoché on the Lion Throne, for the fourteenth day of the first month of the Iron-Dragon year corresponding to the year 1940. Telegraphic invitations were issued to the governments of China, India, King of Nepal and Maharajas of Bhutan and Sikkim.

The ceremony was held in the Si-Shi-Phuntsok, the Hall of All Good Deeds of the Spiritual and Temporal Worlds, in the eastern part of the Potala Palace. The Lion Throne, Sengtri, was built as laid down in the scriptures — square shaped made of gilded wood supported by eight lions, carved from gilded wood, two in each corner. Five square cushions covered in brocade of different shades raised the height of the seat for the child-king by about 7-8 feet. A small table in front held all the seals of office of the Dalai Lama.

30. Dalai Lama: *Autobiography*; pp. 27-28.

The ceremony was long, at times rather frustratingly so, but the child Dalai Lama conducted himself with patience and dignity throughout as if he was used to such reverence and state-ceremonials. After the Dalai Lama was offered droma, a sweet-tasting herb, in a small golden cup and saucer, the retainers offered the same to other guests. This is part of every ceremony in Tibet. Strict protocol was observed throughout. Before presentation of seals of office, the Regent offered Mendel Tensum on behalf of the Government of Tibet. "This was an elaborate emblem of the universe, held on one side by a member of the Cabinet and on the other by the Official Abbot .... After a long search and in consultation with the oracles and high lamas, I was being installed by the Government and the people of the Tibet as the spiritual and temporal ruler of the State ...."[31] Presentation of Golden Wheel and White Conch, the symbols of spiritual and temporal power, came next followed by eight symbols[32] of happiness and prosperity and seven symbols of royalty. The final act of the drama was the presentation of seals of office conveying formal recognition of the four-and half years old Boy as the Fourteenth Gyalwa Rinpoché, the spiritual and Temporal Ruler of Tibet.

The composure of the young Boy Dalai Lama throughout the proceedings was indeed remarkable.

Soon after the death of the XIII Gyalwa Rinpoché, Reting Rinpoché was selected as Regent by lottery. Reting was highly intelligent, progressive minded and a capable administrator; but he was barely twenty when he assumed the Regency, much too young for such a high level job. And he happened to be in poor health — catarrh was his main malady which was further aggravated by his habit of taking snuff, a mixture of strong tobacco diluted with powdered yak dung. He had a weakness for stylish living and dresses which became the envy of his colleagues. His living quarters in Lhasa were decorated with exquisite taste in royal style. He was

---

31. Dalai Lama: *Autobiography*; p. 42.
32. The wheel; the fish; the conch shell; the vase and the flower; the umbrella; the prayer banner; and the woven symbol of the Eight, the Palbu.

always impeccably dressed in robes of the finest yellow silk. To cap it all, he devoted much of his time to financial pursuits rather than to day to day matters of governance. He was therefore under considerable pressure by the nobility to mend his ways. And his poor health made the situation intolerable. Finally, he consulted the Nechung Oracle who advised him to take a break, devote himself to prayer and meditation for some time. Accordingly, Reting resigned his job as Regent and handed over reins of government to his spiritual master, an elderly Lama Taktra Rinpoché who assumed office in 1941 on the clear understanding that Reting would take over again after he returns from his spell of solitude in the mountains. However, when the time came for Taktra to vacate the chair for Reting, he declined to do so.

Reformists and modernists were in for bad times, particularly after the terrifying downfall of Lungshar. It was discovered in 1947,[33] rightly or wrongly, that Reting Rinpoché was plotting a coup d'état against the Government. The powers that be decided to depute Lhalu, one of the senior officials along with another, to arrest Reting who had wielded so much power for so long during all these years of minority of Tenzin Gyatso. Arriving at the Sera monastery, they prostrated before the Rinpoché — that was absolutely obligatory. The Rinpoché blessed Lhalu without the least inkling of what was in store for him. Perhaps, he was absolutely innocent! Meanwhile, a member of the military escort caught hold of Reting at the ankle, dragged him down and informed him that he would have to come with them to Lhasa. Reting was thus arrested on April 15 for having masterminded the evil act of sending a hand grenade-bomb to Taktra's office where a servant was killed while opening the package.

Back in Lhasa, Reting was charged with plotting against the Government by secretly obtaining weapons and troops from the Kuomintang with a view to overthrow the regime of Gyalwa

---

33. It may be recalled that in 1947, India's year of Independence, the free and sovereign nation of Tibet had sent delegates to the Asian Conference organized by the Indian National Congress Party. They held talks with Mahatma Gandhi and Pandit Nehru.

Rinpoché. As soon as the news spread in Sera, there was a resurrection amongst the monks of the Sera monastery's Che (Je) College. They were in a riotous mood. A number of people were killed and the abbot of Sera's Che College was chased across the roof and stabbed to death by his own monk. A mini-civil war had started. The Tibetan army units with their artillery were mobilized. The English radio operator, Reg Fox, who had married a Tibetan lady and settled down in Tibet, helped the Tibetan soldier in loading and firing the cannons. His experience as a gunner during the First World War proved handy. In the battle that followed, three hundred monks and fifteen soldiers were killed before Sera capitulated. Order was once again restored. Reting was put in a cell where he died a gruesome death under rather mysterious circumstances. A subsequent enquiry did not find any foul play in Reting's death and the matter was closed. The twelve years old Gyalwa Rinpoché, Tenzin Gyatso, felt deep anguish for his old master who was not only instrumental in his cognition but had also been responsible for his upbringing and training as the God-King.

5

British Military Expeditions

By the middle of the nineteenth century the British were in firm control of Assam. Under the Charter Act of 1853 Bengal, Bihar, Orissa and Assam were placed under a separate Lieutenant Governor in April 1854. This ensured centralized control of strategic areas of Himalayan foothills. By this action, the British achieved political consolidation besides freeing the Governor General to devote more attention to the larger interests of the Empire. Having established secure bases in the plains of Bengal-Assam the British were on the lookout for lucrative trade opportunities with Tibet and beyond to Central Asia. Meanwhile, the end of Third Anglo-Chinese War was formalized during Chefoo[1] Convention by conclusion of an agreement on September 13, 1876 thereby avoiding the risk of another war between the British and the Chinese. The Chefoo Agreement was divided into three parts, but the part relating to Tibet came under a separate article which, *inter alia*, provided for a British Mission of Exploration to travel to Tibet by way of Peking, or Szechuan, for which the Manchu Government would grant the necessary permission and assistance. Peking also undertook to write to the Chinese Amban

1. Chefoo was a summer resort in Shantung, China. The participants in the Convention held in August 1876 included representatives from Great Britain, Russia, Germany, United States, Spain, France, and Austria-Hungary. They were there as much for business as for pleasure.

in Lhasa to render all possible help to the proposed expedition. However, if the British Mission decided to travel to Tibet from the Indian side, necessary passports etc. would be issued and the Manchu Resident in Tibet would provide necessary assistance. However, the Government of Tibet openly repudiated any suggestions of Chinese suzerainty over Tibet.[2]

First Armed Clash in the High Himalayas

When the contents of the Chefoo Agreement and the Article regarding Tibet became public knowledge, the Tibetan National Assembly, the Tsongdu, categorically declared that the Emperor of China had no authority to permit any one to enter Tibet without prior concurrence of the Government of Tibet. So the British were turned back and the Chinese Government had to cut a sorry figure. However, to assuage the British bruised ego, the Chinese recognized the British unilateral-illegal annexation of Burma. The British greed for territorial aggrandizement was still not satisfied and they went ahead to build a rest-house — locally known as a dak-bungalow — at Kobuk, near Dzelep-la, a border mountain-pass between Sikkim and Tibet. In accordance with the traditional boundary, Kobuk was accepted to lie in Tibetan territory, but the British insisted otherwise and persisted on going ahead with the project. Since the Tibetans wanted to avoid a dispute on a minor point of un-demarcated border, they established a check post in 1887 at Lungthur, further inside Tibet, manned by one officer and twenty soldiers. Although the check post was within Tibetan territory, the British raised objection and complained to the Manchu Emperor that the Tibetans were building aggressive fortifications on the Indo-Tibetan border! They also issued an ultimatum to Lhasa to remove the check post by March 15, 1888, failing which they would take military action to evict the Tibetans. The long and the short of this episode was a disastrous military action on March 21, 1888, in which the Tibetans suffered

2. In 1878 the Russian explorer, Prjevalsky, was issued a passport by the Chinese Government to visit Lhasa. The Tibetan Government refused to accept the validity of that passport and did not allow the Russian to enter Tibet.

heavy losses in men, and whatever little material they had. It is noteworthy that this was the first time in the history of Tibet that they had clashed with the army of a Western power and suffered a humiliating defeat. Unfortunately, it was Sikkim that suffered most in this unequal clash of arms. The class composition of Sikkim being what it was, and ruler being of Tibetan stock, the British took full advantage of local discontent which they themselves fomented through their intrigues, and the British army occupied Gangtok, the capital of Sikkim. The Sikkim royal family underwent many humiliating experiences in their efforts to find asylum. Finally, they were arrested by the Nepalese Army under instructions from the British Indian Government, and handed over to Indian police who imprisoned them at Kurseong in 1893 where they stayed for more than two years. To cut the long story short, the Viceroy and Governor General of India, Lord George Nathaniel Curzon directed that let bygones be bygones and reinstated Thuthop Namgyal who returned to his capital as the ruler on the ninth day of the ninth month of the Wood-Sheep year (1895) subject, of course, to severe restrictions on his powers as the ruler.

British Penetration into Bhutan

While Sikkim was already in the bag, Bhutan was getting ripe to be plucked. Sometime during 1860 a sort of civil war was going on in Bhutan. The Ruler approached the British for assistance while the rival faction requested the Dalai Lama to intercede on their behalf. As usual, the British were fast and the first to react. They soon brought the situation under control. Since there was a proposal by the British to construct a road through Bhutan to connect with Tibet,[3] and also station a permanent representative in the Bhutanese capital, an amicable agreement could not be arrived at. After five long years of frustrating negotiations it was agreed, during the administration of Khenrab Wangchuk (1864-72), that neither a road would be constructed through Bhutan, nor would the British interfere in the internal affairs of Bhutan in any way whatsoever. The British also agreed to pay Bhutan two

3. The valley of the mighty Brahmaputra was, and still is, the only natural alignment for a highway connecting Tibet with India.

hundred thousand rupees for rights to certain forested areas for setting up timber factories. It was generally felt that the agreement was fair enough to all the three parties, namely, Tibet, Bhutan and the British-Indian Government. The Tibetan Government therefore did not raise any objections to the arrangement. However, the resultant peace within opposing factions of Bhutan proved transitory and civil disorders once again broke out in 1885. The ruler sent representatives of rival parties, Alu Dorje and Gongzim Tamdin, to Lhasa requesting the Dalai Lama to mediate in the dispute. At first the Dalai Lama was averse to getting involved for the simple reason that the Government of Tibet had agreed to the British suggestion of non-interference in the internal affairs of Bhutan by either party. However, since it was a request for mediation, the Dalai Lama reluctantly agreed, and succeeded in bringing the dispute to an amicable settlement.

Political Background[4]

The Twelfth Dalai Lama died in 1875. A Regent assumed power. The Regent and a college of ranking incarnate lamas, in a joint session, consulted the State Oracle of Nechung whose pronouncements were given the highest credence. He declared that the true incarnation could only be discovered by a monk of purest morals — specifically by a saintly lama of the Ganden monastery known as Shar-tse Khempo. As advised by the State Oracle, the Ganden Lama accompanied by several Doctors of Divinity visited the Lake known as 'The Wheel of Religion'. It was near a village south-east of Lhasa. A wind arose and dispersed the snow, leaving the ice clear before the Lama, who had his observation post on a nearby hilltop. Then he looked into it, as if he was looking into a glass sheet. He saw the image of the house and the land around it. He also saw a peach-tree in flower, several months out of season for peach blossom. That night in a

4. This part is based on the following literature:
   - *Tibetan Wars through Sikkim, Nepal and Bhutan* by Colonel M.N. Gulati; Manas Publications, New Delhi, 2003.
   - *Rediscovering Bhutan*; Ibid, 2003.
   - * *Tibet: A Political History*, by Tsepon W.D. Shakabpa, London, 1967.

dream he saw a vision of a baby boy about two years old in his mother's lap. The Ganden Lama went to the village a few days later and saw exactly the same house that he had seen in the vision, with the peach tree and the baby boy in his mother's arms. The face of the baby boy was exactly the same as he had seen in the vision and in his dream. The birth place was located at Thakpo Langdun in southeast Tibet where a boy had been born on May 27, 1876 who was eventually declared the Thirteenth Dalai Lama.[5] The Panchen Lama named him Thupten Gyatso. He was enthroned in 1879. It will thus be seen that the Dalai Lama was separated from his parents in infancy. He was brought up by his priest-servants. His mother, or any other woman, played no part in his upbringing, although in a Tibetan household the women are all important and it is they who tend the family-shrine. The Master of the Bedchamber took his mother's place. He fondled him in his arms and looked after him in every way. The same held good for his early education too. The Master of the Bedchamber gave him his first education. No wonder he was so learned! Besides the Master of Bedchamber, the other personal attendants[6] of the Dalai Lama were:

- Chief Butler who laid the food before the High Lama after tasting some himself;
- Court Chaplain who presented food offerings to the deities on behalf of the Dalai Lama;
- Master of the Kitchen;
- Chief Physician;
- The "All Covering Abbot" so called because he was the head of all priest officials.

The Needle of Suspicion

The British Indian Government deputed Sarat Chandra Das assisted by a Sikkimese lama, Ugyen Gyatso, to carry out

5. Bell Charles Sir: *Portrait of the Dalai Lama,* London, 1946, p. 41.
6. Ibid; p. 47

geographical surveys in Tibet in the guise of Buddhist pilgrims. During his stay in Tibet for more than two years, 1881-1883, he managed to collect valuable data about important topographical features in Tibet. The Government issued orders for arrest of the party but they managed to escape taking with them the valuable data about what was otherwise a closed country. The local Tibetans who had given shelter and assistance to the surveyors were suitably punished. There were a few more dare-devils like the famous Nain Singh and his others code-named companions whose efforts were put together to prepare a workable map of Tibet, and approach routes to the forbidden land. Spying remains spying, whatever the motive or technique. Consequently, the Tibetan government became suspicious and cautious in their approach towards the British-Indian Government. Moreover, the traders turned robbers and rulers had already given the British a bad name in political relationships. In fact, the Tibetans had more than one good reason to keep the British at more than an arm's length. As for the British, export of Indian tea from Bengal-Assam to Tibet, China and other parts of Central Asia was the central issue. But this was vehemently opposed by the Chinese for the simple reason that export of Chinese tea to Tibet from Szechwan province alone was to the tune of two million lbs. valued at about one million taels (250,000 pounds sterling) generating revenue of about 150,000 taels. Leaving aside the economic issue, it was also the question of loss of employment to a large number of porters besides creating resentment amongst the monks and monasteries who controlled the tea trade in Tibet. Tea-trade was indeed the crux of the problem.

Sometime during the middle of the nineteenth century the British had connived at making Ladakh a dependency of the Kashmir State, nominally independent but practically under British colonial rule. To sprinkle salt on the injured Tibetan ego, they detached Lahaul and Spiti from Ladakh and merged these territories in British Indian administrative units. Sikkim and Bhutan had lost their sovereign status and had become puppets in the political dramatics of the British. These two territorial units were the gateway to Tibet, straight to Lhasa, from the hot and humid plains of

India. The Government of Tibet had indeed strong reasons to be wary of any British advances from that direction. Moreover, this part of the Himalayan belt was part of ethnographic Tibet; and that was all the more reason for Tibetan reluctance to have anything to do with the British. In short, the British were not only dishonest in their approach towards the frontier areas, but territorial aggrandizement appeared to be their ultimate objective — expansion of the British Empire, its territorial integrity and safety, by hook or crook. To add fuel to the fire, the British occupied the former Gorkha territory of Almora, and sometime later tricked Sikkim into 'leasing' Darjeeling to the British. Soon, they stopped paying rent for the lease, and merged Darjeeling and adjoining areas into British administered territories.[7] The British actions were painted as innocent attempts at stabilizing the Himalayan frontiers as well as to keep away the Russian politico-spiritual connection at a safe distance from Tibet. But the British garb of deceit was much too transparent to escape a discerning eye, more so in the light of their having grabbed the entire Indian sub-continent under similar pretexts of trade and security.

Lest the situation get out of hand, the British decided to apply some soothing balm to bruised Sikkimese ego. The Political Officer in Sikkim, Colonel F.M. Bailey and Mr. Ashley Eden were deputed to hold a border-meeting with the ruler who happened to be away to Chumbi in Tibet — or was it a diplomatic move? He was therefore represented by his eldest son, Sekyong Trulku, who was handed over a twenty-three point agreement for acceptance in toto. The Agreement stipulated, amongst other conditions, that Tibet would not be permitted to interfere in the affairs of Sikkim and the Ruler would not stay in Tibet. If yes: the British would return the six occupied districts and resume payments for Darjeeling including the arrears. By this time Chagdor Namgyal, the Sikkimese ruler, was tired of British shenanigans. He abdicated in favour of

7. A Sikkimese official, Trokhang Dronyer who opposed this deceitful usurpation of his country's territory had to flee for his life and seek asylum in Tibet where the Government granted him an official status and an estate for a living — Shakabpa; op. cit. p. 196.

his eldest son citing old age as the reason. Soon after Sekyong Trulku assumed power, the British resumed payment of rent for Darjeeling and in 1868 they voluntarily raised the payment by three thousand rupees. However, in the same year, Sekyong Trulku, having reigned for seven years abdicated in favour of his younger brother, Thuthop Namgyal.

Younghusband Military Expedition[8]

Lord Curzon's Policies

Right from 1774 when the British made their earliest attempt to woo the Tibetans for trade route concessions, the latter resented these overtures, politely and consistently. Curzon strongly believed that the so- called Chinese suzerainty over Tibet was a mere 'constitutional fiction', a make-believe drama played out by either party as a matter of mutual convenience. His conviction in this belief grew all the more stronger when he found it virtually impossible to deal with Tibet through the Manchu Emperor, or his Amban in Lhasa. The Tibetans would just not respond to any written communication from the British Indian Government; in fact, they would not even receive any such communication from the British. Since Lhasa would not depute an authorized representative, no substantive discussion could be held either. Curzon's inability to penetrate the Tibetan wall of silence multiplied his impotent anger, all the more so when reports reached him that the Russians were having a hey-day in their dealings with the Tibetans. The veracity of these reports hardly mattered to the biased British mind and pre-conceived ideas about the strategic interests of Russia. The resultant frustration became unbearable for the British ego. Therefore, in June 1903, Curzon dispatched a British mission to Khamba D'zong, within Tibetan territory, under the leadership of Major (later Colonel) Francis Younghusband along with a suitable military escort. The objective of the British Mission was to open trade

8. This portion is largely a summary of chapters 6 and 7 of *Tibetan Wars*: op. cit. pp. 224-323, supplemented with excerpts from *Tibet: A Political History*: op. cit. and *India And Tibet* by Francis Younghusband.

negotiations, but the size of the escort — five officers and seven hundred troops — and the venue selected for negotiations were highly provocative, besides being altogether unwarranted.

The Tibetan representatives requested that the negotiations be held at the border village of Giagong. The British declined and continued to march ahead to Khamba D'zong, well within Tibetan territory. Since Khamba D'zong was under the local jurisdiction of the Tashilhunpo monastery, a representative of Panchen Lama and the Abbot of the monastery were deputed by Lhasa to meet the British Mission to persuade them to withdraw from Tibetan territory; but all in vain. However, shortly thereafter, the British voluntarily withdrew from Khamba D'zong to their base in Sikkim. Meanwhile, there were internal differences between the Kashag (the Cabinet) and the Tsongdu (the National Assembly) as to the strategy to be adopted to deal with the British. As usual, the State Oracle was consulted. Some ministers were imprisoned; but the stalemate continued. While the Kashag was in favour of a negotiated settlement, the Tsongdu, perhaps out of sheer ignorance as to the might of the British arms, resolved to fight to the last. In the light of the ancient Prophecy on record, as well as the faith reposed by Tibetans in predictions made by oracles, astrological-planetary influences, et al, the latter approach did not make any sense at all. For all practical purposes, it was an invitation to suicidal disaster. And so the inevitable did happen; it was destined to happen.

Peace Mission or Military Invasion

Towards the end of 1903, John Claude White, the British Political Officer in Sikkim, informed the Government of Tibet that the Younghusband Mission was on its way to Gyantse[9]

---

9. Gyantse is the main wool-trading centre. Caravans bring loads of soft wool of the valley sheep, and coarser wool of the mountain sheep. Some of the finest woolen cloth of Tibet is made here, besides blankets for which they use goat and yak hair. The colourful woolens that we see Tibetans wearing are dyed from natural sources such as grass, roots, bark of trees, stone and earth, but the sophisticated products were dyed with materials imported from India and China.

where a responsible Tibetan official having authority to negotiate should meet with him. On the British side it was no longer a 'Mission'; that was a euphemism for a military expedition of substantial strength. In December 1903 a properly organized military expeditionary force, a brigade group worth of troops, having about five thousand Sikh and Gorkha troops with a sprinkling of a few British gunners, armed with rifles, machine guns and artillery, arrived at Nadaong crossing the 14,390-feet Dzelep-la on December 12, 1903, in biting chill winds laden with whirling snow eddies which cut the skin like spinning ice particles. Colonel Younghusband was the head of the Mission while Brigadier-General James Macdonald was the commander of troops — the former a diplomat and the latter a soldier who 'quarreled daily over the details of the campaign'.[10] Claude White was the Political Officer and Captain O'Conner, a skilled linguist, was appointed as the Intelligence Officer to act as an official interpreter. There were horses for the officers and for reconnaissance parties, about 10,500 ponies and mules, besides 400 donkeys and 9,225 bullocks and yaks, with a train of eight thousand supply and transport porters drawn from both sexes to carry the loads, all equipped with winter clothing to withstand the rigours of the climate. A field hospital and an 'engineer park' were also on the Orbat (Order of Battle). At a later stage, a locally organized cavalry mounted on ponies was added while "*ekkas*" — two wheeled carriages, which were a novelty for the Tibetan landscape, drawn by local ponies — were inducted to ease the supply and transportation problems. In short, it was a well planned military expedition with 'line of communication' troops and built-in supply system, although the columns were required to live off the land as far as possible, but strictly on terms of making liberal payments for whatever supplies they obtained locally. The British officially termed this as a "Peace Mission" — an understatement of the century!

10. Snow blindness added to the woes of one and all. A Tibetan saying aptly described their predicament — There is only one escape from the crowds: Live in the sky among the clouds. *Nowhere Else in the World* by Gordon B. Enders; p. 63.

The Expedition was also accompanied by a host of specialists whose task it was to collect military, scientific, geo-physical, data besides objects d'art, books and manuscripts that would be of interest to western scholars. The officer deputed for this specific task was so successful that he managed to collect four hundred mule-loads of rare treasure for British and Indian museums besides for the personal collection of Lord Kitchener, Commander-in-Chief, India.

The expedition marched on to Phari while the Tibetan army took up 'battle positions' between Tuna and Guru under command of Depon Lhading. Tibetan field 'fortifications' consisted of loosely piled stone-wall across the open-plain. The troops took positions behind the 'wall'. Here it would be of interest to note that the Tibetan army had an ingrained faith in the efficacy of stone-walls not only as an aid to fight a defensive battle, but as a weapon of war itself. This Mongolian inborn faith in a stone-wall dating back to prehistoric times gave an impression that for the Tibetans, the wall was an equivalent of a 'full stop'. Indeed, they were expert-builders of stone-walls. In one case they managed to build an enormous defensive stone-wall eight-hundred yards long, six feet high and four feet thick in just over one night's work. And this wall was different from others encountered earlier in as much as it was much stronger and was ingeniously loop-holed. Meanwhile, Tongsa Penlop Ugyen Wangchuk, grand-father of the then Maharaja of Bhutan, and Kazi Ugyen, grand-father of the late Prime Minister of Bhutan, Jigme Dorje, arrived at Phari to mediate between the two warring parties. They, as well as the Ruler of Sikkim, advised the Tibetans to desist from a totally unequal open contest of arms against the British Army which was far too strong for the ill-equipped poorly trained Tibetan force. The Tibetan senior command was conscious of their inherent severe weakness, and was well aware of the ancient Prophecy and the forebodings of the Oracles. The elite from Bhutan and Sikkim too knew of the Prophecy, believed in it the same way as did the Tibetans. It was therefore a matter of extreme disbelief, and an enigma to all of them, as to why the Tibetans were bent on 'hara-kiri'. That was not all.

The Lamas had issued 'bullet-charms' — talisman against bullets — deluding the poor peasant 'soldiers' into believing that they had divine protection against the English weapons and their projectiles. Thus every Tibetan warrior in the field had one such charm hung around his neck in an amulet box. Of course, none of this junk saved the poor fellows. The Lamas gave them some cock-and-bull story why the bullet-charms were ineffective and convinced them that the new ones issued to them had been rectified, and hence would prove fully effective in the next battle. So they must fight on ....

The advance from Phari commenced on 4th January 1904 and the Force crossed the Tang-La four days later in the face of bitter biting cold winds. As they entered the wilderness of Changtang Plain, they witnessed an interesting spectacle. Wild "horsemen" of the Changtang, in troupes of ten to twenty, "came galloping along in a whirlwind of dust, then executed a perfect wheel-round, then extended out in line at regular intervals, and advanced again; and as if at the word of command reformed into close order and came to an instant halt". These wild "horsemen" ranged in hordes of anything up to fifteen, and in their manoeuvres achieved an uncanny unanimity of movement ... no troop of cavalry was ever more symmetrically ranked, more precisely simultaneous in its evolutions."[11] To cap it all, these were no horsemen of Changtang; they were large wild asses known as *kyangs*, trained by natural instinct into well organized and disciplined cavalry troupes! Although various travelers have described them as wild asses, there is nothing like an ass in a kyang. From his size and fine carriage, he is more like a large mule than an ass. While its belly and legs are white, the upper parts of its body are reddish chestnut in colour, which carries on as a narrow stripe along the middle of its back.[12]

While the process at mediation was on, the Tibetan negotiators at Guru wrote to Younghusband at Phari to withdraw. That came

11. Fleming Peter: *Bayonets to Lhasa*; New York, 1961; p. 123 and Waddell L. Austine: *Lhasa & Its Mysteries*; London 1905.

12. Landon Perceval: *The Opening of Tibet*; New York, 1906, p. 419.

as an unexpected blow to the mediators. The British reacted by crossing the Dang-la, and entered Tuna. On January 12, 1904, Depon Lhading came over to Tuna to see Colonel Younghusband, but the latter refused. The Depon had to return to Guru, empty handed. The fact of the matter was that the British were all out to pick up a fight, crush the Tibetan army for whatever it was worth, and then proceed to the 'Forbidden City' of Lhasa, just for the heck of it, if for no other cogent reason.

The British had a grouse against Tibet for not being given free access to the so-called "forbidden city", forgetting the numerous foreigners including Europeans who had freely traveled in the country. The envoy of Maharaja of Kashmir with his large contingent of guards and military escorts in resplendent uniforms used to periodically visit Shigatse. There were some fifty *sowars* in military uniforms besides about a hundred mounted followers of various nationalities — Sikhs, Mohammedans with flowing beards and white turbans, Ladakhis in their in lambskin dresses, Murmis from Nepal, Dokpas from Chang, a few Nepalese besides some Tibetans from Kirong. It used to be a veritable collection of foreign nationalities whose visit was more like a *demo*, a *tamasha*, a sight worth watching. In addition to this periodic caravan, the Kashmir Government used to send an envoy to Lhasa every three years with a tribute to the Grand Lama for the defeat inflicted by the Tibetan army on the invading forces of Zorawar Singh, the famous Sikh General of Maharaja Gulab Singh.[13]

The stalemate continued. No negotiations; no progress in mediation efforts; no movement; no nothing! Younghusband was indeed tired of waiting, doing nothing. So one fine morning, on March 3, 1904, the Colonel accompanied by Captains O'Connor and Sawyer, just rode off to the Tibetan camp ten miles away at Guru to reason with the military brass there. His stated intention: to avoid unnecessary bloodshed. He was a dare-devil of a man to have taken the liberty of marching into enemy camp, totally unescorted, without any prior notice to friend or foe. "I wanted

13. Das, Sarat Chandra: *Journey to Lhasa and Central Tibet*; London, 1902, p. 52.

to make one last bid to achieve my end without resorting to force."[14] The details of this dramatic action by the Head of the British Mission and its repercussions are beyond the scope of this work, howsoever interesting these might be. Suffice it would be to add that the Tibetan Commander returned the British Chief's 'courtesy call' at Tuna, but the stalemate continued.

The point of no return had been reached

Younghusband informed the Tibetan commander on March 30, 1904, that the British would commence their march to Gyantse[15] the next morning, which they did. However, the same evening the British had surrounded the Tibetan camp at Guru. The next morning the Tibetans were observed having taken defensive positions behind the 'Wall', while the British deployed their troops, machine guns and artillery preparatory to attack. In the ensuing action, the Tibetan force was completely decimated. The first shot was fired 'in anger' by the Tibetan General. All hell was let loose. The Tibetans lost 625 killed and wounded as counted on the battlefield, while another 222 were taken prisoners. Among the Tibetans killed were their generals, Depon Lhading and Depon Namseling, Colonels Rupon Khansar Changma and Rupon Changkhyim. The British casualties: Major Wallace Dunlop slightly wounded, Mr. Candler of the 'Daily Mail' severely wounded and seven sepoys wounded. The resultant action has come to be known as "The Massacre at Guru". The only saving grace for the British was that the wounded were medically well attended, which came as a great surprise to the Tibetans who were used to killing the wounded enemy as a standard practice. The prisoners were photographed, given five rupees and a packet of cigarettes each, and allowed to go home with a warning never to come to battle again. The treatment

14. Younghusband Francis, Colonel: *The Light of Experience*, p. 90.

15. There are three main routes of surface communication to interior of Tibet. They meet at Gyantse in a flat **Y.** The southern leg is the approach route from India, the western one goes to Shigatse and the eastern one goes over the Karo-la to Lhasa. Thus Gyantse occupies a strategic location for military operations.

meted out to the Tibetan prisoners as well as the medical facilities provided to the battle-casualties together with the liberal payments made for firewood, grain and fodder created an excellent impression on minds of Tibetan civilian population. They came to regard Colonel Younghusband as a sympathetic decent gentleman, and not an invading enemy agent. The exemplary behavior of Indian troops and total absence of any looting or willful sacrilege went a long way in creating an all round good impression of the Expeditionary Force.

The Tibetans continued to resist the British advance beyond Tuna, suffering many more casualties. Finally, the British Force arrived at Gyantse on April 11, 1904. The Manchu Amban informed Colonel Younghusband that much as he wanted to come personally to Gyantse, he was unable to do so because the Tibetan Government refused to provide him necessary transport; nor a Tibetan Commissioner had been nominated to conduct negotiations with the British.[16] This one single instance speaks volumes about the Chinese "suzerainty" over Tibet of which our Indian Prime Minister, Mr. Jawaharlal Nehru, and through him the rest of the Western world made such a hue and cry about. Moreover, suzerainty is a vague term. It has not been defined or elaborated upon within specific limitations. It is a mere concept without definitive explanation. Perhaps, the western world could not grasp the fine points of spiritual relationship that existed between the Dalai Lamas and the Manchu emperors. In the absence of a better terminology, suzerainty came into usage to describe the "relationship that existed between Tibet and China from 1720 to 1890. It was very inaccurate, and the use of it has misled whole generations of western statesmen. It did not take into account the reciprocal spiritual relationship, or recognize that the relationship was a personal matter between the Dalai Lamas and Manchu emperors."[17]

Curzon's approach to Tibet was based on the premise that Britain would ultimately have to defend the sub-continent against

---

16. Younghusband: op. cit. p. 184.
17. Dalai Lama: *Autobiography*, p. 75.

Russian aggression. It was not just a pipe dream; he had rational basis for this conviction. The political spectrum of Central Asia was founded on the concept of 'buffer states'. It is a principle of war, a corner stone of strategy, that battles should be fought not on your land but on those of your enemies or neighbours'. Russia was all out to secure its eastern flank, expanding into the vast empty spaces of Central Asia. Cossacks ranged further and further eastwards with the Russian settlers following in their footsteps. Russia grabbed Tashkent in 1864. Samarkand, Bokhara, Khokand, Merve and Pendjdeh fell in the kitty, one by one, at a fast rate. Russian power spread to the Pamirs. Russian and British reconnaissance parties were soon breathing the rarified air of Hindu Kush, Pamir and Karakorums. The two super powers carved out the western borders of Manchu China in favour of Russia such that the latter was on the gates of eastern Turkestan. By then Russia had a number of options towards the Indian sub-continent — across Afghanistan, over the Hindu Kush and through the Khyber Pass; bypass Afghanistan and take the easterly route through Eastern Turkestan and over the Karakoram passes into Baltistan and Ladakh; or go further east from crossing the Aksai Chin desert along the traditional caravan route from Kashgar to Gartok over the Himalayan passes leading to Kumaon and thence to the plains of India. Thus it became a matter of utmost urgency for the British-Indian Government to know the topography, routes of access, seasonal changes, et al, so that suitable defensive measures could be initiated against Russian juggernaut. And it was Tibet that came into prominence in this scenario, since China was in any case too weak a power to reckon with, having already suffered a humiliating defeat at the hands of Japanese in 1895.

The apprehensions of Lord Curzon were therefore well founded, although many knowledgeable authorities scoffed over these as empty excuses to expand the British influence farther into the unknown.

Advance to Lhasa

It must be said to the credit of the Tibetans that, notwithstanding the heavy losses suffered by them to date, they kept up the fight. They gave a tough fight at every position and did not surrender easily. They did not care about the Prophecy, or what the oracle had forecast. Gyantse Fort proved a hard nut to crack. It was captured after some serious fighting in which the invading force suffered some casualties, and artillery was brought into action. The storming of Gyantse fort was "brilliantly planned and gallantly executed; it provides indeed a minor epic in the history of frontier warfare."[18]

In the absence of any negotiations at Gyantse, the British advance to Lhasa was resumed. The irony of the situation was that even if there were any negotiations, Colonel Younghusband had no intention of arriving at a settlement! The British had to enter the sacred City of Lhasa. It was a simple question of prestige and ego. And so they did after crossing the mighty Tsang-po (Brahmaputra) during the first week of August 1904. While the River Crossing Operation was in progress, the Dalai Lama handed over the administration of the country to a Regent, gave him his seals of office, and left Lhasa on July 30, 1904, to go north.[19] Four days after that the British arrived in Lhasa. The Manchu Amban was the first to call on Francis Younghusband and offered his services for a speedy settlement with the Tibetans. It was indeed a strange offer to make. On the one hand he insisted that he could not get transport from the Tibetans to move to Gyantse, while on the other he gave an impression that he had such influence over the Tibetans that he could assist in a speedy solution of an intricate problem. Tibetans were an enigma to the British, and now the Chinese too fell in the same category at least in so far as Lord Curzon and Colonel Younghusband were concerned. The official representative of Nepal, Jit Bahadur, was the next to call followed by the representative of Kashmiri Muslims. But the Tibetans continued to be enigmatic! Discussions went on and on between the Kashag and the Tsongdu as to the future course of action. Finally the Regent, Ganden Tri Rinpoché, took the initiative

---

18. Seaver George: op. cit. p. 236.

19. Finally, the Dalai Lama spent more than one year of his exile in the Outer Mongolian capital of Urga. After many visits and wanderings, the Great Lama returned to Lhasa in 1909.

and called on Francis Younghusband without any fanfare or ceremony, thereby opening the door for negotiations to start. The awakening to the reality dawned on the Tibetan administration rather late, but then they made it up by sending gifts of meat, grains, eggs and fruits to the British camp.

The bonhomie generated by above visits got a rude shock when one of the monks managed to get into the British camp and attacked two officers, Captains T.B. Kelly and A. Cook-Young of the medical service, severely wounding them. The monk was caught, interrogated, but he steadfastly refused to disclose the name of the monastery to which he belonged. Finally, he was hanged in public. In order to ensure that such an ugly incident did not recur, a Tibetan official and a monk delegate from each of the monasteries were kept as hostages in the British camp.

The issues to be resolved before a mutually acceptable settlement could be arrived at were complex having wide implications for the whole of Central Asia. The discussions were therefore tedious and frustratingly long. Fortunately, Younghusband, being a good diplomat, had more than a cup full of patience. He was a good listener, and knew exactly what he and his mentor in India, Lord Curzon, wanted. Diplomatic relations between Tibet and her neighbours as well as with Russia, demarcation of Indo-Tibetan border, the modalities of trade relations between India and Tibet, rights of passage through each others' territory, exchange of prisoners. "War Indemnity", its quantum, modalities and periodicity of instalments, was the trickiest of all. So were the Tibeto-Sikkimese and Tibeto-Bhutanese relations. Since at that point of time Tibet was passing through hard times in its relations with the Chinese who were harassing her in the east and northeast, and worse was yet to come. Nepal was getting impatient over Kyirong and Walung; the Gorkha Kingdom was out to get their pound of flesh when Tibet was in the throes of a politico-military bind. Above all, the top leader of the country and its decision maker, His Holiness the Dalai Lama, was in voluntary exile.

The Lhasa Convention

The poor Regent, Lozang Gyaltsen, was in the most unenviable position. With ever mounting pressures from various directions, a settlement was finally hammered out. The Tibetan proverb: "The stick is greater than the King's command" proved the point. A Convention was signed in the audience hall of the imposing Potala on the twenty-seventh day of the seventh month of the Wood-Dragon year, corresponding to September 7, 1904. Signed it was, but only between Tibet and the English, witnessed by the Manchu Amban, Tongsa Penlop of Bhutan and Jit Bahadur of Nepal. It is noteworthy that the Convention was signed only by Tibet and the British; all others appended their signatures merely as witnesses, and not as parties to the Convention, or the agreement thereof. The Chinese were not a signatory but witnesses to the Convention in which the British were represented by Colonel Francis Younghusband, John Claude White as the Political Officer in Sikkim, and five other British officers while Tibet was represented by the Regent, the four kalons (ministers), four Secretary Generals of the Tsongdu, and representatives of the three "Pillars of State", the monasteries of Drepung, Sera and Ganden. Thus it was a settlement arrived at between two independent sovereign states, each within its own rights. In fact, the Convention made no mention at all of the Chinese. The significance of the Convention lay in Article IX. Under this, Government of Tibet gave a guarantee that without prior concurrence of the British Government, it would allow:

- No portion of Tibetan territory to be ceded, sold, leased, mortgaged, or otherwise given for occupation to any Foreign Power;
- No such power to intervene in Tibetan affairs;
- No Representatives or Agents of any Foreign Power shall be admitted to Tibet;
- No concessions for railways, roads, telegraphs, mining or other rights to be granted to any Foreign Power or to the subject of any Foreign Power. In the event of consent to

such concessions being granted, similar or equivalent concessions shall be granted to the British Government;

- No Tibetan revenues, whether in kind or cash, to be pledged or assigned to any foreign power or the subject of any Foreign Power.

The emphasis on 'Foreign Power' clearly categorized China as a foreign power in so far as Anglo-Tibetan relations were concerned. Thus, the 1904-Convention completely negates any Chinese claim of sovereignty or suzerainty over Tibet. This was in line with the views of Lord Curzon who, in his letter dated January 8, 1903, to the Secretary of State for India, had stated: "We regard Chinese suzerainty over Tibet as a constitutional fiction — a political affectation which has only been maintained because of its convenience to both parties." However, the British Home Government was severely critical of Curzon's aggressive policies. At the same time, the Kashag members were afraid to take any bold decisions, more so because of the treatment meted out to their predecessors. Therefore, the Nechung Oracle rose to be the main decision-maker, since no one could be held responsible if any decision turned out to be adverse. Rational decision-making gave way to hit-and-miss system of prophecies, forebodings by oracles, and utterances during a trance. Thus Tibet turned out to be more and more enigmatic in the matter of governance.

The 1904 Convention contained another article of considerable significance and controversy. Articles VI and VII dealt with the question of war-indemnity and security for payment of the same. The amount of indemnity was fixed at five hundred thousand pounds sterling — equivalent to rupees seventy five lakhs — payable in seventy five annual instalments of rupees one lakh each. As security for payment of this indemnity, and to ensure compliance with other treaty obligations, "the British Government shall continue to occupy the Chumbi Valley until the indemnity has been paid ..." Colonel Younghusband was a farsighted diplomat, a patriotic intelligent man; and he incorporated the occupation of Chumbi Valley for a long period in the overall strategic interest of the British Empire as well retaining the option to build a road connecting the plains of Bengal-Assam with Lhasa and Bhutan. After all, what good is it to have the trading rights without worthwhile surface communications? But the Home Office in London lacked that vision into the future and raised loud protests against these Treaty provisions. "The Secretary of State for India criticized the size of the indemnity demanded from Tibet ..." It was later reduced to 166,000 pounds sterling, equivalent to rupees twenty five lakhs, payable in twenty five annual instalments, and occupation of Chumbi Valley shall end after payment of the third instalment.[20] A few more changes in the Treaty effected at the insistence of the Home Office considerably watered down the provisions of the Convention in so far as long term strategic interests of the British Empire, and later the successor Government of independent India, were concerned.

In so far as the Home Office was concerned, London was as much of an enigma as Lhasa had been for so long. A daring young diplomat in the Political Department at Delhi had managed to achieve what the seasoned cronies in London had not been able to do for decades despite their best efforts. Having got it, the London Office threw it all out of the window. To cap it all, Younghusband was reprimanded. His fault? Over-achievement! Francis was not the type to follow the dotted line blindly. He was a man of initiative, guts and courage. He was determined to make the best of the opportunity for the long term benefit of his country; and he succeeded beyond all expectations. Tibet was in the bag and China had been humbled. In the words of George Seaver, his biographer:

> It is indeed doubtful whether any man could have done more. His genuine friendliness, his unruffled temper, his adroitness in repartee, his unfailing courtesy and patience, his conciliatory address combined with his evident fearlessness and inflexibility on major issues — all these qualities of personality appealed to simple hearted Tibetans.

The entire history of Indo-Tibetan and Sino-Indian relations would have been on a totally different pedestal if only the good

20. Younghusband: op. cit. pp. 337-39.

work of Younghusband had not been undone by London. Above all, Tibet would have been an independent sovereign nation today; the map of Central Asia would have had different contours ... The 'ifs' and 'buts' of history ... The long and the short of this last colonial War waged by the British Empire was *Victory British-India, Advantage China, and Tragedy for Tibet.*

The Question of Foreign Visitors

It is noteworthy, and yet another enigma, that while there was a homeopathic college at Chakpori, there was no institution in Tibet devoted to astrology, a pet subject connected with divination, oracles and soothsayers. However, military training came to be taken seriously in that modern army drill so far completely unknown in Tibet was introduced, while a few selected soldiers were deputed to Shillong and Quetta for artillery and machine gun training. Indeed, the Thirteenth Gyalwa Rinpoché was imbued with progressive ideas. He appreciated the value of English education. At his request, the British-Indian Government established an English school under supervision of Frank Ludlow. Unfortunately, the monastic influence prevailed, and the school was closed in 1926, barely three years after it was started. A similar instance took place in 1945 when an English School opened at Lhasa in 1945 managed by Richard Parker of England was closed down after a few months because of monastic objections on grounds of religion. These were not the only instances of the monastic order creating obstacles in the way of modernization of Tibet. Around the same time the British-Indian Government was permitted to build a motor-road from Yatung to Gyantse to facilitate movement of goods for trade agencies. It was a temporary low-specifications road. Petrol stations were established near the dak-bungalows and three vehicles started plying. But this project too had to be abandoned under pressure of local population applied through the monastic order. It may be recalled that the Dalai Lama had one car in working order, Austin A-40, which he sometimes drove in his residential area. The only other person who owned a car in Lhasa, license-plate TIBET-2, was the powerful business-magnate named Kumphela who created quite a stir while driving around Lhasa. One more instance of the Great Lama's progressive ideas[21] : The British officials from Sikkim used to visit Lhasa on official business every now and then. But the first American to do so was Suydam Cutting who made three trips to Tibet — in 1930, 1935 and 1937. On one of his visits his wife was officially invited by the Government of Tibet, the first Caucasian woman to be so honoured. The Cuttings developed strong friendship with the Thirteenth Gyalwa Rinpoché who presented them with a pair of Apsos, a special breed of Tibetan dogs.[22] Unfortunately, even this friendship and the Cutting's efforts with the State Department did not help when the Chinese communist juggernaut rolled into Lhasa. Yet another instance of "backward isolationism" was the refusal of the Lhasa Government to permit an aircraft to land at Lhasa to evacuate F.W. Williamson, the Political Officer in Sikkim, for medical treatment. Williamson died a few days later. However, when in 1944 a US cargo plane piloted by Lieutenant R.E. Crozier on a supply mission between China and India crash-landed at Doh near the famous monastery of Samye, all hospitality and assistance was extended to the crew. The American crew was guided to the Indian border. The US Diplomatic Mission in Delhi gave an assurance that hereafter no American aircraft shall over-fly Tibetan territory. This is one side of the story. On the other, Father Ippolito Desideri (c. 1714) as quoted by Thubten Jigme Norbu tells us:

> Lhasa is densely populated, not only by natives, but by a large number of foreigners of diverse nations, such as Tartars, Chinese, Muscovites, Armenians, people from Cascimir, Hindustan and Nepal, all established there as merchants ...

---

21. In 1912 the Thirteenth Gyalwa Rinpoché sent Lungshar to Europe as a roving ambassador. He came back in 1914 with progressive modern ideas about reforming the administration and taxation system. His Holiness appointed him as his personal bodyguard. When the Gyalwa Rinpoché left for the Heavenly Fields in 1933, Lungshar presented a petition to the Kashag for putting his ideas into practice. He was arrested, blinded and imprisoned. The priestley class was not prepared to let go its privileges!

22. Shakabpa: op. cit. pp. 267-68.

To cap it all, the "Great Fifth" had himself invited Christian Missionaries to come to Lhasa to teach and practice their religion in freedom. Thus the Capuchins were the first to establish a Mission in Lhasa. Desideri was a great scholar and was willing to study under Tibetan teachers. He was given a private room in Sera monastery and permitted to use one of the chapels for his Christian worship. He translated a number of Tibetan works for the benefit of the western world.[23] Isn't it highly enigmatic that Tibetan Buddhists should go to such length in welcoming Christian missionaries, and on the other totally close the country to all European foreigners? The crux of the problem was that the Government of Tibet did not have an appropriate machinery to deal with foreign affairs, nor was there consistency or continuity in dealing with foreign relations.

23. Tibet did not expel Desideri; he was recalled by the Vatican.

6

Chinese Invasions

The British Military Expedition to Tibet was unfortunate for Tibet in ways more than one. It rendered the Tibetan army totally ineffective against Chinese designs. Tibetan defence potential was completely shattered. Concurrently, the Chinese were jolted into recognition of their total ineffectiveness in Tibet. They could not reconcile to the fact that Tibet could enter into an international agreement without Chinese participation, or assistance. Their reaction was devastating for Tibet. The Anglo-Russian agreement had the added effect of giving the Chinese a free hand in the internal affairs of Tibet.

When the First World War broke out in Europe, there was great anxiety in Tibet as to its outcome, and the effect it would have on the destiny of the landlocked isolated nation. The Dalai Lama assured his people that Britain would be victorious in the end. This was in keeping with the prophecy made in 1915 by various lamas under the leadership of Lord Chamberlain. According to this prophecy, Germany was like an elephant. It would eventually be pulled down, although it would take some time to do so. The Prophecy came out to be true, and His Holiness was pleased to send his congratulations to His Majesty the King. "The enemies of yesterday had become friends of today."[1]

1. Bell, Charles, Sir: *Tibet: Past & Present;* 1924, p.168.

On the outbreak of the War, His Holiness offered one thousand Tibetan soldiers to fight for the Allies, but the British Government politely refused the offer. However, they shipped more than five thousand modern bolt-action rifles to Lhasa for the Tibetan army to be kept ready, if needed.[2] The Tibetan army had one peculiar characteristic. Since nobody was sure as to which foreign army to model it on, the Thirteenth Dalai Lama raised, equipped and trained one regiment on the Russian pattern, another on the Japanese and yet another on the British system. The British system proved to be the best and therefore Tibetan army continued to use words of command and other ceremonials on the British pattern. Meanwhile, with the end of the Great War, Japanese influence started gathering in Central Asia, particularly after Japan came to the aid of Mongolia against the Bolshevists. However, the British kept up their pressure too. The Tibetan army strength was raised from five to fifteen thousand, and the telegraph line from Gyantse was extended up to Lhasa. Concurrently, a local police force was also established with help coming in from Sikkim Police. A mini-hydroelectric station was also established in the Capital. Most of this modernization was the result of visit of Sir Charles Bell and his personal friendship with the Thirteenth Gyalwa Rinpoché.

The British occupation of Lhasa, albeit for a very short period, alerted the Chinese as to how tenuous was their hold over Tibet which had concluded a Treaty with a World Power all on its own without even consulting the Suzerain Power, the Government in Peking. Lord Curzon, the Viceroy and Governor General of India referred to the so-called 'Chinese Suzerainty' as a 'Constitutional Fiction', which indeed it was since Tibet had enjoyed complete independence for centuries and its relations with the Manchus — the second foreign dynasty to rule China — were purely on the model of a spiritual master and disciple, and certainly not as between a ruler and the ruled. Be that as it may, the British Military Expedition and its complete success gave China a perfect excuse to launch a full scale invasion on Tibet. The Dalai Lama returned to Lhasa on Christmas Day, 1909, after his six years self-exile in the face of British invasion.

---

2. Shakabpa Tsepon W.D..: *Tibet: A Political History;* 1967; pp. 257-58.

And the Chinese invasion came on the night of February 12, 1910,[3] forcing the Thirteenth Gyalwa Rinpoché to flee his country once again, and this time ironically into the arms of his erstwhile enemies, the British in India whose hospitality was generous beyond expectations.[4] The Chinese were very disappointed over their failure to capture the God-King of Tibet. To give vent to their anger in frustration, they issued a proclamation on February 25, 1910, deposing the Dalai Lama, as they had done soon after the Dalai Lama fled the country in the face of Younghusband Military Expedition. Eventually, Tibet's small but dedicated army managed to push the Chinese back through Kham to Dartsedo, the original border between the two nations, after which Tibet enjoyed complete independence. It may be recalled that in ancient times, the period of its zenith, Tibet used to be a great military power. In 763 A.D. Tibetan armies had marched right up to the Chinese capital to ensure compliance with earlier treaty obligations of the Chinese to pay an annual tribute of 50,000 rolls of silk. To commemorate their victory over the Chinese, a stone obelisk was erected in front of the Jo-khang on which was engraved the text of the Treaty then concluded between the Emperor of China and King Ralpachan.[5]

Tibet: An Independent Sovereign State

Why was London jealous of Younghusband's brilliant stroke of success? Well, it is not for this work to analyze the clash of

3. It was for the third time that the Chinese Army entered Lhasa on February 12, 1910 — first, following the Dzungarian Mongols invasion in 1720; second, the Nepalese invasion in 1790; and third, after the British invasion in 1904, when in April 1905 the Chinese army crushed Tibetan revolt in Batang monastery in Eastern Tibet. It is noteworthy that there were no Chinese troops in Tibet in 1841 when Dogras of Kashmir invaded western Tibet and were defeated by the Tibetan army fighting under Tibetan generals. In March 1908 Chao Erhfeng was appointed Imperial Commissioner for Tibet. The Dalai Lama was formally deposed and, for all practical purposes, in 1910, the administration of the country was taken over by the Chinese. Chao Erh-feng remained the central figure in Eastern Tibet till his execution by Szechuan revolutionaries at Chengtu in 1911.
4. The Thirteenth Gyalwa Rinpoché arrived at Darjeeling on February 24, 1910.
5. Gulati M.N.: *Tibetan Wars*; p. 30.

personalities. Perhaps, it was the generation gap — Younghusband was young, and so was Lord Curzon; and both had reached the zenith so fast, so early in life. No wonder therefore that the Chinese Communists too followed the British traditional line of blaming the other party for their own failures. Since the Chinese could not win the hearts and minds of the Tibetans after their invasion-occupation of ethnic Tibet, they lay the blame on the doorstep of the Dalai Lama. While inventing invectives against the God-King, the Chinese Communists crossed all limits of decency and called the Dalai Lama "arch criminal who split the motherland", a "tool of western anti-China forces", a "reactionary feudal serf-owner", a "promoter of rape, murder and child cannibalism", a "wolf in monk's clothing", and so on and so forth.[6]

Both Great Lamas, the Dalai and the Panchen, are high incarnates. The first incarnation of both took place in the fourteenth century. Relations between the two have been cordial for generations. However, around the time of Chinese invasion of 1910 a rift developed between the two. The Chinese sensed the cleavage between the two and encouraged to widen the disagreement for their own vested interests. The October-1911 revolution by Sun Yat-sen and its aftermath in Tibet led to widespread plunder by the additional forces inducted into Tibet by the new Chinese regime. Meanwhile, the Tibetans fiercely resisted the Chinese onslaught. Finally, they succeeded in expelling the Chinese forces which had to return to China in disgrace, traveling through India, sans their weapons. Consequentially, the Dalai Lama returned to Tibet from exile in July 1912. He waited till all the Chinese troops were expelled from Tibet and entered Lhasa in triumph towards the end of the year. The Chinese Government once again recognized the Dalai Lama as the spiritual-temporal Head of Tibet. However, the rift between two High Lamas persisted and a few years later the Panchen shifted to the Chinese controlled territory on the frontier to live there for the rest of his life. He died there in 1937. After the expulsion of Chinese civil and military officials from Tibet in 1912, no Chinese had been permitted to enter Tibet in official capacity

---

6. French Patrick: *Tibet, Tibet;* Harper Collins, New Delhi, 2003, p. 112.

till 1934 when a condolence-delegation was allowed to enter Lhasa. And Tibet became an independent sovereign state in its own right. The heading of some ancient Tibetan documents had been: *"By order of the Emperor of China, the Dalai Lama is the Pontiff of Buddhism.* But the Thirteenth Dalai Lama changed that to read: *By order of Lord Buddha* ...

The International Commission of Jurists has analyzed the status of Tibet in great detail. Their verdict in their Report on *The Question of Tibet and the Rule of Law* published in 1959:

> "It is therefore submitted that the events of 1911-12 mark the emergence of Tibet as a fully sovereign state, independent in fact and in law of Chinese control".

The wheel of Fate had moved full circle. In June 1912 the Dalai Lama left Kalimpong for home. The astrologers had fixed the auspicious hour as 02:30 a.m. The Dalai Lama returned to Lhasa in February 1913 and issued a formal proclamation of independence. He decided to implement what he had observed and imbibed about administrative system in India. He directed his officials to attend the administrative matters in their constituency personally rather than deputing some lower level clerical staff to do so. Office timings were fixed, and ordered to be followed. Appointments were given and timings were adhered to. The Thirteenth Gyalwa Rinpoché was the first to have issued paper-currency and postage stamps, besides introducing gold and silver coins. He brooked no delay in implementing his program of administrative reforms. No doubt he was impulsive and short-tempered to get things moving; but he did not 'nourish a grudge'. He was true to the Tibetan proverb:

> Although a lama may be quick-tempered, He does not retain his anger.

India Attains Independence

The prospects of Indian independence should have been a happy augury for the Indian sub-continent and the rest of Asia. But in reality it was a matter of considerable anxiety for all the parties concerned, including Gandhi and Nehru. India was almost on verge of a civil war, which was averted by what turned out to be 'almost a civil war'. The Government of Tibet was particularly anxious on this score. They were not sure what support, if any, they would get from the new Government in Delhi. And their apprehensions proved quite justified. Mr. Nehru made his pro-Chinese stand quite clear through his public utterances, often uncalled for and without any provocation. He was anti-imperialist on the side of leftist imperialists. He was neutral on the side of Russia. He was sympathetic towards Tibet but only if Tibet accepted Chinese hegemony. Tibet was indeed in a tight corner. The centuries old Prophecy was gradually, but inexorably, coming to be true. The assurances given by the British Mission in Lhasa were mere words of consolation with no solid backing. When India attained independence on 15th August 1947, the Government of Tibet decided on 25th August to send a Trade Delegation to India, United Kingdom, United States and China. Tsepon W.D. Shakabpa was leader of the Delegation whose other members were his younger brother, Khenchung Changkhyim, Depon Surkhang and Rimshi Pangdatshang. The raison d'etre for this Delegation:

- Tibet's non-Asian trade to be paid for in hard currency, and not in Indian rupees;
- Investigate possibility of importing machinery for agriculture and wool factories;
- Purchase gold bullion as backing for Tibetan currency;
- To demonstrate Tibet's independent status and sovereignty.

While in the United States the Chinese Ambassador insisted on accompanying the Tibetan Delegation to meet the Secretary of State. Tsepon Shakabpa refused point blank. The State Department also felt that it was not at all necessary.[7]

The treatment meted out to the 1947-Tibetan Trade Mission sent to India, United Kingdom, United States, China and some other countries is not within the purview of this work. Suffice it

---

7. Shakabpa: op. cit. pp. 294-96.

would be to say that, although the Mission established the independent status of Tibet by traveling on documents issued by Lhasa, the conduct of trade and negotiations therefor were obstructed at every stage by vested interests. Procurement of gold by Tibet from the United States was the high point of the Mission, and the Nehru Government went out of its way to create difficulties for the Tibetans in this direction.[8] However, after much wrangling, the Government of India released US $250,000 allowing the Tibetans to buy US $400,000 worth of gold, and eased restrictions on imports and customs duty at Government level, while individual importers-exporters continued to be penalized as heretofore.

The Fall of Tibet

China's Civil War ended in 1949. The Communists emerged as undisputed leaders of the mainland China as well as of the Amdo region which was nominally part of China, but was ethnically Tibetan. In July 1949 they were in full control of Kumbum. However, Thubten Jigme Norbu stayed on as long as it was possible for him to fulfill his obligations as incarnation of Tagtser; but a stage came when he was not allowed even to pray alone. That was the time when Norbu was faced with the greater duty of alerting his younger brother, the Gyalwa Rinpoché, of the impending dangers to the country. In fact as early as 1945, the State Oracle of Tibet had prophesied that great danger loomed ahead from the East. Aggression by the victor and laying claims on the weak neighbour was an inevitable consequence of Communist victory. The Oracle faced East in a trance wildly shaking his head. That was it. Again in 1947 the State Oracle, while in a trance, once more faced East and shook his head wildly, foretelling danger from that direction. Just two years later a bright horse-tailed comet appeared in the sky. The older generation considered this heavenly phenomenon, which lasted several weeks to pass off, as a further proof of impending danger. It was an omen of war, as far as the weak Tibetans were concerned. The older generation recalled

8. Amaury de Riencourt: *Roof of the World*; p. 130 & Shakabpa: op. cit. p. 294.

that a similar comet had made its appearance before the Chinese invasion of 1910. Yet another sign of impending disaster was that the cap-stone of a tall column erected in A.D. 763 to commemorate Tibet's conquest of China was found one morning lying shattered at the foot of the Potala.

The Thirteenth *kachem* had prophesied external threat and internal decay. The latter came to pass much earlier. In 1941, Reting Rinpoché decided to go into religious retreat and therefore handed over the Regency to Dalai Lama's senior tutor, Taktra Rinpoché, with the understanding that when he returns after six years of *Tapasya*, the Regency would revert to Reting. Meanwhile, bribery, corruption and maladministration were rampant under Taktra's regency. His compatriots were averse to relinquishing power that brought them such rich fruits. A conspiracy was hatched by the interested parties and Reting was arrested and detained in the Potala. This treacherous act led to a revolt by the monks of Je college of Sera monastery to which Reting belonged. A local civil war erupted between the government troops and the monks. It lasted nearly twelve days in which more than two hundred monks were killed. The rest then surrendered. And about a week later, one morning Reting was found dead in the prison — a small collection of blue marks on his buttocks were the only signs of abnormality.[9]

The massive Chinese invasion of Tibet came on the morning of October 7, 1950, when 84,000 troops of the First and Second Field Armies under overall command of General Liu Bating crossed the Yangtze in small coracles. The attack came as a complete surprise to the Tibetan field commanders. Destiny had to follow its pre-set course. The *Kachem* and what it forecast had to come true, like it did in the Wood-Dragon Year, 1904 A.D., when the Tibetan army was annihilated knowing fully well in advance that that would be the course of events as pre-ordained by the Wheel of Life. The Chinese announced for the first time on October 25 that their troops had entered Tibet, to liberate Tibet from the clutches of 'imperialists'. The Government

9. Avedon John F.: *In Exile from the Land of Snows*; 1984, p. 26.

of Tibet cabled an impassioned appeal to the United Nations pleading for the World Organization to intercede on their behalf and restrain the Chinese aggression.[10] The General Assembly declined to consider the question of Tibet. The attitude of the Indian representative in the General Assembly was totally negative as far as Tibet was concerned, and that set the tone for the rest of the member states. If only Mr. Nehru had had the courage to take up the matter in UNO on behalf of Tibet .... If only Mr. Nehru had sent a brigade group worth of troops to stem the Chinese advance in order to gain time so that the matter could be taken up in the UN Security Council. If only the Government of Tibet had applied for membership of the League of Nations .... If they had joined the UNO when it was formed after the Second World War .... If they had appointed ambassadors to a few major countries .... The list of 'ifs' and 'buts' of history is a long one indeed.

The second part of the *Kachem* was a far more serious matter. On New Year's Day 1950, the Chinese issued notice to the world at large that they were now all set to 'liberate' Taiwan, Hainan and Tibet; that Tibet was an integral part of Chinese territory; and 'liberation' of Tibet was a pre-requisite for the security of China's western borders. The Government of Tibet on its part was fully aware that it could not possibly withstand the Chinese onslaught. International diplomacy was the only viable course of action to safeguard the security of their country. They sent telegrams to India, Nepal, Great Britain and the United States seeking their assistance to prevail upon the Chinese Government to refrain from resorting to aggression against their peaceful country. Since Tibet did not have any diplomatic relations with any except India, the replies were polite but negative.

Chinese Conspiracy to Replace Dalai Lama

When the Chinese marched into East Tibet in 1950, Tagtser Rinpoché was an incarnate High Lama in the great Kumbum

10. A similar appeal was made on September 9, 1959 by the Tibetan Government in exile.

Monastery. He was captured by the Chinese and taken to China for indoctrination. He was gradually made to 'reform his thinking'. In turn, he gave an impression that he was accepting the communist ideology. He appeared to be a genuine convert; slow, not so staunch, but still leaning towards the new creed. In the heart of his heart, the Kumbum Lama, Thubten Jigme Norbu, was not convinced but he had no option but to cooperate, if for no other reason than for the love of his dear life and his country. When his Chinese masters were reasonably certain, they suggested to him to cooperate with them to depose the Dalai Lama in Lhasa. In return for his collaboration they would dismantle the monastic system of government in Lhasa and appoint him as the President of Tibet in place of the Dalai Lama. Jigme Norbu, the eldest brother of Gyalwa Rinpoché had no option but to agree. He left Chamdo at the head of a five member delegation for Lhasa.

Since it was customary for important visitors to Lhasa to send advance information about their arrival, the Rinpoché sent his trusted personal servant that the approaching delegation was a mere stratagem, a trick of the Chinese Communists, to eliminate the Dalai Lama and thereby take over Tibet, suggesting, inter alia, that the Gyalwa Rinpoché and the Cabinet should flee from Lhasa. Obviously, it was too tall a story to be taken at its face value, and that too from a mere servant. So when the Delegation arrived at Lhasa, the Dalai Lama and his Government was very much there. However, when the Tagtser Rinpoché had a private audience with the Gyalwa Rinpoché and personal meetings with the members of the Kashag, they believed him. It was this information which precipitated departure of Gyalwa Rinpoché and his Government from Lhasa to Yatung. Taktser Rinpoché also accompanied His Holiness to Yatung. However, as soon the news of his flight reached the Chinese, they issued orders to kill him as soon as possible, which in turn made it obligatory for him to flee to India and from there to the United States to escape the dragnet which the Chinese were bound to lay for his elimination.

Gyalwa Rinpoché gave Jigme Norbu two letters: one, to render all possible assistance which Taktser might require; and the other authorizing him to speak on behalf of the Dalai Lama, to conclude any agreement(s) with any power(s) which might agree to help Tibet, and also to make suitable arrangements for the Dalai Lama's escape. George N. Patterson, author of the famous book, *Revolt in Tibet,* was instrumental in making various administrative arrangements for Taktser Rinpoché to meet the U.S. representatives in Calcutta, as well as for his travel plans for going to the States.

After prolonged discussions with the U.S. officials and consultations with His Holiness by a series of telegrams, a preliminary agreement, whose terms are summarized below, was also drawn up:[11]

1. On his escaping from Tibet the U.S. would agree to support the Dalai Lama and one hundred and twenty members of his Government for an indefinite period in any country of the Dalai Lama's choosing, but it was thought advisable that the country should be in the East.
2. The U.S. would take up the matter of China's aggression against Tibet, and Tibet's plea for help, in the U.N.
3. The U.S. would provide finance for whatever was required in Tibet's fight for freedom from the Chinese.
4. Any question of military assistance would have to be left for future discussion, but on arrival in India the Dalai Lama should approach the Indian Government for help, and when this was refused, as it would be, he was to request the Indian Government for permission to approach any other country willing to help.
5. Before leaving Tibet the Dalai Lama shall repudiate the Seventeen-Point Agreement just signed by the Tibetan delegation in Peking, and immediately on arrival in India he would again publicly repudiate it.

Meanwhile, the news of Jigme Norbu's arrival in Calcutta had reached the Chinese authorities. They dispatched an Advisory

11. Patterson N. George: *Tibet in Revolt*; Faber & Faber, London, 1960; p. 82.

Delegation from Peking to Calcutta under the leadership of Chang-Ching-wu. The Rinpoché pretended illness and refused to meet with any body, including the Tibetan members of the delegation. The Chinese finally sent his brother-in-law. Jigme Norbu could not possibly refuse to meet him, but he persisted that he was ill and could not meet any body. Finally, the Chinese Ambassador from Delhi landed in Calcutta and sent Jigme Norbu a message that if he would not come over to the Consulate to meet them, they would come to the Hotel where Jigme was staying. The Ambassador harangued Jigme Norbu for his 'turn-coat' behaviour and assured him forgiveness for his defection. Jigme Norbu agreed with the Ambassador that he should leave India immediately. While the Ambassador had Tibet-China in his mind as Jigme's destination, the Rinpoché intention was to the U.S. By the time Jigme Norbu left for the U.S. Patterson had completed all arrangements for His Holiness to leave Yatung in six days, i.e., on July 12, 1951. Indian Prime Minister had assured political asylum and Khampa fighters had assured protection and safe passage throughout. However, the Abbots of Drepung, Ganden and Sera Monasteries insisted that Gyalwa Rinpoché consult the State Oracle. The advice was: Return to Lhasa. His Holiness did not accept this advice on face value and asked for a second "possession". Again the State Oracle decreed that the Dalai Lama should return to Lhasa. His Holiness had no option but to return to Lhasa. The return journey commenced on July 21. The Chinese Peoples' Liberation Army entered Lhasa on September 9, 1951. They fanned out all over western Tibet and entered Lhasa on March 13, 1952. Meanwhile the Panchen Lama arrived at Lhasa with a strong escort of Chinese troops. The so-called 'Peaceful Liberation of Tibet' was now complete!

Nehru's Appeasement of Chinese

When the Communist Chinese invasion of Tibet came in 1950, the strength of Tibetan army was 8,500 officers and men, fifty pieces of assorted artillery, 250 mortars and about 200 machine guns. This was peanuts as for resisting the Invasion was concerned. The story of Communist Chinese invasion of Tibet on 7th October

1950 cannot be covered in this work. However, the generosity, statesmanship and moral fibre of Mr. Jawaharlal Nehru are worthy of being put on record! His Plenipotentiary, Mr. N. Raghavan, in his letter dated April 29, 1954 addressed, to Chang Han-fu, deputy Foreign Minister of the Peoples' Republic of China voluntarily, without any provocation whatsoever, of course under instructions from Mr. Nehru, agreed on behalf of his Government to unconditionally, without any quid pro quo, decided to withdraw the Indian military escorts stationed at Yatung and Gyantse[12], and also hand over to the Chinese Government the postal, telegraph and public telephone facilities as well as the dak-bungalows (rest houses) and the land in Indian possession along the Kalimpong-Lhasa route. All the good work done by Colonel Francis Younghusband and Lord Curzon was thrown into dust bin with one stroke of pen. This was in consequence of the so-called 'Trade Pact' signed between China and India on April 29, 1954. Trade and commerce was mere excuse for the agreement whose significance lay in the Five Principles of Co-existence enunciated in the preamble: Mutual respect for each other's territorial integrity and sovereignty; mutual non-aggression; mutual non-interference in each other's internal affairs; equality and mutual benefit; and peaceful co-existence. These principles later became the corner-stone of policy of the Afro-Asian Bloc during the Bandung Conference. India gained absolutely nothing out of this plain and simple meaningless rhetoric! And India lost what was bequeathed to her by Colonel Francis Younghusband. Nehru had hoped to obtain a fixed delineation of the hitherto vague border between India and Tibet so as to limit the Chinese expansionist tendencies of nibbling at the neighbouring territories; but in the bargain India gave away what it already had. The poor naïve Indian political leadership took Tibet along with them, down the drain. In a speech in the Lok Sabha, Acharya Kripalani said:

> " ... this doctrine was borne in sin, because it was enunciated to put the seal of our approval upon the destruction of an

---

12. Gyantse is 12,895 feet AMSL. The Tibetan mail carriers used to cover the distance of 147 miles to Lhasa in 2½ days.

ancient nation which was associated with us spiritually and culturally. The Panch Shila was announced on the eve of a nation losing its liberty."

The Indian political leaders made lot of noise about peaceful negotiations, and claiming to have enunciated the Five Principles of Peaceful Co-existence which became the Panch Sheel — Five Principles of Peaceful Co-existence — et al; but this was all empty rhetoric whose futility hit them hard on the head in October 1962 when China launched a full scale attack on India itself. While the fate of Tibet was prophesied by the learned Lamas centuries before the event, the national disaster suffered by India was forecast by Brigadier (later Major General) M.R. Rajwade, M.C., weeks before the blow was struck. The author was personal witness, and the only witness, of that masterly analysis of the then prevailing military situation and the dispositions of Indian troops vis-à-vis the Chinese, along the Thag-La Ridge and the rest of the McMahon Line ...Construction of two major highways linking China with Lhasa — one from Szechuan via Kham and the other from Lanchow via Sining — as well as a full scale military airfield at Dam, about ninety miles north of Lhasa, went a long way in consolidating Chinese control of Tibet, and their subsequent invasion of India.

One of the principles of Panch Sheel was non-interference in the internal affairs of each other. Since India voluntarily abrogated its rights of mediation as well as rights to negotiate directly with Tibet under the provisions of 1904 and 1914 Treaties respectively, China felt free to do whatever she wished to in matters relating to Tibet; and India was totally powerless, willingly and of its own accord, to do anything whatsoever to save the situation. This was the high price Tibet had to pay for the high pedestal of world-statesmanship on which Mr. Nehru stood; and India too paid an equally high price pretty soon thereafter. Nonetheless, Mr. Nehru continued to advise the Dalai Lama to work peacefully with China within the bounds of Simla Agreement of 1914 and the Seventeen Points Agreement. As for the British Government in London, they regretted that owing to Tibet's geographical position in the light of Indian independence, they could not offer any help. The United

States declined to receive the Tibetan delegation with the result that the Tibetans were on their own; left high and dry, all alone to face the military might of a Communist giant. If only India was willing, every one else would have fallen in line. But that was not to be. To say that India betrayed Tibet — that would be an understatement of the century.

In so far as India was concerned, Mr. Nehru and his intellectual elite group of advisers, kept splitting hair over suzerainty[13] and sovereignty, so did Sardar K.M. Pannikar, his Ambassador to Peking and the Defence Minister in his own Cabinet. Perhaps none of them understood the meaning of these terms which they kept using in a loose manner. "More than any other single person the Indian Ambassador to Peking, Sardar K.M. Pannikar, was responsible for the loss of Tibet and the unpreparedness of India to meet the situation."[14] In his presidential address to the All India Tibet Convention held at Calcutta, Jaiprakash Narain, the famous Indian Socialist leader said:

> The policy of Chinese suzerainty over Tibet was born in imperialist sin and the Indian Government is condoning it. India's acceptance of the suzerainty formula has given the Chinese moral and legal sanction and prevented the formation of an Afro-Asian opinion on Tibet. It has prevented the true aggressive character of Chinese Communism being realized by the backward people of Asia, aggravating the danger of their being enslaved in the name of liberation.

---

13. Suzerainty is by no means sovereignty. It is a sort of international guardianship. As long as Tibet was not entering into international agreements independent of China, Chinese suzerainty was applicable, albeit to a limited extent only. However, since Tibet had concluded international agreements with Nepal, Kashmir, the Mongols and, above all, with the Government of Great Britain, all on its own, without reference to China, the question of Chinese suzerainty did not arise at all. Indian Prime Minister and Indian Ambassador in Peking were totally in the wrong in conceding the right of suzerain to China over Tibet, particularly during the period of First World War and thereafter. If only the Dalai Lama had established embassies in a couple of great countries ...!

14. Patterson N. George: op. cit. p. 75.

And as for strategic implications of Chinese actions, the Government of India did not have the foggiest idea what they were in for, more so since they were all out for the so-called "Pancha Sheel" and 'world statesmanship', rather than securing the national interests of their own country from the geo-strategic point of view. Ignorance of military matters was bliss! Mr. Nehru was at his best, standing on a moral pedestal, lecturing the rest of the world about how they should conduct international affairs in a peaceful manner without resorting to force of arms, in the spirit of Pancha Sheel, which was one of his highest and most cherished ideals. But in point of fact, it was mere appeasement of the Chinese dragon, nibbling at Indian territory at will. He was all out to create a niche for himself as a world statesman and go down in history with his name written in golden letters. He readily, voluntarily, without any provocation, gave away to Chinese on a platter what the British Government had earned through Indian and British blood and sweat. He was indeed generous to the point of .... The less said the better. As for the moral pedestal was concerned, Mr. Nehru did not seem to know his history lessons since it was diplomatically obligatory on the part of India, in terms of the 1914-Simla Agreement, to ensure that the Chinese first recognized and respected Tibetan autonomy before they could claim the so-called "suzerainty" over that country, which for all practical purposes, was a fully independent entity in its own right. He sent clear signals to Peking that India, unlike its predecessor British-Indian Government, had no intention of coming to the aid of Tibet, thus delivering a shattering blow to Tibet and her peaceful nonviolent Buddhist population.

During the first years of Communist rule in Lhasa, the only outsider-observer there was a bright young Bengali diplomat, Sumal Sinha. His diplomatic dispatch to Delhi gives a vivid account of collaboration by the old ruling class of nobility making huge profits out of business deals for supplies delivered to the Chinese garrisons. The so-called respectable bunch of Tibetan official class of families went out of their way to imitate the Chinese — to dress, talk, sing, all like the Chinese. "The inroad of neo-Chinese culture into

Tibetan society whether in music, ideology, dress or speech is truly remarkable .... There is not a home in Lhasa where portraits of Mao and his colleagues have not found a place in the domestic shrine ... most officials live smugly in their ivory towers ... the common people find the heavy burdens imposed on them insupportable.[15] They took their revenge during the Cultural Revolution! The stories of that period are gruesome to the extreme, unbelievable but true. Concurrently, new red-light districts came up along the Lingkhor, Lhasa's outer pilgrim walk whose length the pilgrims used to measure by prostrations. Hundreds of brothels mushroomed all over the sacred city, proudly displaying the posters of Bollywood actresses like Madhuri Dixit. However, even brothels have their morals and principles. The Tibetan girls in there would just not have sex with Chinese or Muslims. No wonder therefore that in the twentieth century it took less than forty years for Tibet to win and lose its independence.

With every diplomatic and military success, the Chinese were growing bolder and bolder. The Soviets were backing China in its attempts to grab more and more of Indian territory. The Russian and Chinese journals almost simultaneously published maps showing Ladakh, Kashmir and North East Frontier Area as part of Chinese territory. As for Bhutan, they had already claimed that as extension of Tibet, and hence part of China. While Nehru was extraordinarily generous to the Chinese Communists in handing over India's extra-territorial rights on a platter, there was a glaring contradiction in his policy towards Tibet. Immediately after India attained independence, the Dalai Lama is reported to have approached New Delhi for return of territories expropriated by British colonialism — Sikkim and Darjeeling in particular. But Nehru put forward some lame excuse for not acceding to Tibetan claim.

That was not to be the end of British-Indian Government's and Nehru's Indian Government's parsimonious policy-direction towards Tibet. Wool was a major item of export for land-locked Tibet. Bulk of the wool export trade was carried out through Calcutta port to the United States where it was used for

15. Quoted by Patrick French in *Tibet, Tibet*: op.cit. p. 210.

manufacturing rugs for automobiles. Before the Second World War this trade amounted to about two to three thousand tons a year. However, due to the War, the US had not lifted any wool since early 1940's with the result that wool stocks had accumulated at Kalimpong and en-route to Calcutta in very large quantities. It was beginning to rot. While the Indian authorities permitted the Tibetans to export their wool from Calcutta, they would not let them have the hard currency so earned. Instead, they would convert the hard currency into rupees and pass on the same to Tibetans. That was not the end of step-motherly cruel treatment. The cap-stone was that the Indian Government would charge customs duty for the Tibetans imports! Tibetan economy was thus put to severe strain, particularly for the goods imported from China through Indian ports and land route. This latter trade amounted to about ten million tons of tea alone, besides insignificant quantities of silk, cotton goods, brocades, satins, et al, while exports to China included wool, yak-tails, hides, furs, musk and deer-horns. Consumer goods like matches, soap, buttons and needles etc. came from India. Either way, Tibet was a loser due to the policies adopted by the Indian Government, both under the British and later under Indian Prime Minister Jawaharlal Nehru.

Notwithstanding the above easing of restrictions, Nehru's policy towards the question of Tibet remained flawed. It is not that Nehru was insensitive to the plight of Tibet; in fact, in 1952 he instructed the Director General of Intelligence Bureau, Mr. M.N. Mullik, to keep in touch with the eldest brother of the Dalai Lama, Gyalo Thondup Jigme Norbu, and render help to the refugees in every possible way. But by then lot of water (or blood?) had flown down the Tsang-po. The damage had already been done, beyond repair. His planned visit to Lhasa for September 1958[16] was called off for obvious political reasons of "Pancha Sheel" and "Hindi Cheeni Bhai Bhai". He wanted to maintain the buffer status of Tibet in the same way as he did in respect of Sikkim and Bhutan. On the one hand he was sympathetic to Tibet for obvious traditional and spiritual

16. Coelho V.H.: *Sikkim and Bhutan*, 1970; p. 71.

considerations — and rendered covert military assistance by way of small arms and military advisers on a very small scale — on the other he made every endeavour to maintain friendly relations with Beijing in keeping with his policy of so-called non-alignment. The visit of Indian Political Officer in Sikkim, Harishwar Dayal, to Lhasa did not ease the situation in any way. Nehru's failure to reconcile the policy contradictions cost India heavily. The reality dawned only after the small border clash which left nine Indian and one Chinese dead. Similarly, secret talks continued between Tibet and the United States throughout 1950-52, but nothing concrete materialized out of these lengthy parleys. Tibet remained a victim of its own geographical and cultural isolationism. However, it should be noted that lack of self-sufficiency necessitated a constant trade network, which in turn broke down many barriers of isolation by bringing Tibet into direct contact with Mongols to the north, Han Chinese to the east, Indians and Nepalese to the south, and Kashmiri Moslems to the west, as well as the Europeans. In this connection it might as well be pointed out that as early as 1656, Shah Shoojah, the ruler of Bengal, had sent an envoy to the Dalai Lama with a present of Indian cloth. The Dalai Lama in return sent him a gift of precious stones. Tibet kept itself isolated, as and when it suited their convenience, but broke down the barriers when they found it necessary. That is one way to look at the so-called isolationist policy of Tibet. On the other side of the coin there is a mosque in the middle of Lhasa, over eight hundred years old. It was built when Tibet received a Muslim delegation and helped them build the mosque so they could continue to freely practice their religion. Similarly Hindus and Christians have been in Tibet for hundreds of years. Buddhists (read Tibetans) have always been open to other religions and they are far from fanatical. Furthermore, they did not force Buddhism on the Muslims, Christians and Hindus who settled down in Tibet. For instance, there were more than one thousand Tibetan Muslims in Lhasa itself. They originally came from Kashmir. They married local Tibetan Buddhist women who were converted to Islam; but the Buddhist religious hierarchy took no objection to such conversions. However, no Muslim ever embraced Buddhism, nor did the Buddhists made any attempt in that direction.

With the departure from Tibet of Hugh Richardson for his long overdue retirement, and evacuation of Reginald Fox to India for medical treatment, only four Europeans were left in Tibet — the Austrians Peter Aufschnauter and Heinrich Harrer, the Englishman Robert Ford who staffed the radio station in Chamdo (Kham), and Geoffrey Bull, a former British bank clerk turned missionary.[17]

Seventeen-Point Agreement

Instead of extending a helping hand to Tibet, Mr. Nehru kept nudging the Tibetan Government to negotiate with the Chinese, direct, alone, forsaking India's own obligations and national security interests in the matter. Tibet had no option but to accept the humiliation of sending a delegation to Peking to seek an "assurance that the territorial integrity of Tibet will not be violated" and to "inform the Government of China that the people and the Government of Tibet ... will maintain their independence." The only practical means of travel from Lhasa to Peking and back was via New Delhi. The Chinese diplomats themselves too used to follow this route. So did the Tibetans. But the Tibetan delegation was made to cool their heels at New Delhi with the additional benefit of lectures and advice from the Prime Minister of India! Time was not far off when Nehru, and his India, would be paid back by the Chinese in the same coin — a humiliating national defeat and disaster in NEFA and Ladakh where Chinese would occupy 14,500 square miles of Indian territory in Aksai Chin (Ladakh)[18] claiming it to be their ancestral property! Mr. Nehru learnt a bitter lesson after all. But at what cost to Tibet and India? While India retained its identity, Tibet was reduced to a non-entity.

Meanwhile, the Chinese faked a Seventeen-Point Agreement with the Tibetan Government in Lhasa whereby Tibet's total

17. Grunfeld: op. cit. p. 78

18. Ladakh was invaded by Mongols (Sok-pas) supported by the Tibetans for two consecutive years around 1685-86, but without any success. Ultimately, Lhasa secured the region of Guge through a stratagem by the Incarnate Lama of Bhutan. The Ladakhi King was forced to hand over the entire area east of Lahri stream, Demchog to Lhasa except the village of Missar situated near Mount Kailash — Missar was a revenue village of India till 1962!

surrender and incorporation into the Republic of China was formalized. The Dalai Lama thereafter made a final appeal for support — this time from Harry Truman and the United States. 'Surprisingly, America agreed.' Once again Dame Fate intervened. While His Holiness was preparing to leave Yatung to enter India on July 12, 1951, the abbots of Drepung, Sera and Ganden monasteries — The Three Pillars of State — prevailed upon His Holiness to return to Lhasa to make one last ditch effort for a compromise with the Chinese. Once again the State Oracle was consulted. He advised on two occasions for the Dalai Lama to return to Lhasa. So he did, arriving in the capital in August 1951 after an absence of eight months to undertake the delicate task of co-existing with the new rulers of Tibet.[19]

The Chinese occupation of Tibet, and consequent brutalization[20] of the country and its culture, howsoever painful it might be for the Tibetans, it had one positive aspect. Tibet saw the limelight of the open society in the world at large. Tibetan masters started learning about the western world, its civilization and technological advances. They started writing about their own country to educate the world about Tibetan religion and culture. Centres of Tibetan culture have been established by monastic refugees all over Europe to explain the spiritual attainments of their country. Ignorance about Tibet and its people, its ritual and religious practices are gradually disappearing. The cap-stone is the realization by the West that Tibet was indeed an independent country which has been forcibly occupied by the Chinese. Tibet was never a part of China, and the Chinese claim of full sovereignty over the neighbouring country are false, their military occupation and actions to integrate Tibet with the mainland China are naked aggression against a peace-loving god-fearing spiritual country.

Above all, Tibetans are not Chinese; they never were, nor will they ever be.

---

19. Avedon: op. cit. p. 37.

20. After diligent research, it has been established that during the past forty years nearly 1,200,000 Tibetans have died at the hands of Chinese including 1,000,000 tortured to death — *Tibet: The Facts*, Tibetan Young Buddhists Association, Mcleod Ganj, Dharmsala, 176 219; revised edition 1990, p. 26.

7

Dalai Lama Visits China and India

Dalai Lama Visits China

At the 'invitation' of the Peoples' Republic of China, the nineteen years old Dalai Lama left Lhasa for Peking on July 11, 1954. In Chengdu he boarded an airplane and flew to Xian where he was joined by the sixteen years old Panchen Lama. They arrived at Peking by a private train to a tumultuous welcome by Chinese Prime Minister Zhou Enlai and Vice-Chairman Zhu de, Chief of the Army. The welcome and banquets, et al, were well orchestrated for the consumption of world press. It was an exercise in PR, and no more. The Tibetan party was extremely well looked after and hospitality surpassed all expectations. Nothing seemed to be lacking. The 'picnic' to Peking came to end almost a year after the Dalai had left his country. He was back in Lhasa on June 29, 1955, to find the City an altogether a different place, completely changed by the new world he had just seen abroad.

The Dalai Lama first met the Indian Prime Minister Jawaharlal Nehru in Peking when the two, amongst many other statesmen of the world, had got together to celebrate Chinese First New Year under the Communist regime. At that time Tibet was having serious difficulties with the new Chinese regime, and in view of being the

The Dalai Lama with Chinese Communist Leaders in Beijing

The Dalai Lama with Nehru and Zhou Enlai in New Delhi

The Dalai Lama with Pandit Nehru at Delhi

The Incarnate God of Tibet

successor power to Great Britain, the Government of India was under both legal and moral obligation to come to the aid of Tibet. "I had been looking forward to meeting him. He smiled, but only said he was glad to have met me; and though I saw him on other occasions, those were the only words I had with him in China .... Nor did he ask me whether there was anything India could do to help Tibet. I was very disappointed ...."[1]

Mr. Nehru was much too busy in playing the role of a world statesman to bother about such mundane matters as Tibet, and its strategic value in India's defence scenario! In fact, no other country in Asia has the geo-political military-strategic value for India compatible with Tibet. Its impenetrable mountains, extremely difficult terrain and harsh climate make it ideally suitable for deployment of modern weapons to convert it into an impregnable military citadel. With Tibet as a strong military base, a military power can control the whole of Central Asia, India, Burma, Pakistan, Bangladesh, and the rest of South-east Asia. That is precisely what the Chinese were after. And that is why they built a network of military roads and at least eighteen full-fledged airfields as well as a number of military ALGs (Air Landing Grounds) all over Tibet. Unfortunately the naïve Indian political leadership was gloating over their newly achieved independence, and had their eyes closed to the reality of the situation.

The Dalai Lama also gave a dinner party in Peking to celebrate the Tibetan New Year. It was more to return some of the hospitality that he had received. The Party was done according to traditions and customs of Tibet. But there were no religious ceremonies or rituals conducted at the party. However, there were the usual New Year decorations and a special kind of cake which is made in Tibet for this season. "It is our custom to take a small piece of this cake and throw it up to the ceiling as an offering to Buddha. When Mao Tse-tung was told of this custom, he threw up a piece to the ceiling, and then with a mischievous expression, he threw another piece

1. Dalai Lama: *Autobiography*, p. 120.

down on the floor." Just shows breeding; sheer lack of manners and common courtesy.

During this prolonged visit to China and its countryside, one enduring impression that the Dalai Lama gathered was that the minds of the people had already been 'reformed and reshaped in the pattern of communism'. The same 'strong impression of a uniform mass mind' prevailed throughout the Dalai Lama's tour to various places like monasteries, industrial plants, workers organizations, cooperative farms, schools and universities.

Dalai Lama Visits India

A ray of light appeared when in June 1956 the Crown Prince of Sikkim brought an invitation from the Mahabodhi Society of India for the Dalai Lama to attend the Buddha Jayanti, the 2,500th anniversary of the birth of Lord Buddha to be celebrated in India. But China denied permission for the Indian visit on grounds of security. However, on 1st October, Mr. Nehru telegraphed a personal invitation to Peking that included the Panchen Lama also. The Chinese relented, reluctantly. And at the end of the Indian visit, the Dalai Lama returned home, also reluctantly. Before leaving India he invited Mr. Nehru to visit Lhasa, which the latter gladly accepted. However, when in 1959 Mr. Nehru expressed his desire to make the visit in that year, the Chinese Communist Government told him politely to postpone his visit indefinitely, since they could not guarantee his safety in Tibet suggesting, *inter alia*, the Tibetans might have harmed him instead of welcoming him.

Soon after entering Sikkim, the Maharaja of Sikkim received the Dalai Lama who changed over from a jeep to the Maharaja's car. The car was flying the Sikkimese flag on one side and the Tibetan flag on the other. A great crowd of people was throwing scarves and flowers in greeting. So the car stopped for a little while before entering the town. It was then that a solitary Chinese gentleman, who turned out to be the Ambassador's interpreter, was seen 'furtively removing the Tibetan flag and tying on a Chinese flag instead'. It was indeed a comic incident, noticed by the Indian hosts too, who also saw the funny side of it. The tumultuous scenes of welcome were repeated all along the drive from Kalimpong to Bagdogra Airfield where thousands broke through iron railings and police cordons to have *darshan* of the Dalai Lama. The surging crowds rushed to the *shamiana* (marquee) when a stone tied to a ceremonial scarf struck the Panchen Lama on his face. The Dalai Lama was safe but with thousands of Tibetans convinced that the Panchen was a mere puppet of the Chinese, anything could have happened. The Indian security police promptly evacuated the two High Lamas to the airport restaurant and closed all doors and windows.

On arrival at Delhi by a special plane, the Dalai Lama was received by Vice President, Dr. S. Radhakrishnan and Prime Minister Nehru. The Chinese Ambassador, who was in the plane, insisted on introducing His Holiness first to the two Indian dignitaries and then to the members of the diplomatic corps. Finally they came to the representative of the United States. "It was a delicate exercise in diplomatic manners. At the crucial moment, the Chinese Ambassador suddenly vanished like a magician, and I was left face to face with the American. Somebody from the Indian Foreign Office tactfully stepped in and introduced us."[2]

These comic incidents aside, the God-King of Tibet was soon engrossed in Lord Buddha and in spreading His teachings of the path of enlightenment not only for the people of Asia, but for the entire world.

As soon as the Dalai Lama was free from the main purpose of his visit to India, he had 'first real talk' with Prime Minister Nehru. By that time he had had plenty of interaction with non-Tibetans who expressed true sympathy for the plight of Tibetans. Since he felt that he could not be of much help to his people in Tibet, he had "reluctantly come to a new conclusion: I ought not to go home again." But Nehru was firmly convinced that nothing could be done for Tibet 'at present'. Yes, "at present"; since Mr.

---

2. Ibid; pp. 145-46.

Nehru had already missed the bus! Yes; there was a time when a lot could have been done; in fact should have been done. But 'at present' it was too late not only for Tibet but for Nehru's own country too. Nehru told the Dalai Lama that 'nobody had formally recognized' Tibet's independence. That was quite right, and the fault lay with the Government of Tibet. But the Government of Independent India had also certain obligations under the 1904 and 1912 Conventions. The latter were obliged to ensure the autonomous status of Tibet. What did the Indian Prime Minister do to fulfill those obligations? Unfortunately, India's contribution in that direction was totally negative; their policies were pro-Chinese; they did not wish to annoy the Chinese Giant in the least lest ... and the 'lest' did happen: And it happened pretty soon too. Did Aksai Chin require any external recognition that it was part of Indian territorial jurisdiction?[3] Did McMahon Line require any recognition from an outside power? — In short: India was afraid of China, and Nehru was not prepared to risk his status of a world statesman. But was he really a world level statesman? "Power flows through the power of the gun". But the power of India flowed through .303 bolt-action unwieldy rifles!

The Dalai Lama and Prime Minister Nehru were back to 'square one' — "Go back to Tibet and work peacefully to try to carry out the Seventeen Point Agreement". However, before going back, the Dalai Lama wished to visit Kalimpong since the people of that town very much wanted him to come there. But the Chinese Prime Minister had advised against the visit. As was to be expected, Nehru agreed with Chou Enlai's advice but added that if he really wanted to go there, the Indian Government would make suitable arrangements. So the Dalai Lama did visit Kalimpong contrary to Chou's advice. The people up there strongly advised the Dalai Lama not to go back to Tibet; but the

3. Sir Girija Shankar Bajpai, Secretary General to the Ministry of External Affairs, had suggested that India should continue to hold the old Consulate at Kashgar in Sinkiang. It is well on the cards that Chinese infiltration to Aksai could have been frustrated, if the said Consulate had not been abandoned by India — J.P. Mitter: *Betrayal of Tibet*, Calcutta, 1964, p. 10.

Dalai Lama had made up his mind to go back home. And so he did. As he crossed over the Nathu-la into Tibet, he was astonished to see large red flags of China with portraits of Mao-Tse-tung instead of the traditional small prayer flags Tibetans always put up at high places. "No doubt this was meant as a welcome, but it was a melancholy welcome to my own country." A Chinese general was waiting at the other side of the Pass to officially welcome the Dalai Lama to his own country.

On his way up to Lhasa, Tibetans gathered in large numbers at Yatung, Gyantse[4] and Shigatse to warmly welcome the Dalai Lama back to his own home. He took these opportunities to do some 'plain-speaking' in the light of the promises that had been given to him and his brother during their visit to Delhi. He emphasized in his speeches that "the Chinese were not our rulers, and we were not their subjects ... We had been promised autonomous government, and every one should do his best to make it work". He told his people that the rulers of China had assured him that "the Chinese were only in Tibet to help the Tibetans ..." As for help and learning were concerned, Tibetans had no doubt that their technical and cultural development was much behind that of China and India. They were keen to learn, to improve. They adopted almost everything in the way of Chinese material culture, but for knowledge and learning they turned to India.

There are wide gaps between spoken Tibetan and the written language. The latter is the language of religion. Efforts are now afoot to standardize the two. There are four different forms of Tibetan script. The form used for printing is known as *U-chhen*. Originally, Tibetan language had no script. It may be recalled that in the second decade of the seventh century, the Tibetan King Srontsan Gampo sent a delegation of sixteen students led

---

4. Before the Second World War, the British-Indian Government was empowered to issue entry permits to travelers going up to Gyantse without any reference to Lhasa. However, after the War, Lhasa had requested that they be informed of any visitors entering Tibet, even if it was only up to Yatung. Beyond Gyantse, Tibet was totally forbidden to foreigners — *Roof of the World* by Amaury de Riencourt; p. 15

by one of his ministers to India to learn so that the *Nyanpo Sangba*, the "books of hidden greatness" could be translated into Tibetan. Unfortunately, the low altitude and hot climate of plains of India took a heavy toll and all the students died. The minister, Thonmi Sambhota, who worked in Kashmir, was the lone survivor. He devised a new alphabet based on the Kashmiri Sharada alphabet. The new script had thirty characters, based on classical Nagri script, suitably modified to meet different phonetics of the Tibetan language. The minister gathered a number of local students and scholars and got many Buddhist and Hindu scriptures translated into Tibetan. Thus an old prophecy regarding spiritual learning spreading in Tibet came to be fulfilled.

King Srontsan Gampo recognized the value of a political marriage. He married the Nepalese Princess Bhrikuti. She was a devout Buddhist who spread Buddhism in Tibet in place of the old Bön religion. Similarly, the King took Princess Wong Shen Konjö from the Imperial family of China as his wife. She too was a devout Buddhist. Thus the King had politically allied himself with Nepal and China besides getting the benefit of Buddhism as the main religion of Tibet. He had also fulfilled the prophecy made to his ancestor, Lhato Thori, by unlocking the secrets of the 'Hidden Greatness'. Buddha's ten 'Golden Precepts' became law of the land, so did a civil code of sixteen articles devised by the King. King Srontsan Gampo thus became the founder of Buddhism in Tibet.

Notwithstanding the above developments, Tibet continued to look to India for spiritual and intellectual guidance.

8

Revolution

A Mass Up-Rising

The PLA came to Kham in strength in the mid-1950's. At first they appeared quite friendly. But in 1956 they suddenly ordered all Khampas to hand over all their weapons. The Khampas are a class by themselves — well built, powerful martial race who love their land and their liberty. Above all, they love their rifles and other personal arms. A Khampa is a born warrior and will not part with his weapon, not voluntarily of course. He will fight and die, but not surrender his rifle. They are also excellent horsemen and take a great interest in looking after their sturdy riding mules[1] and horses. So they love their saddlery too. The Chinese reacted viciously.[2] They destroyed their monasteries, religious books and humiliated them and their women no end. When they humiliated their religion and images of Lord Buddha, the Khampas' cup of tolerance went over the

---

1. Tibetans' own mules were of poor quality. Good riding mules came from Sinning, near the Chinese border. And they were expensive too — say about fifty pounds sterling plus per piece. And that was the price in the 1960's when one pound sterling was approximately one hundred sangs (Tibetan currency unit).
2. For instance, in just seventeen days in 1966, 69,000 Tibetans were executed in and around Lhasa alone — *Tibet: The Fact*, op. cit. p. 29.

brim. One thing led to another, resulting in full scale organized guerrilla warfare. The Khampas fought the Chinese all over Eastern Tibet under command of their leader, Asuktsang.

Suspicious Invitations

On March 1, 1959, two junior officers from PLA headquarters called to extend an invitation on behalf of their commanding general for the Dalai Lama to attend a theatrical performance in the Chinese military camp. His Holiness politely declined since he was busy preparing for Geshé Lharampa, Doctor of Divinity. The invitation was repeated and the Gyalwa Rinpoché reluctantly fixed the date for 10th March. The performance was to be held inside Silingpu itself, the local headquarters of the PLA, 'an unprecedented location for the Dalai Lama's presence'. A day before the proposed performance, Brigadier Fu called P.T. Takla, officer commanding the 500-man Kusung Magar, the Dalai Lama's Bodyguards, to his office and told him: "Now I want to make this thing clear to you: There will be none of ceremony you usually have. None of your armed men are to come with him, as they do when he goes to the Preparatory Committee. No Tibetan soldier is to come beyond the Stone Bridge ..."[3] The Stone Bridge was the limit of the vast army camp which also contained the Chinese headquarters. It was located within two miles of the Norbulingka and hence was an eye sore not only to Gyalwa Rinpoché but also to the rest of Lhasa-Tibetans. Furthermore, the instruction that the customary guard of twenty-five armed soldiers — a custom that was always observed as an obligatory ceremonial— was to be dispensed with, made the whole affair look extremely suspicious.

Takla was further informed that this entire thing was to be kept strictly secret.[4] It was strange that the Dalai Lama alone was invited; none from his Cabinet was shown this courtesy, nor any of the prominent local citizens. "By custom, my Senior

---

3. Dalai Lama: *Autobiography*; p. 166.
4. Barber Noel: *The Flight of the Dalai Lama*; p. 75.

Chamberlain always accompanied me wherever I went, as the Chinese knew very well, but neither he nor any other officials were included in the invitation." The suspicion that the Dalai Lama may be abducted gained further ground since three airplanes were standing by at Damshung Airport, 70-miles northwest of Lhasa. That added fuel to the fire since the Chinese radio had already announced, without the consent or concurrence of the Dalai Lama, that His Holiness would be attending the meeting of the Chinese National Assembly due to be held in Peking shortly. The curious invitation was therefore taken by the people as a ruse to kidnap the Dalai Lama and fly him out to China against his will. Similar kidnappings and murders had already taken place in the eastern region when high lamas had been invited to parties by Chinese commanders, thus lured away and eliminated.[5] If that was the Chinese plot — which most people had reasons to believe so — it was indeed a very crude stratagem.

"During the evening and night of the ninth of March excitement and agitation grew, and by the morning most people of Lhasa had decided spontaneously to prevent my visit to the Chinese camp at any cost." In the morning the situation took a serious turn. About 30,000 people collected in front of the Norbulingka, making sure that none could enter or leave the Palace. When Phakpala Khenchung, a known collaborator, rode up firing two shots from his revolver to scare away the crowds, he was stoned to death and his body, tied to a horse, was dragged through the city streets. This incident caused profound anguish to His Holiness. Lest the crowd get out of control thereby providing the Chinese army with an excuse to intervene, Prime Minister Surkhang told the crowd that if they had any grievance, "why don't you choose some men as your representatives and I'll let them inside the palace to talk with us, and work with us". This was the genesis of the 'Freedom Committee' of about sixty persons representing various classes-categories of people.

5. Dalai Lama: *Autobiography*, pp. 168-69.

It would be wrong to assume that all Tibetans were against Chinese occupation of their country. There was a microscopic minority that was collaborating with the occupation forces, working against the interests of their country. It would not have mattered if this group of people were from the lower or middle classes; it was the ministerial level as well as senior monks who were working for the Chinese forces against the Dalai Lama. Phakpala mentioned above was one of them. Another prominent person in this category was Ngabo, a senior monk. The Prime Minister, Surkhang, got information from a spy planted by him in the Chinese military camp as a cleaner that 'some sort of abduction was being discussed at Yutok'. Outside the Place there was near rioting. The leaders of the crowd made it clear that in no circumstance would the Dalai Lama be allowed to leave the palace grounds. Surkhang and Phala thereafter confronted His Holiness and bluntly told him that he must not visit the Chinese military camp, then or any time thereafter. The Gyalwa Rinpoché reluctantly agreed to abide by the wishes of the people.

A cabinet minister soon announced that the Dalai Lama had cancelled his appointment for the evening show, and that he would not accept any invitations to PLA headquarters in the future. General Dan Guansan was absolutely furious and promised severe reprisals. Concurrently, the local leaders declared an end to the Seventeen Point Agreement. There were mass demonstrations against the Chinese regime. The spirit of freedom inspired the people all over. Kusung Magar revolted. They discarded their Chinese uniforms and donned their own old Tibetan ones. They took up positions around the Jewel Park. The Dalai Lama's family was moved from Yabshi House to a small pavilion in the Norbulingka as a precautionary measure.

Lhasa in Turmoil

The revolt against Chinese rule had reached its flash point. Anything could happen any moment. The Gyalwa Rinpoché was terribly upset, not for himself but for his people. The consequences of a clash would be catastrophic for the people of Tibet in general, and of Lhasa in particular. During this period the correspondence exchanged between the Chinese Headquarters on the one hand, and the Dalai Lama and the Cabinet on the other, makes interesting reading. The Chinese used these letters to tell the world that the Dalai Lama was kept under duress by a "reactionary clique", and finally abducted out to India against his own free will. It was indeed preposterous for anyone to assume that the Dalai Lama required any protection from the Chinese against his own people, whose sole concern was the safety and wellbeing of the Gyalwa Rinpoché. The Chinese had already fired the first salvo and were preparing to reduce the Norbulingka to smithereens thereby endangering the life of the 'Precious One'. The crisis in Lhasa had passed the pint of no return.[6] The events were inexorably moving at break-neck speed adding new chapters to the history of Tibet. Meanwhile, the Chinese were sending additional reinforcements and heavy guns to Lhasa. The Sacred City was under severe military threat as never before. The Kashag ministers therefore called for a hurried conference in one of the houses in the compound of the Summer Palace. They had this well appointed house for such emergencies only. The object of the meeting was to devise ways and means for the Dalai Lama to escape from Lhasa should that become necessary. However, the consensus at the meeting was that the Dalai Lama should leave Lhasa at the earliest and set up his Government outside Lhasa, possibly in the South, the Khampa controlled territory. At this point of time, there was no thought of fleeing to India. In view of the extreme urgency and delicacy of the matter, Surkhang left the meeting and went straight to

---

6. That was not all. Repeated protest demonstrations and riots broke out in Lhasa during 1987 and 1989. Refugees kept streaming into Dharmsala with hair-raising stories of Chinese atrocities. Nonetheless, many well to do Lhasans continued to console themselves with the thought that it was not the Chinese that were the problem, it is the Communists! The situation had gone bad to worse with Mao's catastrophic Great Leap Forward to the famine of 1958-62.

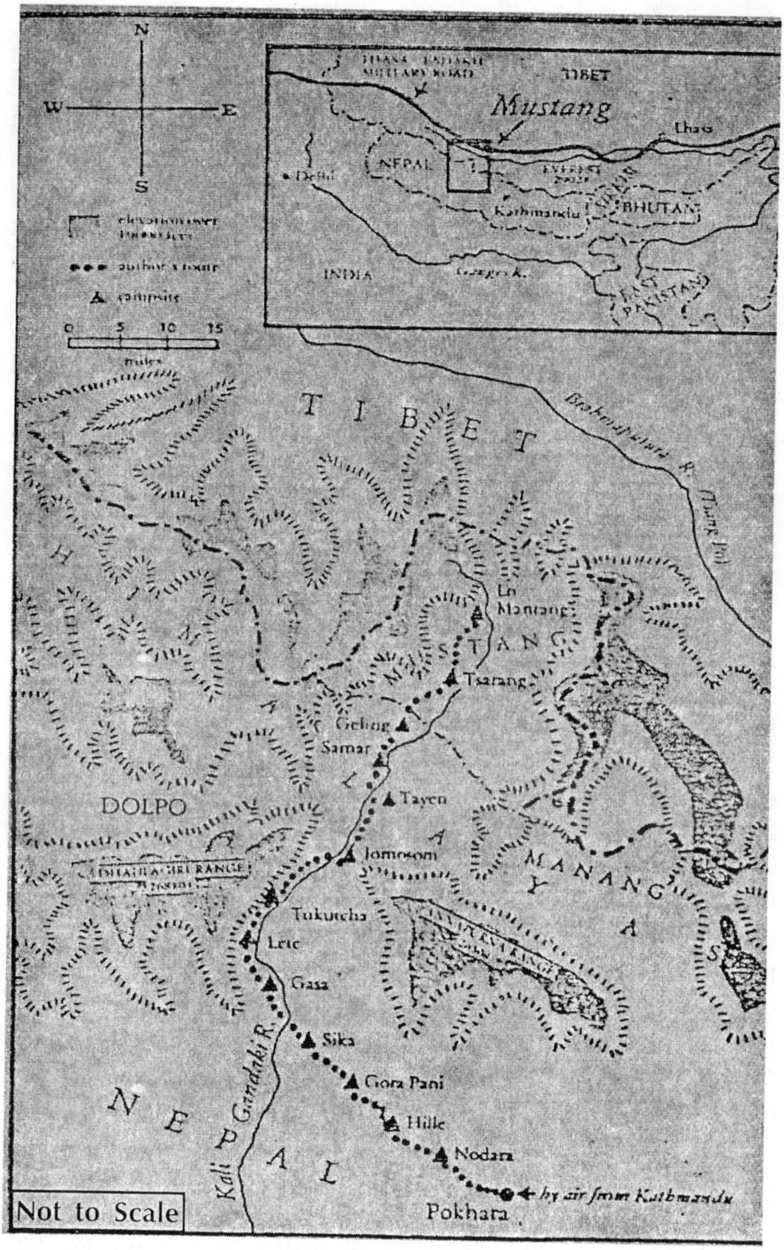

Map of Mustang

private apartments of the Dalai Lama and told him bluntly that it was the advice of his government that the Dalai Lama should leave Lhasa as soon as possible and set up his government outside Lhasa till help could come from India or the Western countries. Since India and the West had so far shown brutal indifference to the plight of Tibet, His Holiness did not expect any help from outside. He was silent for a while, deep in thought, and then said: 'I didn't think it was as serious as that. I don't want to leave my people, but I do agree that I may have to'. However, by 16th March the situation had reached flash point. There was a sort of 'corporate tension' in the air. The writing on the wall was 'bloodshed'. The Chinese were fully prepared to bring down an artillery barrage on the Norbulingka irrespective of whether the Dalai Lama was there or not; whether he would be killed or survived — that was none of their business.

Notwithstanding the severe turmoil that had engulfed Lhasa and its surrounding areas, the Chinese were all out to keep up the pretence that there was nothing wrong anywhere in Tibet; it was all quiet and peaceful. The Chinese were indeed an enigma to themselves and to the outside world. In this game of make-believe, Peking radio had a most powerful and trustworthy collaborator. Name? Mr. Jawaharlal Nehru, the venerable Prime Minister of India who, in a rather lighthearted manner, informed the Indian Parliament that very day that reports of trouble in Lhasa were 'bazaar rumours' adding that the situation in Tibet was a 'clash of minds rather than a clash of arms'. A typical pigeon and cat tale! To say that he was ignorant of the true situation would be a travesty of the highest order. After all, the Indian Consulate in Lhasa was in constant radio communication with Delhi. This was yet another instance of deliberately misleading the Indian Parliament, the Lok Sabha, of appeasement of Chinese in the vain hope of gaining their friendship. Mr. Nehru denied any large scale violence in Lhasa, or anywhere else in Tibet for that matter. But ironically, the same Mr. Nehru did not blink an eye when he announced two days later that the Indian Consulate in Lhasa had been shelled by Chinese artillery![7] As far as the Dalai Lama was concerned, he was quite prepared to make a last desperate effort to go to the Chinese military camp and 'throw myself on the mercy of the Chinese if that would have prevented the massacre of my people'. The letter was smuggled to Ngabo who acknowledged it with a promise of a detailed reply later, which never came.

Guerrilla Base in Mustang

Mustang was a tiny 750-square-miles 'kingdom' jutting out like an elevated wedge into western Tibet, the highest kingdom[8] in the world with a mean altitude of 15,000-feet. In 1802 F. Buchanan describes Mustang as a 'Lordship in Tibet'. Although an island of ethnic Tibetan culture[9], the sparse population was not mongoloid. It was a vassal state of Nepal since early nineteenth century. Its only obligation to Nepal was payment of annual tax of about $100/-;[10] otherwise it had practically no contact with Kathmandu because of its geographical isolation, being about three weeks trek from the Nepalese capital. Nonetheless, access to Mustang was controlled by Kathmandu. The only approach to Mustang was from the south through the extremely narrow and deep Kali Gandaki Gorge — the greatest canyon on earth. It was the world's deepest gorge since it was located between two of the world's highest mountain peaks, 26,504-foot Annapurna and 26,801-foot Mount Dhaulagiri towering 18,000 feet above the

7. It may be recalled that earlier Mr. Nehru had tried to mislead the Parliament and Indian public regarding the Chinese incursions in the Aksai Chin area and the casualties suffered by an Indian patrol doing its duty within Indian territory.

8. Phag Ri in Tibet is the highest habitation in the world; altitude around eighteen thousand feet — Brennan J.H.: op. cit. p. 4.

9. Like in Tibet, polyandry was common in Mustang also, for exactly the same reasons.

10. The Raja of Mustang used to pay the tax to the king of Jumla; however, when the Gorkha defeated Jumla, the tax payment was shifted to Kathmandu. The Raja was obliged to pay a certain amount of tax to Lhasa also. He was called a Raja by the Hindus; otherwise his designation was Lo Gyalpo — *Gyalpo* in Tibetan means King.

river, an almost three miles high perpendicular walls! — an excellent natural defensive position, virtually impassable. Mustang had tremendous strategic value in that it was situated very close to the Chinese newly built Xinjiang-Lhasa highway. It was one of Tibet's two main arteries, originating in Kham and running along the entire northern scarp of the Himalayas through Indian territory of Aksai Chin region of Ladakh.

In so far as taking liberties with neighbours' territories was concerned, the Dalai Lama had an innate sense of Chinese[11] mental calisthenics. At one time he had confided to Sir Charles Bell — "The Chinese way is to do something rather mild at first; then to wait a bit, and if it passes without objection, to say or do something stronger. But if we take objection to the first statement or action, they urge that it has been misinterpreted, and cease, for a time at any rate, from troubling us further. The British should keep China busy in Tibet, holding her back there. Otherwise, when the Chinese obtain complete hold over Tibet they will molest Nepal and Bhutan also."[12] How very perceptive and insightful on the part of a young man whose exposure to the outside world and diplomatic antics was so extremely limited. The Dalai Lama's prediction proved to be correct. Soon after the Chinese had consolidated their position in Tibet, they announced that Nepal and Bhutan are feudatory to China. Not only that, in so far as Bhutan was concerned, the Chinese Amban in Lhasa issued a directive to Bhutan that Chinese coins would be legal tender in Bhutan and shall be given free currency there. Indeed, Chinese were experts par excellence in nibbling at the next door. The Tibetan proverb was most apt to describe this: "When one has seen a scorpion, one looks on the frog as divine."

The then un-surfaced highway and its rickety single telegraph line connected various Chinese garrisons along the 1,500-mile sensitive border, most of which had come under illegal occupation of China over the past about one decade. The guerrillas operating from Mustang had the benefit of an inaccessible cave-monastery,

11. Tibetans call the Chinese as *Gyami*.

12. Bell, Charles, Sir: *Portrait of the Dalai Lama*; London, 1946, p. 99.

Nyphu Gompa, tucked away in a cliff dotted with dozens of small black holes, set one above the other, about a thousand feet above a small village. It was more like an underground hive, snug and full of activity like in a nest for birds.[13]

The Rebellion

The conditions in Tibet deteriorated rapidly under the rule of PLA. Famine, physical torture, forced compliance with so-called democratic reforms, separation of children from their families to be brought up in communes, confiscation of property, collectivization of private farms — the list of atrocities, brutalities and executions was endless. The PLA implemented the so-called democratic reforms in Central Tibet in a rather gentle manner; but in the Kham and Amdo regions they were ruthless. Violent intimidation and enforced socialization was the order of the day, with children being abducted to be brought up not as Tibetans, but as Chinese under State control. The Khampas reaction was violent. Thousands of them took up their arms and overwhelmed the Chinese garrisons at Derge, Kanze, Nyarong, Po, Lithang, et al, who retreated to safety. During the summer of 1956 the PLA once again resorted to highhandedness thus giving birth to Tibet's formal guerrilla resistance movement, christened *Chushi Gangdrug*: 'Four Rivers, Six Ranges" after the rivers and mountains of Tibet. Gompo Tashi Angdrugtsang, an important trader from Lithang took charge of field operations while Dalai Lama's second elder brother, Gyalo Thondup, who lived in Darjeeling, looked after the intelligence gathering work. With the assistance of his Chinese wife, he had already enlisted the aid of Taiwan in para-dropping in Eastern Tibet a limited quantity of arms and ammunition for the guerrillas. Since requests to Taiwan were passed on to CIA, the US authorities told him to get in direct touch with them for better coordination. Thus contacts with CIA were established. A base for training Tibetan guerrillas in modern weaponry, commando techniques and parachuting was organized at Guam. In the first instance six

---

13. Michael Piesel: op. cit. p. 252.

Tibetans were smuggled to Guam via India and Thailand, given short intensive training, and then air dropped in Tibet at night to organize local resistance group. These small groups of Kham fighters operating from horsebacks made frequent forays on small PLA outposts and ambushed Chinese convoys, so much so that even the road between Lhasa and Yatung became unusable for the Chinese due to Khampa guerrilla activities.

At this point of time, Gyalwa Rinpoché was firmly opposed to armed opposition to the occupation forces. They were much too strong for the Tibetans to be able to make any headway. Gompo Tashi then approached the CIA if they would support the Tibetans if active hostilities break out. Their answer: Certainly; but only if the Dalai Lama approached them direct in clear cut terms. By then the cat was out of the bag and Gompo Tashi left Lhasa for the love of his life. He established Chushi Gangdrug headquarters at Drigu Thang in Lhoka. About five hundred cavalrymen were enlisted. On June 16 an impressive cavalry parade was staged. The first battle lasted good part of three days in which about two hundred Chinese were killed for forty of the guerrillas.

The Chinese reaction was severe and devastating. Entire villages were obliterated by air bombardment. Mass executions took place. Crucifixion, dismemberment, vivisection, beheading, burying, burning and scalding alive, dragging the victim behind galloping horses, pushing people out of airplanes, forcing children to shoot their parents, monks were made to publicly copulate with the nuns, desecration of sacred images — such atrocities and brutalities became routine treatment against the suspects, proof or no proof; that was immaterial indeed. The prophecies by State Oracles and the Thirteenth Gyalwa Rinpoché himself proved more than accurate. The PLA laid siege to large areas of Tibetan habitation, and then systematically annihilated them in small pockets, one by one. A mass exodus of refugees took place westwards, seeking shelter under the protective wings of the Dalai Lama at Lhasa. It was not long, therefore, that the rebellion spread to Central Tibet. The inevitable had to happen. On 16th June 1958, *Danglang Tensung Makhar* (Volunteer National Defence Army — VNDA for short) was formed at Drigu. By this time there were three resistance organizations: Chushi Gangdruk, the original Mimang Tsongdu, and now the VNDA. All three assembled under the banner of VNDA in a plain about one hundred miles from Lhasa. About 5,000 cavalry raised VNDA flag before the portrait of His Holiness. The rebellion had the blessings of Tibetan Government. The level of fighting escalated. There were 80,000 Khampa horsemen in U-Tsang alone, within about thirty miles of Lhasa. Soon they over-ran the 3,000 man PLA garrison at Tsethang. The Chinese ordered the Tibetan Government to deploy Tibetan Army to put down the rebellion. They declined. There was no question of Tibetans killing Tibetans. In any case the task was beyond their capability, more so since the Tibetan Army units were being integrated with the PLA.

One of the side-effects of the Rebellion in the East, and its spreading westwards to Lhasa, was movement of large number of Khampa refugees taking shelter in and around Lhasa, and seeking protection of the Government. Since the revolt had started in the eastern Khampa and Amdo regions, these people were mortally afraid that the Chinese would take revenge on them. So they petitioned the Cabinet seeking state protection. The Chinese commanders told the Cabinet to assure these refugees that they would not take a general punitive action against the people from the eastern region. This mollified the refugees for a while. However, soon they were back to the Cabinet requesting for a formal written assurance from the Chinese commander that the Khampas and Amdo people would not be punished. But the Chinese refused to give such an assurance. Their reasoning was all the more irrational — they said that if such an assurance became public and reached Indian ears, China would lose face. Sounds curious indeed, and totally unconvincing. Indeed, the Chinese had an extraordinary way of mixing matters of the highest importance with totally trivial details. When this matter of security of the eastern people was being discussed at the government level, the Chinese demanded that these people should always be referred to as "reactionaries". Since the authorities in Tibet did not attach any emotional significance to this phrase, it came to be synonymous with guerrillas, and its nuance had a sense of admiration for the freedom fighters as far as the Tibetans were concerned.[14] However, the Chinese lacked the necessary depth of understanding to know this inner voice of the Tibetan people. Ironically, the Chinese were 'haunted by a similar spectre' of non-existent 'imperialist forces' in Tibet. If there were any imperialist forces in Tibet, it was none but the Chinese themselves!

The guerrilla resistance under the auspices of Chushi Gangdruk continued well after the Dalai Lama's escape to India. The young and healthy Khampas working in road-gangs in India continued to be recruited for training and guerrilla actions in Tibet to harass the Chinese forces and cause disruption. During early stages they were taken to East Pakistan where Pak Army conducted the Tibetan volunteers in army trucks to Dacca from where they were airlifted to Okinawa military base. After four months training in Guam/Okinawa the volunteers were dropped in Tibet to keep up the resistance movement. However, a few weeks after the March uprising, the CIA[15] decided to train the Tibetans in the United States. The scope of training was enlarged, so was the strength of a working-unit increased to 500 men. Utmost secrecy was maintained so much so that the Tibetans were never told that they were in the United States, nor did they have any means to know this fact on their own; they were completely isolated. The training base was located at Camp Hale in the middle of the Rocky Mountains. The training period was

14. Dalai Lama: *Autobiography*, pp. 161-62.

15. In 1960 CIA changed the training base from the US to Mustang in Nepal Himalayas. The weaponry was 55mm recoil-less rifles, mortars, carbines and explosive devices. CIA was spending nearly US$2million annually on this operation, besides paying US$180,000 to the office of His Holiness. Due to various reasons, American support for Tibetan guerrilla operations was gradually withdrawn. It came to a complete halt after President Nixon's rapprochement with Beijing in 1972. On the orders of National Security Adviser Henry Kissinger, all covert funding to Dalai Lama also ceased. His first visit to Chengdu was code-named 'Polo I'!

fixed as six months after which the volunteers were to be air dropped in the regions to which they belonged. By the time this large batch of volunteers had finished their training, the entire balance of power in Central Asia had undergone complete metamorphosis including the CIA-Tibetan link. However, 5:00 a.m. October 20th, 1962, opened Nehru's eyes. The irrationality of his government's policies at the national security level, in geo-strategic military planning and international diplomatic relations, et al, came staring in his face. India suffered a humiliating national disaster of horrendous proportions.

Guerrilla Training

By the middle of 1960 training of Tibetan volunteers by the American Central Intelligence Agency (CIA) successively in Okinawa-Guam-Camp Hale in the Rockies was well under way. The National Volunteer Defence Army (VNDA) of Tibet decided to locate their main base less than two hours north of the principality of Mustang waging a fierce fight for Tibet's freedom. Mustang was indeed home ground for the Khampas who could operate from there against the Chinese with almost complete impunity, as well as support guerrilla activities in southern and eastern Tibet. In the early stages, Mustang as a base was established by men of the VNDA who had retreated from Lhoka under 'General' Gompo Tashi whose troops fought main rearguard actions to facilitate Gyalwa Riposte's escape from Chinese clutches. Soon they were joined by other guerrilla groups many of whom had reached India as refugees working as road gangs.[16] They were mostly Khampas who managed to reach Mustang following the route Darjeeling-Gangtok through thick jungles of southern Nepal—up

---

16. While superintending the construction of Hindustan-Tibet (HT Road) along the Sutlej Valley in Kinnaur district of Himachal Pradesh, the Author had a few thousand Tibetan refugees working as road gangs. They were given generous assistance in various ways which attracted the attention of the personal office of His Holiness, the Dalai Lama. A couple of letters of appreciation issued by his Private Secretary in 1968 now proved useful to the Author to get autographed photo of His Holiness along with some other excellent pictures.

the Kali Gandaki Gorge—finally making it to the Tibetan Plateau at Mustang's border. 'General' Baba Yeshi — illiterate but highly intelligent and extremely ruthless — was Mustang's Tibetan commander who developed a well organized support base, flying Tibetan flag, for covert operations against the Chinese, *Gyamis* as the Tibetans call them.[17] About two hundred Tibetans were deployed in Mustang under arrangements of the CIA. They were soon reinforced by forty trained volunteers from Camp Hale, para-dropped along with badly needed weapons, ammunition and communication equipment. "Death-pills" were also part of the consignment! Twelve additional trained men arrived on foot via India. These guerrillas fought their first action in 1961 when they raided a Chinese convoy killing six of the enemy against loss of one of their own. The raids against the Chinese convoys continued for many years. Initially, the guerrillas were paid Rs. 5,000 per month, later increased to Rs. 11,250. All the money was routed through Gyalo Thondup in India. There were ten war-camps in Mustang sending out raiding parties against Chinese supply columns.[18]

Like all bubbles burst, so do all good tidings come to a dead end. Henry Kissinger made a secret visit to China leading to rapprochement between the two super powers. Tibet took a back seat in international arena; in fact no seat at all! CIA connection snapped as quickly as it had come into being. Nepal saw the warning signals and declared all Tibetans in Mustang as *persona non grata*. Out they went. Nepal's own survival came first. Meantime there were internal internecine squabbles amongst the guerrillas themselves. Baba Yeshi broke with the main organization, accepted Kathmandu's offer of political asylum and spilled the beans. That was the end of Mustang episode.

Establishment Two-Two

A belated sense of responsibility dawned on Indian political leadership. A Special Frontier Force code named "Establishment

---

17. Tibetans always called the Chinese as 'beggars', behind their back of course.
18. Grunfeld: op. cit. p.156.

22" was founded in the remote Chakrata area in the Garhwal Hills. It was raised on November 13, 1962, under Cabinet Secretariat (Research and Analysis Wing — RAW) supervised directly from the Prime Minister's Office with the primary object of training Tibetans as commandos to fight in their own country in furtherance of India's security environment, besides guarding the world's highest borders. The nucleus of training shifted from the Rockies to India's own backyard without the earlier complications of Pakistan-link. CIA[19] assistance by way of technical know-how, supply of weapons and equipment and financial support continued much against covert protests by the Chinese Government. Indian officers formed the core of instructional staff while a few Gorkha officers were later co-opted. Even in the face of blatant denials by the Tibetan Government-in-Exile as well as the Indian Government, the headquarters of National Volunteer Defence Army (VNDA) were located at Delhi, which hereafter controlled its activities. A special communication centre was set up in Orissa to maintain contact with the operatives in Tibet besides collecting intelligence. Orissa was particularly suitable since the area was free of dense radio traffic.

A meeting of senior officers of VNDA, RAW and CIA was held at Delhi every Monday night, intelligence transcripts from Tibet were analyzed and directions given accordingly. By 1970 the CIA support had totally dried up because of American deep involvement in South East Asia resulting in India being the sole support of Tibetan guerrilla movement. The Indian Government established the Indo-Tibetan Border Police (ITBP) for which the Tibetans were directly recruited as part of the Indian Army. These recruits were trained at Chakrata, Dehradun, for eventual deployment for liberation of Tibet from the Chinese yoke. Para-jumping training was imparted at Air Force Station, Sarsawa, in

19. Initially, CIA started training Tibetan guerrillas in a highly secret operation on the remote Pacific Island of Saipan, and later shifted to Camp Hale in the Rocky Mountains in Colorado. They para-dropped into Tibet by night from US planes dressed in chubas and equipped with rifles, mortars and hand-cranked Morse radios, plus of course cyanide capsules.

conjunction with the Para establishment at Agra. In fact, some ITB personnel, the Tibetans, "were used in the Bangladeshi War, in which forty-one were killed" in action.[20]

Defection by a Chinese General

The Chinese military camp at Lhasa held weekly cinema shows for the benefit of its soldiers. They would assemble in their respective unit areas and march to the camp cinema filling the long single-storey building. The officers were the last to come in and they occupied the front seat. On Tuesday, February 24, 1958, all the front seats were occupied, except one reserved for General Chang Hwa-ting, Commander of Artillery, who had sent a message to say that he was not well. In fact he was hale and hearty and was sorting out his things, getting ready to defect to the Tibetans, Khampas to be more precise. To the Tibetans, it came as an unbelievable bolt from the blues — certainly a most unexpected development.

General Chang had given this grave matter a deep thought, and only then come to this momentous decision. He was a sensitive man, cultured and sincere, a man of personal convictions. For him, ideals mattered more than creature comforts or material gains. An introspective man, he could not reconcile himself to the atrocities being inflicted on the Tibetans by his countrymen. His conscience did not permit him to be a party to outrageous treatment being meted out to the people of Tibet. In fact, he was convinced that his army, his country, had no business to be in Tibet. "I am perfectly certain that many of them would have liked to help us, but they were all subject to strict communist discipline ... One of them, however, felt so strongly that he joined our guerrilla forces in 1958 and fought with them for nine months, and is now a refugee in India".[21] It was not a simple matter to cast away an unblemished military career for a cause which had no prospect whatsoever of success; Tibet could never be free, but the General listened to the voice of his inner conscience and cast his lot with the guerrillas. When the cinema show was well on its way, he drove

20. Grunfeld: op. cit. p.157.

21. Dalai Lama: *Autobiography*, p. 155.

over to the main Tibetan army camp near Sera monastery, about four miles north of the capital city. It took him about half an hour to reach the gate of Tibetan army camp where the sentry was startled when he faced a full fledged Chinese general in uniform. Chang knew very little Tibetan, really none at all. He came out of the jeep, raised both his arms above his head, and said: "General Tasha Paran" — the name of the (Tibetan) Camp Commandant.

While sipping ceremonial tea, Chang told Paran that he wanted to join Tibetan guerrillas. It came as a bombshell to Paran, since it had grave political implications. "Why this change of heart?" Chang told Paran: "Under Communism I have no liberty. The Communists treat all human beings as animals, and I don't believe we Chinese have any right to be in Tibet."

Tasha Paran (or Tashi-Para) ordered his horse to be saddled immediately, placed Chang under arrest, and at 11:00 p.m. at night set off alone for the Summer Palace where he knew he would find Phala, the Senior Chamberlain of the Dalai Lama. Over the inevitable cups of buttered tea, Paran told the entire story to Phala. Phala had known Chang earlier. Both men agreed that 'the Chinese general could be trusted'. Phala decided to accept Chang as a guerrilla whose value in fighting the Chinese in the South would prove most useful in the long run. Phala also decided that His Holiness must not be told anything about this episode, since it would put him in an awkward political situation. He further told Tasha Paran that even the Kashag must not be given any hint of this matter. Secrecy was of the utmost importance if they were going to be able to make use of Chang's military capabilities. Moreover, it was absolutely essential that Chang must be taken out of Lhasa immediately, this very night, before the Chinese authorities realized that one of their senior generals was missing.

Chang was kitted out as a Khampa guerrilla. His new name was Lobsang Tashi. Phala asked Paran to tell Chang: "I admire his courage ... one day when I am in the South, I'll surely meet him". The Chinese general was now one of the Khampa guerrillas in whose company he crossed the Tsang-po around dawn. The Chinese Chief, General Tan, accused Kashag and every one else that mattered of having abducted one of the senior officers of the Chinese Army. He warned them of dire consequences and gave them one week to return the Chinese general ... the week would be up on March 3.[22] While Chang saw the present and the future, the Indian saw only the past and the present; they just did not think of the future implications of strategic developments of the present and how they would affect the future security scenario. Indeed, we Indians were true to the proverb:

If he drinks beer, his head aches;
If he does not drink, his heart aches.

Indian political thinking on matters of military strategy was invariably in a limbo. And we have been paying a heavy price ever since, for the inability of our political leadership to see beyond their nose.

After Tasha Paran had accepted the surrender of the Chinese General, certain incidents of wanton killing of some Tibetan soldiers by the Chinese soldiers in the nearby Chinese camp had generated anti-Chinese feelings in the mind of Tasha Paran, so much so that he started looking at every Chinese as a spy of the PLA. It was about six months after the Chinese General's defection that a young Chinese captain approached Tasha Paran for asylum on the grounds that he had fallen in love with the daughter of the gardener at the Lingka Sarpa (New Park) on the north bank of the Kyichu. Initially, his superior officer permitted him to marry the girl; but when it transpired that she was a Tibetan, permission was promptly revoked. That is when the young captain approached Tasha Paran for asylum. Tasha refused the request. For all one knew, the Captain may be a PLA spy being planted by the clever Chinese. He therefore decided to send the Captain back to the Chinese camp. It was then that the Captain told Tasha to shoot him rather than send him back because in any case he would have to face execution, besides torture, in the Chinese camp. Now Tasha was convinced that the Captain was not a mole. He gave him a new name, Lobsang Tashi and took him in his régiment. It turned out that the Chinese Captain was far more knowledgeable in guerrilla tactics than anyone else in the Tibetan Regiment.

---

22. Barber Noel: op. cit. pp. 59-63.

9

The Great Escape

The first shots were fired at 4:00 p.m. March 17, 1959. Two mortar shells fell in the Norbulingka palace gardens where the Gyalwa Rinpoché was holding a cabinet meeting, causing no damage. It was a clear enough warning of the bloodshed yet to come. However, the Chinese consistently denied that they fired any shells at all on the Norbulingka. Surprisingly, there was no further bombardment. The Gyalwa Rinpoché was not afraid of becoming a victim of Chinese shelling; for him 'the end of one mortal frame was of no great consequence.' But the people and officials did not share this view. "To them the person of the Dalai Lama was supremely precious". For the people of Tibet, the Dalai Lama represented Tibet and the Tibetan way of life, their history, heritage and culture. "They were convinced that if my body perished at the hands of the Chinese, the life of Tibet would also come to an end ..." There was a compelling anxiety amongst 'all my people to get me away before the orgy of Chinese destruction and massacre began'.[1] Therefore, the first salvo resulted in the momentous decision: Flee Lhasa that very night. It was a unanimous decision of the Cabinet. "I prayed for guidance and received it", recalls the Gyalwa Rinpoché. For all practical purposes, the Dalai Lama had no option. His immediate

1. Dalai Lama: *Autobiography*, p. 195.

family was the first to go; they left at 9:00 p.m., properly disguised of course. Meanwhile, Tenzin Gyatso, the Dalai Lama, wrote a letter formally certifying the names of people's leaders. He completed his disguise quite ingeniously, with the sacred painting of the Protectress Palden Lhamo in the special container slung across his shoulder. Watches were synchronized. The last moments of waiting for the exact time of departure were the most agonizing. Phala was getting worried lest they be recognized. And that is when a miracle took place! One of the worst sandstorms Lhasa had ever experienced wrapped the city. Visibility was down to barely a few feet. In the words of Heinrich Harrer: "As I see it, their miraculous escape could not have been achieved without the astonishing and timely intervention of this sandstorm .... They obliterate every thing."

Shrouded in the severe but most welcome sandstorm, the Gyalwa Rinpoché left the Norbulingka in the company of Kusung Depon (Officer Commanding the Bodyguards), Master of Religious Ceremonies and the Lord Chamberlain. As he left the gates of the Palace, no one recognized the rifle wielding soldier! It was absolutely essential that the fleeing party was well away from Lhasa before dawn. There was no time to waste, not even time enough to go to the treasury to get some funds, or the Potala to collect a small part of the immense wealth of jewels and assorted treasures. Most state papers were in the Potala together with the 'immeasurable wealth of jewels and treasures I had inherited'. All had to be left behind.

Finally they reached the ancient Ramagan ferry site. The party crossed the river in coracles. "Now we are refugees".... The Dalai Lama later recalled: "The day after I escaped from Lhasa, I felt a tremendous sense of relief. Actually the danger was still very much alive. But despite this we were moving freely, on our own, and we had finally come to the point of openly criticizing the Chinese. 'I have the right to say bad things about them', I remember thinking. That feeling of freedom was very vivid: my strongest reaction following the escape." Their immediate objective was to put the wide turbulent Tsang-po behind them but they dare not follow the main tracks lest they meet some Chinese patrol. Therefore, they made for a lesser known ferry site at a small village known as Kyishong, or 'Happy Valley'. After crossing the great river whose valley is the lifeline of Tibet, they would be in the security of Khampa stronghold.

The entire party was totally relaxed, more so with the sense of security generated by the tough looking big, tall powerful Khampas armed with pistols, rifles, swords, and of course their colourful charm boxes. Phala had taken good care of logistics of the escape — the horses, the ferry, food, protection parties, et al. The "refugees" could sleep in peace for a few hours at night since they were well guarded by the devoted Khampa warriors. The fleeing party reached the foot of the Che-la about eight in the morning where they halted for a quick cup of tea. Che-la means "Sandy Pass". It was a long steep climb towards the Pass and the track was rough and weary. A dignified old man, Tashi Norbu, joined the party when they were climbing up. He offered his graceful white horse to Gyalwa Rinpoché. "I accepted it gratefully, and all my party was happier, because Tibetans consider such a gift as a very good omen. In Tibet, it is customary to ride uphill but to walk downhill. An old Tibetan proverb, aptly describes the custom:

> *If you do not carry him up a hill, you're no horse,*
> *If you do not walk down the hill, you're no man.*

Not that the fleeing party was out of danger; far from it. The Chinese were literally hunting for the Dalai Lama, from the air and by fast moving ground troops. There was no time to rest. A quick cup of tea and off they left, leaving behind three hundred picked Khampas of the Khelenpa, or 'Suicide Squad', to guard the ferry site against Chinese crossing. Soon a ferocious battle was fought here to ensure that the Chinese could not cross to cut off the Gyalwa Rinpoché route of escape. Meanwhile, Norbulingka was shelled at 2:00 a.m. March 20th, just over forty-eight hours after the Dalai Lama had left the City, but before the "Chinese had discovered that I had gone." The Chinese artillery kept up their bombardment of Norbulingka for the whole of that day, knowing fully well that the Dalai Lama was there, and might as well be killed in the process. In other words they were least concerned whether the Dalai Lama lived or died, better dead than alive. Concurrently, they turned their artillery on the Potala. Thousand upon thousands of Tibetans were killed and wounded in this wanton act of destruction. The streets of Lhasa were littered with bodies. Of course, there was no one to provide any medical aid to the wounded; they too would have died. What was the Indian Consulate, the guardian of liberty doing? And what could a poor major in-charge of the Indian Consulate do under the circumstances! After all, the cardinal principle of Indian Government's policy in respect of Tibet was appeasement of the Chinese. Whatever they wished to do in Tibet, they could go ahead and do it without any fear or qualms. The Indian Government had voluntarily abrogated their rights and privileges with respect to Tibet, and was now totally powerless to intervene. By dawn on Friday, 20th March, Lhasa was ringed by heavily armed men of the PLA. Every main exit was blocked. To cap it all, even after the Chinese had come to know that the Dalai Lama was no longer in Lhasa, that he had escaped, they still continued to bomb Lhasa. What for this continued wanton and senseless destruction of life and property with its ancient treasures ...?[2] Although success crowned the Tibetan efforts in hand-to-hand fighting in which they were far superior to the Chinese, the glory was a mere passing phase, albeit morale-raising all the same. The Chinese were much too strong for the Tibetans to make much of a dent in their fortified positions. Nonetheless, by Saturday the world press was full of stories of Tibetan heroic resistance to Chinese occupation forces, and their success in close-quarter battles in narrow by-lanes of Lhasa. Destruction of the Tibetan offices of the New China News Agency was a notable success for the guerrillas. The Chinese news media did not make any mention of shelling of the Indian Consulate nor the severe damage inflicted by Chinese artillery

---

2. One stray shell knocked out the ancient plumbing system for the Dalai Lama's English bath, leaving the bath itself undamaged — Noel Barber: op. cit. p. 133.

Tibetan Army contingent on Parade in Lhasa

on the Nepalese Consulate in the Inner City. Indeed, they gave very little coverage to the turmoil and bombardment of Lhasa. Unfortunately, even the shelling of the Indian Consulate did not open the eyes of our worthy top political leader(s), and none had the moral courage to focus on the danger lurking in this apparently innocuous action of Chinese artillery. The Chinese had taken the liberty of violating Indian diplomatic precincts and got away with it without the slightest protest, thereby proving what the Gyalwa Rinpoché had earlier told Sir Charles Bell — 'they' would do something, and if there is no reaction, they would become bolder and do something bigger.

By 23rd March, the fighting had died down to left over embers of a conflagration. Lhasa had fallen to the enemy. The estimates of casualties varied. The Chinese claimed that more than four thousand rebel troops were taken prisoners. If that figure be taken as the base, it would be reasonable to assume that about ten to fifteen thousand Tibetans were killed in and around Lhasa. The Chinese claimed to have captured about eight thousand small arms of different types, eighty light and heavy machine guns, twenty-seven 81-mm mortars, six mountain guns and ten million bullets. Of course, they did not mention how many bullets were of Chinese make which the Tibetans had bought in the flourishing black market of Lhasa!

The news of fall of Lhasa coupled with safe escape of the Dalai Lama was a signal for mass exodus of Tibetans, rich and poor, to the South. They packed whatever little they could take along and set out on a perilous journey whose end they could not visualize. Lhasa had gone; so had their Gyalwa Rinpoché. Tibet was on the threshold of an unprecedented reign of Chinese terror and brutalities. The risks involved in attempted escape were great indeed. But the prize was certainly worth the effort — FREEDOM!

Government in Exile

Zhou Enlai announced dissolution of — what was in name only — the so-called autonomous Government of Tibet and replacing it with the Preparatory Committee for Tibet Autonomous Region. Ngabo, the traitor par-excellence, was appointed Secretary General and Vice Chairman of the Committee. After that, the Dalai Lama naturally felt free to reconstitute his own government which he did on 29th March 1959 at a brief ceremony in Lhuntze D'zong, a sort of Potala in miniature. A Proclamation of the establishment of a temporary government was read out before the assembled gathering. The Dalai Lama "formally signed copies of it to be sent to various places all over Tibet. The ceremonies ended with the staging of the Droshey, the Dance of Propitious Fortune". Back in Lhasa, the city was heavily bombarded and the ill-armed untrained Tibetans were slaughtered in their thousands. They knew the consequences, the end result, but still they put up resistance, an exact repetition of various massacres when the Younghusband Expedition advanced to Lhasa half a century ago. As the Dalai Lama and his entourage neared India, it was decided that the religious and political leaders who had accompanied the Dalai Lama would go with him to India, while the military personnel who had come to provide protection would return to Tibet to fight the enemy. However, there was one signal exception to this rule: Lobsang Tashi, the Chinese General who had the courage of conviction to defy the Chinese, joined the Tibetan guerrillas and fought shoulder to shoulder with them till the Dalai Lama reached the Indian frontier. Lobsang Tashi also got his taste of freedom on Indian soil. Lobsang Tashi's credentials were impeccable, vouched by none other than the Dalai Lama's Chief Chamberlain.[3] Since the Dalai Lama was ill, his followers helped him onto the broad back of a *dzo*, the cross between the yak and Indian cow, which is an equable animal with an easy gait. The God-King of Tibet left his country on that 'primeval Tibetan transport'.

Since domesticated yak is unquestionably the most useful animal in Tibet, the reader would bear with a little digression on the subject. Wild yaks are called *drongs*. They are fierce and dangerous. Wild yaks are dark brown, almost black; but

3. Lobsang Tashi, originally General Chang-Hwa-ting of Chinese Army, was moved to Switzerland where he was appointed head of the Tibetan Office in Geneva.

domesticated ones have varying degree of white. The more the white portion, the more valuable the animal is. They have long shaggy black hair and usually manage to find their own forge. In fact, they seem to require very little for sustenance. Yaks cross-breed easily with any females of the ox family. The female of the species is called *dri* and provides abundant quantities of milk, cream, cheese and butter. Butter, butter and butter; the less said about the butter, the better. It is used even for polishing stone floors! A *dri* crossed with a bull produces a hybrid of immense strength called *dzo,* most useful for agricultural work. The female hybrid is called *dzomo* and it gives more milk than even a *dri.* The dung of the species is used as fuel as well as manure. A yak is valuable both dead and alive — excellent meat, good hide for boots and coracles, saddlebags, ropes, tents, blankets, clothing, snuffboxes from its horns. Indeed, "the yak is the most extraordinary animal Nature has provided. He carries 160 lbs. and consumes nothing. He subsists solely on stray blades of grass, tamarisk, and tufts of lichen, that he picks up on the road. He moves slowly, and bears the look of ineffable resignation ..."[4]

Now back to the trail — When they reached Pa-ri, said to be the dirtiest town in the whole world (!), they were close to the border-demarcation between Bhutan and Chumbi Valley. On the crest of the mountain range that separates Chumbi Valley from Bhutan, there used to be, and perhaps still is, a strong square building, 50×50 feet and forty feet in height, made of large heavy dressed stones, placed one atop the other, without any mortar or mud, and roofed with flat stone-slates. It denotes the boundary mark between Bhutan and Tromo, erected after many territorial disputes and conflicts. The structure is called Pang-kar B-tsi chö-ten. Legend has it that inside this building is a chö-ten, or stupa, and inside the stupa is a copper urn. During the construction stage a boy and a girl, each about eight years old, were slain and their blood poured into this urn. The corpses were then placed in the urn, head downwards and feet pointing towards the roof. A demon took possession of the

---

4. Candler Edmund: *The Unveiling of Lhasa*; New York, 1905; pp. 93-94.

chö-ten after he got the scent of blood and the corpses. The chö-ten lies south-east from Upper Tromo, an inauspicious direction. Thus it comes that, while Bhutan goes unharmed, the devil grievously afflicts the Chumbi Valley."[5]

A decision was to be taken whether to seek safety, and refuge, in Bhutan[6] which was barely two miles way; or to take the long route down the Chumbi valley, climb another five thousand feet over the Dzelep-la into Sikkim and then on to mainland India — a walk of another forty miles. The Dalai Lama used a simple form of divination: Eyes shut; he put the tips of his two forefingers to meet across his forehead. The tips met; so he decided to face the forty miles instead of only two. In the heart of his heart, the Dalai Lama wished to come to India even against the advice of his ministers who, at that point of time, were more concerned with safety. But the Dalai Lama knew that while in India he could bank on diplomatic intervention of the Western world, if not of Mr. Nehru. Moreover, India was a spiritual home to the Tibetans. In the process, they missed the famous nine-storied temple, which Milarepa was ordered to build by his teacher Marpa, as a punishment for Milarepa had been a very sinful person.

The decision having been made, a fast moving advance party was moved ahead to ask for Dalai Lama and his party for political asylum in India. The request was readily granted. The Dalai Lama and his immediate entourage entered India at 4:00 p.m. March 31st through a newly built bamboo welcome gate at the Indian border check-post at Kanzeymane near Chuthangmu, where six Gorkha soldiers presented arms while the guard commander presented a scarf in greeting — welcome to a prolonged exile! After the Dalai Lama left his country, about sixty thousand Tibetans followed him into exile, and thereafter, the trickle continued; it still does.

---

5. Bell: op. cit. p. 81.

6. Potatoes are grown in Bhutan as a sort of cash-crop. Credit for that goes to Warren Hastings, the then Governor of Bengal (1772-1785), who gave specific instructions to George Bogle to plant potatoes during the various stages of his journey into Tibet. How far-sighted, meticulous and wise!

It is virtually impossible to arrive at an accurate figure as to the number of Tibetan refugees now settled in various parts of the world. They are spread all over Asia, Europe and America, the maximum concentration being in India, about 70,000 or so, while the minimum number might be in Japan or Taiwan, the total adding to about 90,000. Whatever be the numbers, the fact remains that the Tibetans have left their homes and hearths to face the harsh realities of refugee camps in alien lands of which they were totally ignorant. Thus they have cast their vote against the Chinese, their communism and way of life, not through a ballot box or an EVM, but literally by their feet by walking out of the country of their birth. The Tibetan refugees have been in their adopted countries for nearly half a century. They have imbibed modern education. Many intellectuals amongst the highly educated refugees have become critical of their elders and the 'Shangri-la' image of historic Tibet that they had presented to the outside world.

Indians were ecstatic over safe exit of His Holiness, the Dalai Lama. China was venomous in its denouncements both of India and Tibet, while Nehru continued to harp on his favourite spineless theme of 'Pancha Sheel' with the oft-repeated resolve that India would never support the cause of Tibetan freedom. However, he announced in the Lok Sabha that the Government of India had granted political asylum to His Holiness the Dalai Lama and other political refugees from Tibet. They were temporarily settled in the northern Indian hill resort town of Mussoorie where Prime Minister Nehru met the Dalai Lama on 24th April. The Indian supporters of Tibetan independence led by the Sarvodaya leader, Mr. Jayaprakash Narain, held a convention in Calcutta on May 30th. How one wished that some one like Lord Curzon was at the helm of affairs with a diplomat of the calibre of Younghusband to handle the day to day knotty problems faced by Tibet and India! The Indian sentiments were aptly conveyed by K.M. Munshi: "For a young independent nation like ours, with its spiritual heritage, our handling of the Tibetan situation has been a crime in history." — A historical blunder of Himalayan proportions right in the midst of the

Himalayas, where traditional butter lamps were replaced by electric 'butter' lights.

Mussoorie was a stop-gap arrangement. The Government of India was on the lookout for a secluded permanent hill-town location for the Dalai Lama and his entourage. The choice fell on Macleod Ganj, established in 1856 when British troops moved up from Jallandhar in the wake of the 1857-Mutiny. It was named after Sir Donald Macleod who later became Lieutenant Governor of the Province. Its cool climate, greenery and altitude were an added attraction. So was the good old name plate — "Nowrojee & Sons Inc., General Merchants." A seventy-one year old Parsi, Nauzer Nowrowjee, was instrumental in persuading the authorities concerned to accept his offer when, in 1960, initial steps to establish the Tibetan Government in Exile at Dharmsala were initiated. Its isolation and distance from Delhi was certainly a negative point. But then the Dalai Lama recalled a Chinese proverb:

As long as it stays among the mountains,
the snow leopard keeps all of its dignity,
but if it descends towards the plains,
it is treated like a dog.

In April 1960 when the move to Macleod Ganj was commenced, there was little rejoicing amongst the exiles. The former bungalow of the district commissioner was almost totally engulfed by the encroaching forest; it was retrieved, so to say, repaired and renovated, and renamed "Swarg Ashram" (Heavenly Abode) to welcome the God-King. However, down the road Macleod Ganj has evolved into a prosperous thriving community, a veritable Lhasa in India, and the focal point for all Tibetans in exile. To add to the aura of the new settlements, there is a beautiful lake, about ninety miles from Dharmsala. The Tibetans call it Tso Pema — Lotus Lake — sacred in the eyes of the Tibetans because, according to tradition, it has a link with Guru Padmasambhava. It is also equally revered by the Hindus and Sikhs too.

Political activity was expressly forbidden by the Indian Government. However, some sort of agitation-hunger strikes did take place every now and then. Soon these mushroomed into hundreds and became regular feature during visits of VIPs, even though they were generally on a small scale. However, one terribly shocking incident in one such demonstration that left an indelible mark on me occurred in 1998, when six Tibetans were sitting at Jantar Mantar, a central location of New Delhi, on hunger strike protesting against complete neglect of Tibetan question by the United Nations as well as abuse of human rights by the Chinese occupation forces in Tibet, Lhasa in particular. The condition of the hunger strikers had deteriorated considerably. The Indian Government did not interfere with such small scale quiet peaceful demonstrations. However, on April 27, 1998, Chief of General Staff of Chinese PLA was scheduled to pass that way and the Indian Government, in keeping with their policy of appeasement of Chinese, did not want the General to be greeted by those famished hunger-strikers. So the Delhi Police went into action with lathi-charge, kicking and abusing the starving demonstrators. One Tibetan could not stand this ill-treatment of his people. He poured gasoline all over his body and set himself aflame. It caused deep anguish to all those who watched the tragedy and saw it on TV all over the world. The disgraceful behaviour of Delhi police and Indian Administration drew public hue and cry. Before the enflamed demonstrator collapsed, he shouted: '*Po Gyalo*' (Victory for Tibet) and '*Po Rangzen*' (Free Tibet).

Instead of ensuring that the demonstrators and hunger-striking persons are kept out of media-public gaze, the Indian Government inadvertently gave them the benefit of international publicity. And that is precisely what the Tibetans wanted.

10

The Oracles

In the heart of Asia lasts to this day the one mystery which the nineteenth century has still left to the twentieth to explore — the Tibetan Oracle of Lhasa.

Lord Curzon, Viceroy of India, 1905.

There is hardly any nation or culture in the world that does not indulge in forecasting the future, in one form or the other. It is a common feature in resolving personal-domestic problems, particularly so when one is in a complicated difficult situation, or the options open are contradictory making the choice all the more difficult. Under such circumstances one may follow the line of least resistance and consult an astrologer or some one like that, before taking the plunge. In India, this practice is particularly significant where matrimonial alliances are concerned. Comparing of '*janam-patris*' (birth charts) is the first step before deciding on the suitability of a proposed matrimonial relationship.

Role of Tibetan Oracles

So far so good, as far as personal matters go. Individual consultation of astrologers on personal matters is understandable. However, when it comes to collective, political or national level it is a different matter altogether, and defies rational understanding. But in the case of Tibet, the State Oracle is an institution by itself. The nation's leaders consult him on practically all matters concerning the State; the practice has been in vogue for the past over 1,300 years. And this does happen in India too, albeit on a very much restricted scale.

When sacred matters are involved, the performance of the oracle is an open affair. There may be hundreds in the audience to watch the performance. But when it comes to matters of State, it is strictly a confidential matter and the audience is restricted to those directly concerned with the official business.

There are hundreds of oracles in Tibet. Practically every monastery has one, if not more. Every town worth the name has its oracle. They specialize in telling the future, or in exorcizing specific evil spirits. For routine work, they would go into a trance and speak in strange words which only a trained assistant could decipher; like the mother does for her baby's talk. During this period their bodies get twisted, constricted, allegedly taken over by a spirit. When the trance is over, they are back to almost normal state, a bit weak and quite tired of course. However, they are not the only institution of divining the future. While every monastery has its oracle, the oracles of the three great centres of learning — Ganden, Sera and Drepung — are accorded a high status. Amongst them, the oracle of Drepung is considered the most powerful. The Oracle from Nechung monastery, about four miles from Lhasa, is generally known as the Nechung Oracle and is accorded the status of the "State Oracle". His pronouncements carry supreme value. Except in exceptional cases, personal matters are not referred to him. The identity and functioning of the Nechung Oracle are generally not divulged. However, with Tibet's entry into world affairs, His Holiness decided to permit some details of the Nechung Monastery, its most important resident, the *kuden*, as well as working of the State Oracle be made public. When he is consulted on matters affecting the State, the question may be written down, sealed in scrolls and silently handed over to the Oracle.

He may not even open the scroll to read the question, but still must answer the question. In fact, this procedure was followed when there was a rival claimant to become the Fourteenth Dalai Lama, Gyalwa Rinpoché to the Tibetans. Although Gyalwa Rinpoché is the head of Gelug-pa sect, he is spiritual and temporal head of the whole of Tibet. It is not necessary that his rebirth must take place in the Gelugpa sect only; he might as well be born in a Nyingmapa family. In such an eventuality he will be educated and trained as ordained in the Gelugpa tradition. Nonetheless, he is obliged to take initiations of other sects also, so that he is truly the spiritual head of the whole of Tibet. But Gyalwa Rinpoché is not God; he is the reincarnation of Chenrezig and he is a human being like everyone else. The Tibetans do not worship the human body of Gyalwa Rinpoché; they worship Buddha through the manifestation of Chenrezig. This may tantamount to "*moorti pooja*", idol worship. But in this case, the "*moorti*" is a living being, part of the living world.

It sounds absolutely fantastic that the oracle must answer the question without even being told of the question, and the astonishing thing is that he does answer. In other words, in the first place he is required to decrypt what is written on the scroll, and then find the answer through his spiritual access to the unknown. The art (or science?) of 'mind reading' certainly comes into play. Perhaps it would be more appropriate to refer to this phenomenon as 'clairvoyance' or ESP. A similar forecast, without knowing the question, was made for The Prince of Sikkim who was perturbed by a personal problem. He wanted to consult the *Gomchen* of Sekyong to seek his advice; but he was away in the high mountains to spend the summer there in meditation. The Daling *Gomchen,* to whom he had mentioned his desire to meet his master to seek advice, was right there in the Palace. He told the Prince that if the subject was very serious he could perhaps receive the advice even without taking the trouble of going all the way to Sekyong *Gomchen*. Meanwhile, the Daling *Gomchen,* without asking or knowing anything about the problem, closed his eyes and went into immediate trance. "Gradually his features changed, his face wrinkled, taking on an expression I had never seen before." The *Gomchen* opened his eyes, lips contorted and, after some difficulty in articulation, said in a very different voice: "Do not be disturbed. This question will never have to be considered by you." The subject troubling the young Maharaja was about his fiancée and an affair — which he did not want to break off after his marriage — with a girl who had borne him a son. The answer did not make any sense at that time. But the young Maharaja died a few days before the proposed date of marriage. David-Neel Alexandra personally witnessed this episode.[1]

The aforesaid episodes are just a couple out of hundreds that modern parapsychologists have logged. One of Dr. Brian Weiss's patients had the uncanny knack of anticipating the question the Doctor was about to ask her, and she would start answering without even listening to the question. Intuitive ESP? In another instance she picked up the winner for every race on the track, every single race for the entire afternoon, and collected a sizeable amount. It could not possibly be a coincidence. In fact, she had just acquired intuitive psychic ability but she did not want to use the same for financial gain. That would be highly unethical. So she gave the entire amount to the first poor person she came across outside the racecourse.[2] However, intuition and ESP should be within certain rational limits and bounds. One single instance in the life of Dr. Brian and his patient went so far beyond the bounds of rational thought that it left no doubt about the existence of certain supernatural powers in the 'Spirit World', which too existed like our own world — unseen, unfelt and unperceived by average human beings. The oracles emanated from that spirit-world.

Dr. Brian had a son who died in infancy from a one-in-ten million heart defect. Dr Brian's father had a Hebrew name. The details of death of his father and the naming of his daughter — all these personal details were spurted out by Dr. Brian's patient

---

1. David-Neel Alexandra: *Magic & Mystery in Tibet*; London, 1967, p. 60.
2. Weiss Brian Dr.: *Many Lives, Many Masters*; 1998, p. 44.

when she was under hypnotic regression. There was absolutely no way she could have found out these facts of private life of the Doctor. So he asked her who had provided her with all this personal information. The answer: "The Masters — the Master Spirits tell me. They have told me that I have lived eighty six times in physical state."[3] Thus the enigma of Tibetan oracle which Lord Curzon left for the twentieth century to unravel was resolved during the last two decades of the twentieth century; that is, only if you believe in the veracity of the foregoing tales. The Nechung Oracle certainly had outstanding knowledge and ability.

Divination

The Sixth Gyalwa Rinpoché[4] proved to be a misfit. He composed some very good romantic verses and enjoyed wine and women. His nocturnal forays in the town became notorious. His Prime Minister (the *Desi*), Sangye Gyatso, came to know that one Thargyanas was acting as the go-between the High Lama and the women. He therefore arranged for Thargyanas to be eliminated but, as a case of mistaken identity, it was the servant who got killed. The Dalai Lama consulted his oracle. The assassins were identified and legally executed. From then on the relationship between the Dalai Lama and his Desi became indifferent.

For all practical purposes, the oracles appear to have been the backbone of administration, if not the decision makers.

---

3. Ibid. p. 56

4. The Sixth Dalai Lama was born in India at Towang, in the Kameng Frontier Division of NEFA, now Kameng district of Arunachal Pradesh. Of course, at that point of time Towang was part of Tibet. McMahon Line awarded Towang region to India and the Tibetan Foreign Minister, Shatra Paljor Dorje, accepted without demur. Within a month after that, the British secretly sold five thousand rifles and half a million rounds of ammunition to Tibetan army. Independent India too sold new rifles, Bren guns, Sten guns, mortars and explosives; but then Hugh Richardson, Bell's successor, was India's representative in Tibet, and Krishna Menon's influence had not penetrated that far. When the British Government refused to recognize Tibet's independence, Richardson wrote: "The British Government sold the Tibetans down the river ..."

Nonetheless, by and large, they did prove their worth. While they did not make decisions, they indicated the guidelines for the decision. And more often than not, the line of action adopted by the administration or the individual was the same as suggested by the oracle — the medium in trance. Lord Curzon was quite convinced of the role played by the oracles in Tibetan affairs, and that too generally on the right lines. Their role in the daily life of individual Tibetan and the Government was all embracing. The oracle was consulted on every decision of any significance, and his advice, even if not binding, was generally accepted.

After a Gyalwa Rinpoché had left for the 'heavenly fields', how and where to find his incarnation, the next Dalai Lama: that used to be a major problem for the Tibetan science of divination. We have already gone over this process, very briefly, when we covered 'making the recognition' of the Fourteenth Dalai Lama. This system proved a tremendous success in dealing with the problems of succession and leadership at various levels that there came to be hundreds, if not thousands, of reincarnations at all levels. However, there was one major snag: Who ruled the country during the long period elapsing between the discovery of the new born reincarnation and his reaching the age of maturity? It was the Regent, selected by common consent from amongst the top elite — less than a dozen at the most — from the ecclesiastical order. This practice proved of immense advantage to the clerical elite who wielded full powers for prolonged periods, giving rise to all sorts of malpractices and intrigues amongst the 'contenders to the throne'. Consequentially, only three of the fourteen Dalai Lamas have actually ruled Tibet while the Regents wielded full powers for the rest of the period. In fact, the possibility that some of the Dalai Lamas were eliminated through intrigues and murders before they reached the age of maturity cannot be ruled out. "From 1751 to 1950 regents ruled for 77% of the time (94% if we exclude the exceptionally long reign of 13th Dalai Lama)".[5] This was a basic flaw in the Tibetan system of government —

5. Grunfeld Tom A.: *The Making of Modern Tibet*; Delhi, 1987, p. 10.

the long periods of Regency were inherent in the structure of the government and that caused weak fault lines.

Upon the death of a Gyalwa Rinpoché, the most important lamas in the country would meet in solemn conclave to consult the oracles. In the case of cognition of the Thirteenth Dalai Lama, that is, in or around 1878, the Nechung Oracle fell into a trance as is usual in such situations. In this state, the Oracle is "gesticulating, gyrating, and beating his breast, hissing, groaning, and gnashing his teeth, foaming at the mouth like an epileptic." Then the Oracle actually revealed the names of the father and mother of the baby, the future Gyalwa Rinpoché. However, since the system of surnames does not exist in Tibet except amongst the nobility, and practically all the Dalai Lamas have come from ordinary families, the names as such do not help much. The Oracle of Samye Monastery — one of the oldest in Tibet founded in the eighth century by Padma Sambhava — announced that 'the mountain near the house of the re-born Precious Protector has the shape of an elephant'. Various groups of lamas gave differing views. So goes a Tibetan proverb:

Every village has its own dialect,
Every lama has his own doctrine.

So the Nechung Oracle was consulted again. He gave the name of the place as Tak-po. Concentration of thought on one single point together with complete 'emptying' of the mind of all extraneous thoughts is the essence of 'trance'. Silence is golden, so is blankness. Unless these fundamentals are mastered trance cannot be achieved; otherwise the 'medium' would continue to shiver in the cold. The Nechung Oracle's pronouncements were subjected to stringiest tests. The Baby which the Nechung Oracle had pronounced as the rightful reincarnation was finally enthroned as the Gyalwa Rinpoché. Just goes to prove the vital role the Oracles of Lhasa used to play in matters affecting the destiny of the nation as well as in administrative matters.

After prophesying a disaster-in-making for his country, and forecasting a warning to his people, the Thirteenth Gyalwa Rinpoché left for the 'heavenly fields' on December 17, 1933.

The Great "Earthquakes"

In 1947 — the year of Indian Independence and rise to power of Mr. Jawaharlal Nehru — the State Oracle of Tibet, while in a trance prophesied that Tibet shall face great difficulty in the year of the Iron-Tiger, 1950 A.D. "On the evening of August 15, 1950 (third anniversary of India's independence) while Tenzin Gyatso was taking a small meal of tea[6], yoghurt and homemade bread delivered once a week by his mother — Gyalyum Chemo (The Great Mother)[7], a handsome clear eyed lady of sixty with fine bones, a one in a million type worthy Mother of Gyalwa Rinpoché — an earth tremor suddenly shook the Norbulingka. It was followed by forty tremendous reports resounding in rapid succession across the sky. The Gyalwa Rinpoché and his attendants ran out into the garden of his residence, looking east towards Sera Monastery, from which direction the sounds of explosions had come. ..." The picture became clear a day later when All India Radio announced that a massive extremely powerful earthquake of magnitude 8.6 had struck a sparsely populated area along the Indo-Tibetan and Sino-Indian border with its epicenter in Arunachal Pradesh. It had rumbled across southeastern Tibet and that sounds of its aftershocks had traveled twelve hundred miles across Tibet, all the way to its western borders. Even most of the aftershocks were also of the magnitude of around six.

It was no ordinary earthquake. It was the fifth most powerful quake in the history of civilization, lasting about four to eight minutes. Mountains became valleys and where there were valleys, mountains made appearance. The mighty Brahmaputra (Tsang-po in Tibet) River was completely re-routed causing immense

---

6. The tea plant was introduced in Darjeeling area by Dr. A. Campbell of Indian Medical Service (IMS) while he was appointed as Superintendent of Darjeeling. He was also instrumental in bringing in large number of Gorkhas from Nepal since he was earlier Political Resident in Nepal — *Among The Himalayas* by Maj. LA Waddell; op. cit. p. 39.

7. The Great Mother was the one Lady in Lhasa who dressed in the Amdo style and wore her hair in three plaits.

havoc of horrendous proportions to life and property all over Assam, Bengal and adjoining areas in India affecting an area of about 4.5 million square miles. The pungent smell of sulphur prevailed over the area.[8]

It was not merely the pent-up natural forces inside the earth that caused an earthquake in Tibet; the Chinese invasion of Tibet was another kind of earthquake that shook the country during 1950. When that occurred, the Tibetans resorted to their traditional remedial measures reserved for such dire situations — the medium of Gadong Oracle was called to the Norbulingka. An official trance was conducted. The protective deity took possession and the body of medium "reared up from its seated position, hissing loudly and shuddering with tremendous force." A secretary to the Cabinet read the formal request from a scroll, addressed to the Gadong Oracle for guidance to face the dangerous situation arising out of unprovoked naked aggression by Communist China. The Oracle came before the Gyalwa Rinpoché, clearly saying, "Make him King", he collapsed. The trance came to an end.[9]

At age fifteen, Tenzin Gyatso was still three years short of the prescribed age for the Gyalwa Rinpoché to assume temporal powers, to exercise the powers vested in the Gyalwa Rinpoché in his capacity as the King of Tibet. But these were no ordinary times. The Government consulted the State Oracle and high lamas. Guided by their advice, the Cabinet appealed, and the people demanded, that Tenzin Gyatso lead them in this hour of national emergency. He agreed, reluctantly. Consequentially, on 17th November 1950, in a stately ceremony conducted in the

---

8. The great mountains of Tibet are the source of Asia's major rivers: the Brahmaputra ('Son of Brahma'); the Mekong which flows into Burma and Laos; the Salween which also flows into Burma; the Yangtze, the fifth longest river in the world, and the Yellow River which flow into China; the Sutlej into India and Pakistan; the Indus into Ladakh and eventually into the Arabian Sea through Pakistan. Every river having its source in Tibet carries with its gold dust. There is also a gold field at an altitude of 16,340 feet. The place is called Thokjhalung, perhaps the highest inhabited place on earth, situated about 200 miles from Ladakh.

9. Avedon: op. cit. p.33.

Potala, Tenzin Gyatso was invested with full powers as the Supreme Temporal Ruler of Tibet — His Holiness the Gyalwa Rinpoché of Tibet. Just about a month later, at 2:00 a.m. on the night of December 19, 1950, His Holiness surreptitiously slipped out of the Norbulingka in the garb of an ordinary Tibetan soldier, and thus was on his way to exile in India following the path of the erstwhile Younghusband Expedition of 1904.

The Nechung Monastery was formally called 'Nechung Dorje Drayangling' — The Immutable Island of Melodious Sound — situated about four miles west of Lhasa in a groove of juniper and fruit trees, just below the Drepung Monastery. It had an establishment of 115 monks and was totally supported by the Government of Tibet through what was known as *Lhatrel*, or God-Tax. Once a year the country's 120 district governors collected offerings from the mediums in their region on behalf of the spirits and forwarded the same to Nechung on the third day of the New Year[10] as ritual offering to Pehar Gyalpo. This was part of the system through which the human and spirit worlds were connected. The primary duty of the 115 monks was to keep intact a daily link with Tibet's main spirit Protector, Pehar Gyalpo, who lived in the spirit world invisible to humans. Dorje Drakden is his principal emissary to worldly Tibet. Contact was maintained with the Protector and his Emissary regularly on a daily basis. The eight-hour ritual used to begin at 6:00 a.m. and end at 10:30 p.m. every day, conducted in four sessions, with suitable breaks in between. Lobsang Jigme was (or is?) the twelfth medium of the State Oracle borne in a middle class family of shopkeepers.

The family — *trompa* meaning 'household' in Tibetan — is the basic unit of Tibetan society. Since cultivable land was extremely limited, of necessity therefore, when a son got married he could not go away to live on his own since the arable land was not enough to create new fields. The house and all the land therefore went to the eldest son. The second son usually became a monk and the other son(s) must either live with the elder

10. Tibetan New Year is flexible similar to the Christian's Easter.

brother, or take on to some other profession. That is why there were so many monks in Tibet, and why so many young men lived with the elder brother sharing not only his house and the land, but his wife too. That is why polyandry was widely prevalent in Tibet. All said and done, it was an intelligent and practicable solution to the socio-economic problem whereby parceling out of limited arable land was avoided. Another significant factor leading to prevalence of polyandry was highly unbalanced demographic ratio. While in most parts of the world the number of females exceeds that of the males, in Tibet it is the other way round. One estimate puts the number of healthy surviving females at only one against an average of fifteen males. The data appears to be highly exaggerated, may be to prove the point; but it does prove the basic point. This appears to be the case in most high altitude areas too. After all, polyandry is common in Tibet and the neighbouring high altitude regions.

Marriage was not considered a religious matter in Tibet; the primary consideration was matching of the astrological signs of the couple. Once that was alright, everything else got in place. The date and time of marriage was also a matter of astrological decision. Since the holding of a wedding was a costly affair, most poor people just started living together rather than getting involved with ceremonial considerations. In fact it was considered more important to have children, even outside the marriage, rather than wait for the wedding to produce children. For the same reasons, extra-marital sexual relations were also generally condoned. However, amongst the nobility, men were free to have sexual intercourse outside the marriage, generally with servant-girls, but the wives were expected to remain faithful. Under the circumstances no wonder that divorce was also a simple quick affair of mutual consent. If the husband wanted a divorce, he paid the wife a small sum of money and they parted. However, if the wife wanted a divorce, she gave a fixed amount and a suit of clothes; and that was the end of the marriage.[11]

---

11. Waddell L.A., Major: *Among the Himalayas*; Delhi, p.108.

Tibetan weddings were typically like Indian Hindu marriages with the astrologers playing a major role in decision making — the suitability of the match; the horoscopes; date, place and time of marriage; etc. Horoscopes and consultations with astrologers are not an Asiatic peculiarity. They are common all over the world. While in the West, and a large part of Asia, casting of a horoscope is a simple matter of place, date and time of birth to determine which constellation is in ascendancy, and its relationship with other planetary influences. But in Tibet, China, Japan, Korea, et al, it is a fairly complicated affair. In these countries the ancient calendar is divided into a sixty-year cycle. Taking the case of Tibet — they used to follow the lunar calendar in which the first day of the new moon is the first day of the month while the full moon is the fifteenth day of the month. The years fall into various cycles while in each cycle there are constantly recurring years, each bearing the name of an animal — Mouse, Bull, Tiger, Hare, Dragon, Snake, Horse, Sheep, Monkey, Bird, Dog and Pig. A further cycle of five pairs of years occur. These five couples bear the names of elements — Wood, Fire, Earth, Iron and Water. The individual element is used in its male aspect in the first year while the female aspect follows in the second year. These double cycles are completed once every sixty years.[12] Thus according to Tibetan reckoning, we are now living in the seventeenth cycle of our modern era, which lasts from 1987 to 2047 A.D. It would have been noticed that the Tibetan months do not have particular names; they are merely counted as numbers.

Since the lunar month-year is shorter than the solar one, 360 days against 365¼, an intercalary, or extra, month is added every third year to bring the lunar year at par with the solar year, and thereby coincide with the seasons. To further complicate the issue, the intercalary month is not added consistently at any point, but anywhere among the twelve regular months that is considered lucky for the year. This makes conversion of the Tibetan

---

12. This system of chronology results in many complications. For instance: a date referred to as Shing Druk, the Wood-Dragon Year, could be 1964, 1904, 1844, 1784, 1724 and so on.

month-year to the corresponding Western month all the more difficult, if not impossible. The situation becomes still more enigmatic because of the need to adjust the theoretical 360-day Tibetan lunar year with the actual lunar year of 354 days. So the adjustment is made by omitting certain days! The calendar itself consists of pages marked off in six squares with a number in each square representing the day of the month. But the six squares do not correspond to a Tibetan week; instead, five such pages make a lunar month of thirty days. When a day is omitted from the calendar, the number is omitted from its proper square and the word *chad* (cut off) inserted. That day of the month thus ceases to exist, as if it never dawned! The final calendar may appear as 1, 2, *chad,* 4, 5, 6, etc., or as 1, 2, 3/3, 4, 5, 6, etc. While Tibetan-months do not have any names (they are merely consecutive numbers), the days of the week do have names based on the visible planets. The word Sa (Planet) is prefixed, thus: Sa nyi-ma (Sunday), Sa da-wa (Monday), Sa Mik-mar (Tuesday), Sa-Lhak-pa (Wednesday) Sa Phur-bu (Thursday), Sa Pa-sang (Friday), Sa pen-pa (Saturday).

Since the Tibetan Calendar provides for innumerable combinations, the astrologers have a hey-day! And astrologers in Tibet, as in many other parts of world, are a respected lot. Those who distinguish themselves in the field of astrology, they rise to an esteemed position of a *Tsipa*; and every fair sized monastery has at least one Tsipa, a fairly well paid respectable position in life and society.[13] In any case, there are no bad days in the Tibetan calendar! They have a very sensible custom under which they just strike out any bad day — for instance the thirteenth of the month; it is struck out of the calendar and they count the fourteenth twice. An enigmatic characteristic in itself!

Each year is designated by associating one of the twelve animals with one of the five elements. The various animals and elements are allocated a certain degree of significance to work out the proportions to obtain the data-base for the horoscope. The inter-se relationship between the animals and the elements,

13. Norbu Thondup Jigme: op.cit. pp. 77-78.

affinity and antagonism between them, and a host of other factors are taken into consideration. Thus the Tibetan horoscope is an extremely complicated, and therefore an expensive affair.

It is customary amongst the Tibetans for the groom's family to pay a certain sum of money to the bride's mother. It is called *Nu-rin* (Breast-price). Even if the bride's mother is not alive, this amount is obligatory payment to the bride's family. Like the Indian Hindu system, the groom's party proceeds to the bride's house as a reception party for the bride. But this reception party is mostly comprised of horsemen. And here comes a major departure from the Indian Hindu system: The groom's party of horsemen is accompanied by a fully saddled mare, which has already been foaled and which the bride will ride from her home to the bridegroom's house.[14] However, if the parents of the bride have no sons, the bridegroom might go to live with his wife as a member of that family so that her family line will not die out — like the *"ghar Jamai"* system of India.

Appointment of a New 'State Oracle'

The Lobsang Jigme was destined to occupy the exalted position of Nechung Oracle. His family had the choice of sending the young boy to Je College or Namgyal Dratsang[15] Monastery. To decide the issue, his mother sought a *mo* (divination) from

14. Ibid; p. 18. In the Indian system, the groom rides a mare to the house of the bride.

15. Some Dratsang, meaning colleges, specialize in certain scriptures. A student is generally at liberty as to which *Dratsang* he would like to join; but he is given his place of residence, or *Khamtsan*, according to his place of birth. The *Khamtsans* are all regional. All the *Dratsangs* in a university come under an apex body called *Lachi*, an academic council. Studies fall into five groups, each one taking several years. First is Namdrel, study of logic; then comes Parchin, study of Buddhists scriptures followed by Oumah which teaches avoidance of extremes; Sunyata, the study of nothingness, non-existence comes next followed by Dzö, the one year course in metaphysics. After complete revision of the studies done so far, the final course of study is Dulwa, expounding of the Vinaya philosophy. This last course takes at least nine years to complete — Thubten Jigme Norbu: op. cit. p. 265.

a renowned lama who said that the child should not be sent to either of those two. He had "very important work" to do at Nechung Monastery and hence should be sent there only. After some years of study and meditations, Lobsang Jigme soon learnt that "advanced practitioners whose psychic channels had been opened by years of meditation, would see Dorje Drakden, garbed in the robes of a stately monk, during daily prayers. The rest, however, received their only glimpse of the Renowned Immutable One during the five official trances held each month."[16]

Meanwhile, Lobsang Jigme suffered serious mental illness. The doctors of Mendzekhang and Chokpori could not cure him. However, their diagnosis was quite clear — it was spirit possession and not mental illness. By age fourteen his condition became so serious that he was no longer able to attend to daily rites of Nechung. He suffered frequent fits, seizures, sleepwalking, hallucinations, high fever, and was bed-ridden most of the time. He was shifted to Ganden Monastery where he was put up in the room of Samling Rinpoché, an incarnate lama. He saw images of scorpions of the size of yaks and frequently dreamt of scorpions. During one of his seizures, the spirit in possession gave a clear cut message heard by Samling Rinpoché and those around him: "On the fourth day of the sixth month, as the sun rises above Wongpo Ri Mountain, the Choekyong Dorje Drakden will take possession." And fourth was the following day. So Samling and Jigme's teacher came over to Jigme's room early in the morning. Soon both men noticed a ball of red and yellow string. No sooner Jigme's teacher picked it up, it turned into a scorpion. As the teacher threw it to the floor, Jigme went into a trance, his face and body totally attenuated. As the sun's first rays struck the summit of Wongpo Ri, Lobsang Jigme collapsed; the trance ended as abruptly as it had begun. Of course there was no sign of the string or the scorpion in that small room. Soon thereafter, they discovered that the current medium of Nechung Oracle had suffered a stroke and was close to death. Taking all factors into consideration, Samling Rinpoché and Jigme's

16. Avedon: op. cit. pp. 200-201.

teacher came to the conclusion that Lobsang Jigme was being taken in the employ of Tibet's main protector.[17]

Jigme's bouts of 'illness' continued as did Dorje Drakden's possessions leading to frequent seizures preceded and followed by severe pain. However, one fine morning Lobsang Jigme suddenly felt that he was well. The next day he felt still better. He was no longer ill. His recovery was as sudden as his illness had been. Concurrently, a messenger brought the news that Lobsang Namgyal, the *kuden* of Nechung had died. The day he died, that was precisely the day Lobsang Jigme recovered from his 'illnesses. The messenger had been dispatched by the abbot of Nechung Monastery with instructions to get Jigme back to Nechung. Meanwhile, on the death of the *kuden*, the Regent Taktra Rinpoché was informed by the Gadong medium that the prospective *kuden* was a young child of fifteen born in the year of the Iron Horse. He belonged to Nechung Monastery and his name: Lobsang Jigme. He was ushered into the presence of the Regent. As he was about to offer the scarf, Dorje Drakden instantaneously took possession and greeted the Regent through the new kuden thus establishing Jigme's validity. The trance lasted about five minutes during which the Protector spoke to the Regent in private. As the trance ended, Jigme collapsed and was returned to Nechung where he was subjected to further tests to make triply sure that the Kuden was absolutely genuine. Since delicate internal and foreign relations matters were involved, it was imperative that there was no possibility of leakage, and that the trance was thorough and complete under the possession of true and genuine Dorje Drakden. "Such a possession could occur only if the 72,000 psychic channels upon which, according to tantric theory, consciousness[18] is mounted in the human body were clear of all obstructions." Having established that Lobsang Jigme was a pure

17. Avedon, John: op. cit. p. 207

18. There are eleven kinds of consciousness recognized in the Tibetan system. While the Tibetan language has three different words to describe the same, English language has just one word, the 'mind', to collectively express the same.

"vessel", the next requirement was to establish the true identity of Protector in that it was really the genuine and true Dorje Drakden. This part involved complicated long procedures. After he had successfully passed all the prescribed tests, early in 1945 Lobsang Jigme was publicly proclaimed to be the new medium of Tibet's State Oracle — an honourable and high position which was also potentially dangerous.[19]

Divine Protection

The abbots of Drepung Monastery attended a regular monthly audience with the Protector on the second day of every lunar month[20] to seek guidance on various issues affecting their vast estates of their Monastery. They did so when the medium was in trance before the two-storey high statute of Hayagriva, "a ferocious multi headed, multi armed tutelary deity". Similar sessions with the Protector were conducted for the four government departments on a weekly basis. These sessions were conducted openly and members of the public, or those directly concerned could attend the same. Thus there was an intimate connection between Nechung Monastery and the government of the country, the latter being invariably guided by the Oracle's prophecies-predictions. It was an institution of prime importance in conducting the day to day business of the administration as well as rendering advice at the time of national emergencies of whatever nature. However, private trances were often conducted at the request of the Dalai Lama and these were totally personal and secret. The secretary of Nechung Monastery was required to keep meticulous record of prophecies made at various sessions. The predictions were first recorded in shorthand, keeping pace with rapid utterances of the oracle, on blackboards using inkless bamboo pens, and thereafter

19. The very first Kuden appointed at the founding of the Monastery was executed.

20. Tibet has two calendars — the official lunar calendar that begins in February and has twelve months of thirty days, and an agricultural calendar that varies from region to region. As the lunar calendar is shorter that the solar year, a month is added every three years to make up for the difference.

The Nechung Oracle

Monks Playing on Long Horn

The State Oracle in Preparation

The Nechung Oracle

The State Oracle in Action

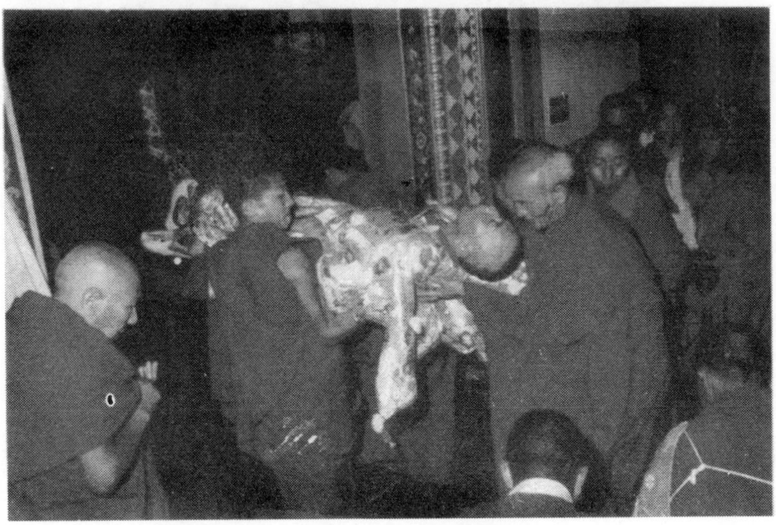

After the Trance

Lobsung Jigme, the Medium of the State Oracle of Tibet

transferred to permanent records in large wood-framed books in the presence of the departments concerned. These books were wrapped in brocade and stored in cupboards. In addition to these wood-framed books, there were a number of "sacred vessels through which the Protector, without the use of a medium, was believed to communicate directly".

The Thirteenth Dalai Lama reached the age of majority in 1893. He was the first one to do so in over a hundred years and therefore quickly consolidated his position by replacing officials who aspired to be his rivals in exercising power. When he took over from the Regent, a plot was hatched against him. However, the Dalai Lama himself discovered the plot through a dream. The plotters were reported to be the nephew of the outgoing Regent and the Chinese Amban.[21] Thus the Protector exposed an assassination attempt by directly challenging the Regent, thereby revealing Nechung Oracle's miraculous abilities. Similarly, at the end of his reign, the Oracle bid farewell to the Thirteenth by facing him while he was leaving after a public trance, an act of final parting. This was contrary to the usual practice, and hence an enigma by itself, which made its meaning clear after about four months when the Thirteenth left his mortal body unexpectedly.

The State Oracle is not a myth, nor the Protector a mere superstition. They do take a practical interest in mundane matters of the State and convey their appreciation or otherwise of the performance of various organs of the government, as well as of important individuals. For instance: during the late 1940's when the Dalai Lama was a minor, corruption was rampant in the administration under the Regency. Dorje Drakden was unhappy with the government and conveyed his displeasure in no certain terms by knocking out the Gadong medium that the administration had decided to consult, thereby instantly ending the trances. In the words of the Dalai Lama: "... dealing with Nechung is not easy. It needs time and patience. He is very rigid, almost like a

21. Bell Charles Sir: *Tibet: Past and Present*, p. 124. Also pp. 104-105.

great man of the old society. He is not talkative, he is reserved. Very much reserved. He does not bother with minor things. He takes a tremendous interest only in the bigger issues." In 1948, two years before the Chinese invasion, the Protector had directly warned that that in the year of the Iron-Tiger (1950) Tibet would face extreme danger. And mark you; this was not the first time such a warning had come from the Spirit World. The palliative measures advised by Dorje Drakden were ignored; and when the invasion did become imminent, the Protector repeatedly advised that the Dalai Lama take over temporal powers of the State. Finally, in November 1950, the government felt so confused and defeated that they had to agree to the Dalai Lama, still a minor, to assume full temporal powers. In 1956 the Protector advised that the Dalai Lama visit India to establish contact with Nehru for the long term welfare of the Tibetan people. Again in 1958 the Choekyong prophesied that the Dalai Lama must flee the country for which the Protector would provide necessary assistance against Chinese troops. Dorje Drakden again informed the abbots of Drepung that although Sera had been shelled, no harm would come to Drepung, and that all the fighting would be over in three days. Both prophecies came out to be absolutely accurate. On being specifically questioned, he also advised that the *kuden* should start marching southwards immediately.

Protection of Dorje Drakden continued well into the Exile

During early 1970's the Nechung Oracle had predicted a period of decline for the Chinese. Another prophecy recorded that the death of Mao Zedong be followed by rapid disintegration of all that he had built over the debris of death and destruction that he had wrought on millions of innocent citizens of his country. As luck would have it, Zhou Enlai died on January 8, 1976. Chu Thé — a close associate of Mao based in Yanan and was instrumental in large scale distribution of the little 'Red Book' — went thereafter; and Mao Zedong himself passed away on 9th September the same year. Thus there occurred a clean sweep of China's triumvirate that had ruled Chinese Communist Party for nearly four decades, causing all round havoc, particularly on the minorities and the intellectual elite. To cap it all, the Tang Shan earthquake at the end of July took a heavy toll of life and property. The Tibetans were naïve enough to take these tragic events for good omens for their country. They proved right, albeit to a very limited extent only. The truth was hidden in the old Tibetan proverb: "The clouds of summer float by, but the sky stays where it is for ever." However, there was an exception. Dr. Tenzin Choedrak having suffered nearly two decades of severe privations in Chinese prisons was released on account of his exceptional ability in Tibetan medical science, and was ultimately allowed to join the Dalai Lama in Dharmsala in India as his personal physician. Dr. Choedrak had received the formula of one of Tibetan medicine's most powerful drugs from Khenrab Norbu, the Master of Mendzekhang, and he was keen to pass on this personal knowledge before it was too late. The Dalai Lama was quite enthusiastic about the project and a staff of eighteen full-time pharmacists was employed for three months to prepare the largest quantity of *tsother* manufactured in the history of Tibet. It was indeed a lucky omen that Dr. Choedrak was one of the four of a group of 176 prisoners who were sent to suffer horrendous brutalities in Chinese prisons managed to survive, so that lineage of *tsother* could also make its mark in the world of modern medicine. Incidentally, penicillin in a disguised form had been known in Tibet for centuries before its invention in the West.

There appears to be a tendency amongst western travelers to, and writers, on Tibet to exaggerate the negative aspects of traditional Tibetan medical practices. Since the sanitary conditions and health care facilities were rather primitive, it was but natural that infectious diseases, small pox, gastro-intestinal, leprosy, venereal diseases, et al, would be prevalent on a large scale. Indeed they were. But that does not grant a license to modern medicine to describe the traditional Asian systems in pejorative terms. Tibetan medical system was quite advanced in its own way and their diagnostic techniques proved to be more accurate and to the point without the aid of modern technology and instrumentation. However, this aspect is much beyond the scope of this work; suffice to say that while pills rolled out of excreta of venerable high Incarnations and their urine are merely superstitions and certainly not part of the Tibetan system of medicine, their drugs formulated out of medicinal herbs have proved their worth. After all, what are Aloe Vera and all the rest of products developed and being marketed in the United States and Mexico? Some odd instances of a piece of paper with a prayer written on it being ingested; touch of a monk to cure a headache; wearing blessed rosary made out of human skulls; et al, should not be generalized to represent Tibetan medicinal system. There is no denying that the doctors of Tibet were monks, and most of them were well qualified professionals. They were not surgeons, but in the fields of diagnostics and internal medicine, they were certainly worth their weight in gold — and that too without the benefit of modern instrumentation.

Ceremony of Trance in Dharmsala on February 14, 1981[22]

After extensive preparations and personal cleansing by the principal monk lasting for a few days, on the appointed day four attendants helped the monk to dress for the elaborate ceremony. It is a very complicated heavy armoured type martial dress that by itself weighs nearly one hundred pounds. It is not that the monk was going in for combat. Instead, within a few minutes of his being seated beneath the bright lights of the cathedral, his consciousness is replaced by that of Dorje Drakden — "the Renowned Immutable One". He is chief spirit minister and bearer of the counsel for the State Oracle of Tibet, the Nechung Oracle.

In the Central Cathedral the Gyalwa Rinpoché sat on his throne, completely engulfed in silence. The ministers of his Cabinet, the Chairman and Vice-Chairman of the Peoples' Deputies and their secretaries were all seated on low cushions to the left of the Gyalwa Rinpoché. A select group of abbots and lamas were seated opposite on the other side, their demeanor

22. Avedon, John F.: op. cit. pp. 189-199.

serious and subdued as was that of the rest of the congregation. These proceedings are totally secret and of immense significance, particularly so when matters of State policy are to be gone into. No outsider, Tibetan or otherwise, is allowed in. In fact, the very fact of the proposed ceremony was not even known except to those directly involved. It was indeed a well kept secret.

The ceremony began with two ten-foot *thungchen* (long horns) producing a shattering blast, followed by shrill notes of *gyaling*, accompanied by cymbals, drums, and monks' recitation, invoking the oracular deity to descend into the *kuden*, the "receiving body". As the curtains part the 'medium' appears, supported by three assistants; he can barely walk weighed down by more than forty kg of eight layers of clothing. The helmet weighs another fourteen kg. But it is not only the weight of his accoutrements that makes it difficult for him to walk; he is already in the first stage of the trance. His breathing is short and loud. His cheekbones jut out fiercely and his eyes wear a wild and startled look. His face is severely distorted. He is made to sit on a brocade-covered camp stool, facing the Dalai Lama, about twenty feet away. The various cycles of prayers are being recited, invoking the Protective spirit of Dorje Drakden to enter the body of the medium. The *thungchen* produce another wall-shattering blast and the trance deepens. Possession commences. It appears as if the breath and mind is being pushed out of the medium's body, which visibly expands by about two inches. His legs suddenly start leaping up and down the floor.

The Protector has now entered the body of the medium. The heavy helmet is placed on the medium's head. His face turns bright red. Recitations are abruptly ended. The body of medium is as if it is dead. The tiny golden bells atop the helmet produce a jingling musical sound, not from the shuddering of the medium's head but on account of the presence of Dorje Drakden himself. As soon as the helmet is finally secured, "the Protector shows himself to be in full possession. Leaping up, he swings a long sword in his right hand and begins to dance ... interspersed with bows offered out of respect to the Dalai Lama.

Three bows are completed within thirty seconds. Dorje Drakden throws down the sword and rushes up the steps to the Dalai Lama ... a polished silver cup on a long silver stand, containing dark black tea, is given to him. He raises it to the Dalai Lama who takes a small sip. In communion, he drinks the rest himself and steps to the right side of the throne, so that the Dalai Lama can lean over to whisper in his ear. This is the first most secret question asked." Answering quickly, the Protector offers a scarf hurling it twelve feet into the air, directly on to the Buddha's begging bowl, with an astonishing force and aim. The offering is repeated to other images.

While the Protector continues to sip tea, the VIPs from the government congregate around Dorje Drakden. Dalai Lama's Chief Private Secretary, Venerable Tara, reads from a two-foot long scroll. It is the official petition, composed in verse. In essence, these are three questions concerning the future of the Dalai Lama, the Tibetan people and their government. While the earlier question(s) were highly secret, the ones from Tara along with their answers were heard by other members of the congregation, all specifically invited for the purpose. The answers to such questions are generally open to the public, but in this instance no outsiders or members of the public are present. Dorje Drakden speaks humbly, answers the three questions, slowly, enunciating each word distinctly. The Gyalwa Rinpoché repeats them back slowly, followed in chorus by the secretaries who note down every word. The atmosphere for this transmission is warm and informal. Dorje Drakden takes hold of the Dalai Lama's hand with an utmost refined and intimate gesture, in lilting metered verse. The prophetic answers to the three questions are completed in this manner, after which the long horns emit another resounding boom.[23] The trance ends.

---

23. The details of ceremonial trances and what transpired in the same were a well kept secret. It is only after the Dalai Lama has settled down in India that some outline of the ceremony have been allowed to be divulged. The foregoing description is entirely based on what information John F. Avedon gathered from His Holiness The Dalai Lama. Since the Dharmsala ceremony, like the rest of them, was not open to the media, the answers to the three public questions are not available for dissemination.

The curtains part again. The medium of Gadong Oracle supported by attendants enters. The trance has already set in. The spirits possessing him are known as Shinjachen. He is also one of the main protective deities of Tibet — Pehar Gyalpo, the ultimate source of oracular pronouncement. The session with the Gadong Oracle was beset with some difficult moments. The Dalai Lama had to intervene with a sharp command when normalcy was restored. When it is all over, there is complete silence. The mediums lie in the recovery room wrapped in golden brocade blankets. After changing their costumes, the two *kudens* and their staffs walk to the front door of the Cathedral, enter and prostrate three times before the Dalai Lama.

The trance concluded. Tea is served. The Dalai Lama drains his cup and leaves the Cathedral after a couple of minutes.

11

Psychic Phenomena

Prevalence of psychic phenomena on a large scale was one of the primary mainsprings for Tibet's fame in the western world. Its geographical isolation, enigmaticism and extreme remoteness added to the exotic lure that enticed the rich and the vagabonds to its borders, as much as its present occupation by Chinese nationalism and fanatical communism repel them. Tibetan mystic doctrines, magical-occult practices, 'supernatural' occurrences which defied rational explanation, abundance of prodigies, art of divination, 'wind-wireless technology', sonic power, super-speed levitation, et al, whetted the appetite to run innumerable risks involved in the adventure. Such enigmatic occurrences added to the fountainhead of Tibet's reclusive and exclusive philosophy.

The American Society for Psychical Research (ASPR) was established in 1885. Their very first project for scientific study was telepathy. One of the conclusions of this study was that telepathy occurred independent of hypnosis. Another important finding was that changes in blood volume occurred while sending telepathic messages while electroencephalogram monitoring indicated changes in pattern of brain waves such that the sender and the receiver were on more or less compatible wave lengths. The environment for telepathic communication was not regressive either, nor did it involve trance like condition. Since there were thousands of bereaved families as a result of the First World War, telepathic experiments were undertaken on a mass scale in Britain and the United States. The crisis situation faced by the families led to spontaneous telepathic communication in many cases. The traumatic emotional state of the bereaved families was an added factor, since telepathy is essentially related to the emotional state of the individual. Women proved to be better receivers, while geriatric telepathy was found to be fairly common. During the present space age technology an unauthorized experiment conducted by Astronaut Edgar D. Mitchell on board the Apollo 14 mission in 1971 proved that distance was no bar in telepathic communication, which in this case was 150,000 miles from the earth. Telepathy certainly transcends time and space. All said and done, telepathy like all other psychic phenomena is 'elusive and difficult to test systematically'.

Tibetan psychic phenomena may be produced consciously, or unconsciously. The former is generally a one-man show while the latter may involve more than one person. In either case, the phenomena are produced in accordance with the laws of nature; no miracles are contemplated. Just as milk is present in cheese or butter, so is psychic phenomenon pre-existing in the laws of nature. However, talisman or charms usually defy rational explanation, besides being ineffective most of the time. The bullet-charms issued by clever monks to credulous Tibetan soldiers fighting against the British-Indian Military Expedition of Sir Francis Younghusband prove the point. And the explanation given by the lamas for their ineffectiveness, and measures taken by them to make the next lot really effective — just goes to show to what length the lamas would go to further their vested interests. Thus, Tibet's psychic phenomena had its negative aspects too, which the doubting toms exploited to the hilt: But the skeptics hardly made much headway in running down Tibet's spiritualism.

Experts in psychic phenomena do not easily fall victim to a sorcerer's actions. In the 'battle' of psychic forces between two antagonistic parties, the targeted party becomes aware of forces generated, and released, by the 'enemy' force and is in a position to take counter-measures to escape the ill-effects of the released force. The targeted person who is adept in psychic training can detect the harmful 'waves' and deflect them. Such well trained persons are said to be capable of creating any kind of phantoms which are not mere mirages but are tangible beings and possess the characteristics and faculties of actual beings that they are supposed to represent. Sounds like fairy tales; however, parapsychologists have verified a number of cases and found at least a small fraction to be factually tangible. Single-minded thoughts concentrated on an object generate the requisite energy in that object and make it appear as the real object, even though it may still be a mere phantom only. The crux of the matter is the power of the mind, and one's faith in spiritual matters. Tibetans had plenty of both attributes, and hopefully they would continue to nourish the same while in exile, if not under communist domination. While in the Bardo, the mind is mobile and vulnerable to the extreme. Since there is no anchor, like the body framework, thoughts may turn into reality; and if they happen to be unpleasant, the consequences could be quite dangerous. In this connection it is worth recalling the phenomenon of "unseen companion" in high altitude mountain climbing. So a phantom may be something more than a mere fairytale!

Over the millennia high altitude-mountains have evoked a sense of awe, bordering on worship, amongst the people who have lived and worked in that environment. A number of peaks in the Himalayan mountains have been named after the gods — Kailash[1], Parbati Parbat, Gurudongmar, Gaurishankar, Swargarohini, are some of the prime examples which immediately come to mind. The local inhabitants, being simple by nature, naturally associate the awe-inspiring mountains with gods, goddesses and deities which they worship, albeit from a distance but certainly with a sacrosanct feeling in their hearts. They seem

---

1. The upper reaches of Chamoli and Uttarkashi including the sacred Mount Kailash and sacred waters of Mansarovar Lake were called 'Tangan'. The altitude of surface water of the sacred Lake is 14,950 feet and its water is saline. Its circumference is 54 miles and it covers an area of 200 square miles. Surprisingly, most lakes in Tibet are saline, and in the Mount Kailash region all lakes are saline.

to exercise an 'unseen power' on the local inhabitants as well as on the climbers. A number of mountaineers have recorded that while under great physical and mental stress they have received a helping hand from an unseen power. They have felt the presence of an "unseen companion" who has guided them out of dangerous situations, particularly on the upper slopes of Mount Everest (29,028-feet). In their attempt to reach the top of the world, over two hundred climbers have lost their lives. In fact, one of the climbers who died from an accidental fall is still hanging from a rope, so says Pemba Dorji Sherpa who climbed the Peak on 21st May 2004 in eight hours and ten minutes. "When I stopped at a mound of rocks I saw some spirits in the form of black shadows coming towards me, stretching their hands and begging for something to eat." Another member of the team, Robert Cluny, a professional guide with American Summit International, says: "During one climb we all had this feeling we were being watched all day long. There were only three of us up there, but as the sun was setting, we definitely saw a fourth figure sitting in our Camp, leaning over our stove."[2]

The veteran mountaineer, Dr. P.M. Das, Inspector General in Punjab Police has vividly recorded his experience when he and his two companions were faced by a disaster while descending from the Bhagirthi (20,184-feet) summit. One of them slipped pulling the other two along with him. The fall could not be arrested. One of them died and the other was badly wounded while Das had some superficial injuries, half buried in snow without any equipment or additional clothing. Throughout the night "I felt the presence of a Being. This Presence was around me and at times I talked to him and it urged me to concentrate on my survival ... It was not a ghost-like apparition, but like a companion. A presence. Eventually the Presence disappeared from my consciousness as I sighted the rescue party ..." This is not a solitary instance; hundreds of such experiences have been recorded by climbers in distress both in the high Himalayas and in the Alps.

---

2. *Himachal Times*: August 26, 2004.

Mind-Power

Power of the mind is creative in its own peculiar way as illustrated by Lady-Lama Alexandra David-Neel through her first hand experiences. She had become an apprentice under *Gomchen* (Great Hermit) of Lachen and learnt the technique of *tumo* whereby she could generate enough heat in her body to stay alive in the freezing cold of icy Tibet. After staying for almost two years in the monastery of Kumbum, in 1921 she set out on a three-year long perilous journey to the capital, Lhasa. In preparation for that long journey, she granted three weeks leave to her servant Wangdu, after which he was to return with fresh supplies. The man did not return for more than two months. Then one night she saw him in a dream wearing an unusual hat. Next morning other servants told her that Wangdu was seen coming down the hill. She too saw him coming up, dressed exactly as she had seen him in the dream, with a peculiar headgear, and without the caravan of supplies. But after he reached the Chörten, he just disappeared. There was no sign of Wangdu after that. She sent two servants to look for him near the chörtens, but there was no trace of Wangdu. Puzzled, she gave up the search. However, a little before dusk Wangdu appeared in the valley with his caravan of supplies, wearing exactly the same unusual headgear. Subsequent enquiries established beyond any doubt that Wangdu had not come anywhere near the Chorten that morning.[3]

The Lady-Lama had a similar experience when she perceived the 'somewhat nebulous shape of one of the fantastic beings' behind a painter, an artist who had come to meet David-Neel. The artist had been hard at work that day painting a particular deity. The Lady-Lama had noticed the phantom of the deity of which the artist was not aware of. In another similar instance David-Neel saw a Lama who used to visit her sometimes. He was sitting on the camp chair beside the table. The servant went to the kitchen to make tea for the Rinpoché while the Lady-

3. David-Neel: op. cit. pp. 308-09.

Lama advanced towards the tent outside which the Rinpoché was sitting. As she approached the tent, she did not see the lama on the chair. Instead, she perceived a 'flimsy veil of mist'; the Rinpoché had suddenly vanished.[4]

After the above two episodes with phantoms, David-Neel undertook a personal experiment. She shut herself in *tsams* to perform the prescribed concentration of thought and other rites. After a few months of thought-concentration the phantom monk was formed in her mind. He became a part of the traveling party and used to undertake the usual tasks expected of a member of the team. In due course the phantom-monk became bolder, troublesome and out of control of the Lady-Lama. His presence soon 'turned into day-nightmare'. So she decided to dissolve the unwanted traveling companion, the phantom-lama. It took her six months of hard struggle to get rid of the mental image of the monk-companion. "There is nothing strange in the fact that I may have created my own hallucination." These instances were creations of mere suggestions, "the creator's thought impressing others and causing them to see what he himself sees."[5] The Lady-Lama survived the hazards of journey from Kumbum to Lhasa where she arrived in February 1924. She was quite disappointed with Lhasa and left in April, reaching France in 1925. She died in 1969 at the age of one hundred.[6]

In yet another instance of suggestion, auto-suggestion and thought-control, the Panchen Lama wanted the consecration ceremony of the huge image of Buddha Maitreya to be performed by his spiritual adviser, the Kyongbu Rinpoché. But the hermit declined as he would be dead by the time the temple-complex would be completed. However, the High Lama earnestly requested the hermit "to delay his death till he had blessed the new building". The hermit acceded to the request and promised to perform the consecration ceremony. It is astonishing, and of great interest that

4. Ibid. p. 312
5. Ibid. p. 315
6. Brennan: op. cit. p. 21.

high mystics of Tibet possessed the power 'of choosing the time of their death'. When the temple was ready, the Panchen sent a beautiful sedan chair to fetch the hermit for the consecration ceremony. The Kyongbu Rinpoché sat in the chair. The porters started for Tashilhunpo. Thousands of people had collected for the religious ceremony. They were completely confounded when they saw the Rinpoché coming alone on foot. The door of the sedan-chair was opened when it arrived; it was empty! — The readers may draw their own conclusions from this astounding episode.

Telepathy and Clairvoyance

Essentially, telepathy and clairvoyance are two facets of the same human faculty. Both are extra-sensory perception in nature, ESP in short. Telepathy may be defined as the extraordinary faculty by virtue of which, under certain conditions, the thought of one person, the sender or agent, is directly transmitted to another person, the receiver or percipient, without using the usual sensory channels of communication. It is mind to mind communication. It is not some kind of magical process peculiar to Tibetans; it is a world-wide phenomenon, having just about crossed the threshold from the field of magic into the domain of science, although transformation is still not complete. If Tibetans have better telepathic ability, it may be because of the clear pristine peaceful environment of that country. Magic is an art, not a science; but telepathy is akin to a scientific process in which thoughts are conveyed from one mind to another through spiritual means. It is a subtle way of sending messages 'on the wind'. The respective 'minds' have to be on the same wave-length to be able to communicate without physical contact. There could be variations in application of telepathy. One could have the power of sight and appear to the 'receiver' in physical form. Or it could be the power of movement whereby objects could be telepathically moved. Like any other science it can be learnt through knowledge, training and constant practice. In fact, it is part of parapsychology in which field scientifically trained minds have done considerable research with abundant measure of success. However, it requires perfect command over the mind, concentration on 'one-pointedness of thought'. The natural environment of Tibetan countryside, the quiet and peace that was characteristic of life in those mountains, emphasis on spiritual rather than material, et al, were contributory factors for telepathic transmissions amongst like-minded Tibetans. Single-minded concentration of mind is the crux of telepathic communication, and through constant practice and frequent meditations they often acquired this extra-sensory capability.

Over a period of last half a century or so, telepathy has come to be recognized as part of scientific psychology, in one form or the other. The word 'telepathy' is derived from the Greek terms *tele* meaning distance and *pathe* meaning occurrence or feeling. The term 'telepathy' was coined in 1882 by a French psychical researcher Fredric W.H. Myers. The original definition of the term, "thought-transference' or 'thought-reading', did not convey the intrinsic sense adequately; hence the new phrase, which en-compassed "mind to mind" communication in its entirety, to include thoughts, feelings, sensations and mental images. Thus in keeping with the Tibetans, amongst aboriginal tribals of India, Australia and many other similar communities, telepathy came to be accepted as a human faculty. It is instinctive by nature and involves mind to mind contact beyond the frequencies of wave-lengths of the five sensory perceptions — sight, hearing, touch, taste and smell. Two other psychic phenomena work in conjunction with telepathy. One: 'Clairvoyance' — It is almost the same phenomenon as telepathy except that here only one brain, that of the clairvoyant, is involved. The clairvoyant mentally sees what is out of sight. Often, it is also called 'second sight' and is believed to be deeply connected with the 'subconscious' mind. Two: 'Precognition': Although this faculty is part of ESP, it is different in as much as 'Precognition' is supernatural knowledge or perception of future events. It emphasizes prediction rather than causing events to occur through mental energy. By implication, it means that the event is predestined to occur; the clairvoyant only foretells the event but has no control over the event or sequence thereof.

We are aware of a world of experience *within* us, a psychic world; and outside of us there is the vast physical world. The psychic world exists not only inside our own selves, it does so in other fellow beings too. Therefore, "we may regard the psychic as existing, so to speak, like islands in separate individuals, these islands being directly connected by (psychic) bridges from one to another"[7]. Furthermore, there is an essential homogeneity amongst these so-called psychic islands.[8]

Telepathic communication is more easily established between members of the same family, particularly during times of distress. Naturally, twins can communicate telepathically far more easily than others. Focusing thoughts and deep concentration go a long way in helping to establish communication. Crisis-situations trigger telepathic communications without even the knowledge of the subject. Death of a family member often gets communicated through telepathy. A Mother has a knack of getting to know when her child is in serious trouble. She is instantly on the same wave-length as her child and knows that there is trouble around. Conversely, two persons in love-bond find it much easier to get into telepathic mode. Surprisingly, pets too have a knack of telecommunicating with the master of the household. In fact, pets are generally aware as to who is the master of the house.

From the above it will be seen that telepathy means connecting to the wave-length which you wish to watch — like switching on a TV channel to watch the programme you wish to. When you no longer wish to remain in telepathic communication, you just switch off the connection.

From a Military Power to a Spiritual Giant

The ancient history of Tibet tells us that the Tibetans were a great military power so much so that at one time they had occupied the Chinese capital. The Chinese were indeed afraid of

7. Sünner Paul: *The Brain and the Mind*; London, 1926, p. 80.
8. These psychic islands could be collectively referred to as a super-personal mind.

Tibetans. However, some 2,500 years ago Lord Buddha had prophesied that Chenrezig would come to Tibet, and transform the warlike people into such a peaceful race that they would not like to even kill an animal. This encouraged the enemies of Tibet to take their country and make the people captive. "Several times they nearly succeeded, but Chenrezig gave us strength ... we were never conquered."[9] The advent of Buddhism in Tibet had such a strong influence that they abandoned their war-like ways and took to spiritualism in a big way. Over a period of time, their spiritualism advanced so much that one person out of every four of the entire population became a monk or a nun, and the rest considered themselves as a support system for the monasteries. It was a complete transformation of their cultural mien. On the one hand the new found spiritualism gave a remarkable fresh insight to power of the mind, on the other it led to cultural imbalance, weakness in administration and inability to maintain their identity as a free nation due to serious deficiency in defence capability.

An ordinary person is not expected to be able to concentrate on 'nothing'; some specific target is needed to achieve the necessary depth of concentration. In order to achieve absolute concentration of mind on a single point, some sort of mantra or formula is a pre-requisite. The devotees may be repeating it millions of times over extended time periods. Amongst the Hindus, the Sanskrit mantras are generally unintelligible to the person who is repeating it; so is the Tibetan one, albeit to a lesser extent — the most ordinary and well known: *Aum mani padme hum!* — the mantra of compassion and peace. Aum is a mystic word, a creative sound. Its vibrations spread far and wide. It is neither easy to understand nor can it be explained away in simplistic terms. There is immense amount of literature in Hindu philosophy to dwell on the esoteric, exoteric and mystic meanings of this one syllable. The entire Hindu Trinity of Brahma, Vishnu and Shiva are condensed in Aum, often written as Om. Indeed it is mere symbolic, after which there is nothing

9. Jigme Norbu and Turnbull: *Tibet: Its History, Religion and People*; p. 37.

but silence. It cannot be expressed in concrete terms: "It is Inexpressible Absolute." However, there is no magical connotation about Aum; it is pure as pure can be.

Mani padme are Sanskrit terms, meaning 'jewel in the lotus'. That is the simple literal meaning which is merely superficial. However, that is also the correct interpretation. "In the lotus exists the precious jewel of Buddha's teachings." In this context 'lotus' stands for the world. In yet another interpretation, lotus is taken as the mind in whose depths one may find various intangible jewels like knowledge, truth, nirvana, et al. However, according to current interpretation, the jewel represents Chen-re-zi, or the Gyalwa Rinpoché, the Dalai Lama. This is the universal mantra of Tibetans. It is painted in vivid colours hundreds of times on the rocks beside the mule-tracks. It is written down thousands of times on tightly rolled paper fitted in hand-held miniature drums. One could never get away from signs of religion in old Tibet. A variation of the mantra, as prevalent amongst those who follow the ancient cult, is: *Om matri salei du.* Yet another variation is *Oma-swa-sato-hum.* From the philosophical point of view, the six syllables of the mantra[10] are intimately connected with 'power of sense-perception', the six sentient beings. Each one of them is related to one of the mystic colours as follows:

Aum is white and is connected to gods.

Ma is blue and relates to non-godly beings.

Ni is yellow connected to human beings.

Pad is green and is connected to animals.

Me is red. It is connected with those miserable beings who are perpetually tortured. They are not humans.

Hum is black, connected with those undergoing spiritual purging for their sins. It is like a mystic war cry.

The above mantra, or any mantra for that matter, being a sequence of words acts as an aid to concentration. It excludes

10. Maraini Fosco: op. cit. pp. 89, 161.

all extraneous thoughts from the mind. The style of its chanting is the essence of spiritual development. Its chanting is circular in style 'like a snake swallowing its own tail' — "Aummm manee padmeh hummm aummm manee padmeh hummm", and so on with the 'humm' of the final syllable running into the beginning of 'aummm'. It runs to a particular rhythm, and rhythm is hypnotic. Thus it stills the mind and aids meditation and concentration of thought to the exclusion of all else.

The above formula is slightly enlarged by the addition of syllable *hri!* And this is not the only formula; Aum vajra sattva, Aum vajra guru padma siddhi hum! etc. are also used by certain sects.

Mind and Body

What is mind? This million dollar question has engaged the attention of millions, and shall continue to perplex us for times to come. Mind is formless. Therefore, its source must also be formless. Matter cannot create mind, and mind cannot create matter, even though the two are interconnected. Mind is not the brain, in the brain; that is certain. This brings to mind the frequently asked question: "A flag moves. What is it that moves? Is it the flag or the wind?" Neither! "It is in the mind that moves." Lama David-Neel — the only European woman to have been honoured with the exalted rank of a Lama[11] — answers in her characteristic style quoting Tibetan mystics: "The whole

11. Born in Paris in 1868 and brought up in Brussels, she made her first trip to the Far East at the age of twenty-three, visiting Buddhist centres in India and Ceylon (Sri Lanka). In 1904 Alexandra David got married to an engineer, Philip Neel. They separated after two years, but otherwise remained married. It was his money that financed her expensive and extensive trips to the east and in the deep Himalayas. She is reported to have had an affair with the Crown Prince of Sikkim and that became her passport to travel to Lhasa, and to have an audience with the Thirteenth Dalai Lama who advised her to learn Tibetan, while a *naljorpa* (Tibetan magician) advised her to seek initiation from a spiritual master. For her memorable adventurous work, she was awarded the French Legion of Honour, Gold Medal of the French Geographical Society, Silver Medal of the Royal Belgian Geographical Society and Insignia of the Chinese Order of the Brilliant Star.

universe is a mirage which exists in the mind." That is what Hindu philosophy loudly proclaims. So what is mind? — Most people all over the world believe that our mind is located inside the skull behind the eyes. The Tibetan view point is much different. They believe that the 'absolute essence of mind pervades the entire body' thereby establishing a direct relationship between mind and body's subtle energy system. This complex doctrine was very briefly explained by the Dalai Lama at the Fourth Biennial "Mind & Life Conference" held at Dharmsala (India) in 1992. In his view, neither mind nor consciousness was of any consequence in themselves since there were a number of subtle levels and degrees of consciousness. Our every day consciousness is 'gross' in nature; it depends on the brain for its existence. As long as the brain is functioning, so is the 'gross consciousness'. When a person is brain-dead, gross consciousness is also dead. In other words, the subtle "essence of the mind" continued to exist since its existence is independent of the brain. And it did so notably in the heart chakra. It continued to exist as long as the energy system continued to function.

The Tibetan tradition has carried the concept of 'mind being the only reality' much too far. It has gone to the extremes. But that is precisely the essence of Tibetan occultism, its great secret. The whole world, indeed the entire universe, is purely a mental construct. "It has no existence outside of the mind that made it." If that be so, then what is the big idea of returning to the world that does not exist in reality? The Tibetan mystics have gone to great lengths to imbibe this great truth as the key to liberation from the eternal cycle of birth, death and rebirth. For the Hindu mystics, this is all '*Maya*', (The Buddhist Doctrine of Maya, like the Hindu one, is a separate study by itself) merely a phantom reality, the make-believe state without a solid base, an illusion only. The Tibetans call it *Gyûma* meaning a magical or illusory show. The *Brahmanical* system also refers to Maya as the *Shakti* of Brahman, and claim that it has "seven worlds or seven degrees within the *Samsara*, an antithesis of *Nirvana*, constituted as seven globes of a planetary chain having seven rounds of evolution on each globe making forty-nine stations of active existence ... the sacred number seven whose square is forty-nine, the symbolical number of the *Bardo*.[12] At this stage it is worthwhile reminding the reader that Hindu mythology is the source of Bardo symbolism. Since this world is a mere illusion, one must not fall in this trap of illusion being perceived as reality. A dream shall remain a dream; it cannot turn into reality. Since our world is the product of the mind, and it is all in our mind only, then control of mind must also lead to control of our environment. What is made by mind can also be changed by mind. These extraordinary ideas have originated in Tibet; their after-death ideas are the product of their single-minded concentration of thought process. Their development and practice of concepts of '*tumo*' and *lung-gom-pa* are the result of many decades of rigorous training of mind, forsaking the comforts of life, and self-denial to a degree which only intellectual mystics can resort to. Such ideas and practices are beyond the capacity of ordinary humans. Generations of Tibetan monks, lamas, mystics, hermits and 'magicians' have fine tuned the secrets of human mind through personal diligence and renunciation. The people of Tibet have thus earned the reputation as being the most gentle, spiritually advanced nation in the world. "They became 'psychonauts' exploring the deepest reaches of inner-space."[13]

In Lhasa there used to be a class of magicians known as Ngak-pas. They are supposed to be armed with occult powers. Two of them are assigned the job of ensuring that hail is not allowed to fall on the Potala, the Jewel Park or the Great Temple. They are armed with a special horn, red in colour, which has been taken from a bull or bull-yak that has killed another bull in a fight. The horn is filled with seeds of white mustard. The

---

12. The word 'bardo' is commonly used to denote the intermediate state between death and rebirth. The original text provided for four bardos: The natural bardo of life; the painful bardo of dying; the luminous bardo of dharma; the karmic bardo of becoming. Lately, Sogyal Rinpoché has added two more bardos: The bardo of sleep and the bardo of dream, thus making a total of six bardos — Sogyal Rinpoché: op. cit. pp. 11 and 112.

13. Brennan: op. cit. pp. 126,128-29.

Ngak-pas blows incantations into the horn and in the process the seeds acquire great power. The figures of scorpions engraved on the horn are in turn transformed into thunderbolts when thrown against the hail-storm. This was all very good, but when Sir Charles Bell happened to be in Lhasa and there was a hail-storm, the plantation in all three sites was damaged. The Ngak-pas had failed.

The Spirit World

Dreams have played an important role in the religious, political and social life of Tibet. The well known Milarepa was earlier known by the name of Phopaga and was expert at performing evil acts. But after he was reformed by a saintly spirit, he became a powerful force in doing good deeds and came to be known by his new name, Milarepa.[14] He foresaw the death of his mother in a dream. After she died he resolved to attain nirvana, the ultimate spiritual goal of liberation from the cycle of birth, death and rebirth, through karmic action. In the process, he attained a high degree of proficiency in the art of *tumo*[15], a mental discipline that generates great body heat so much so that in the extreme cold of his high mountain cave, he could survive in a light cotton robe called *repa*; hence his new name Milarepa. The modern science has also come to accept the veracity of dreams forewarning of events yet to come, and such other strange phenomena. Here is a story claimed to be true by the reputed Italian traveler-photographer, Fosco Maraini — The Abbot Ken-rab dreamt that he heard a voice saying: "Go to such and such a mountain and walk a hundred paces beyond the first waterfall. There you will find a revelation." At first the Abbot took no notice. But when the

14. Milarepa= Cotton-clad Mila. He was a wizard, hermit and poet whose thrilling life story written by his pupil Rechung has moved Tibetans for nearly a thousand years. — Maraini Fosco: op. cit. p.202

15. *Tumo* is actually 'psychic heat', but it is not ordinary heat or warmth. It is of three types; it is the esoteric version that keeps the body physically warm. It is a subtle fire which warms the generative fluid and runs all over the body along tiny channels of vein, artery or nerve — David-Neel: op. cit. pp. 216-17.

voice became more persistent, he finally decided to obey. He climbed the *kang-ri* (snow-mountain) "walked a hundred paces beyond the waterfall and found a smooth, flat stone, which looked as if it had been shaped by a man, where certainly no-one had ever been before. His monks raised it, and underneath they saw an ancient wooden box. They opened it and found a book. It was *termá*[16] ... Once upon a time I did not believe in these things ... but now I am convinced of them. Just when the Abbot Kenrab was about to turn the pages of the book terrifying screams were heard, and green fire started issuing from the hole in the ground, threatening to burn them all alive...." It is alright as far as the story goes. But the root of the issue was: Why did Kenrab have that dream at all? After considerable research and study spread over a long time, it came to light that one of the monks had been stealing the offerings made by worshippers to the tutelary deity of the monastery thereby depriving the deity of his legitimate altar offerings. The deity did what he did to avenge. Of course, no one knows what is written in that book. Some things are left to themselves, unknown, and not worth knowing. But the misdeeds of the guilty monk are best explained by a Tibetan proverb:

"Gods, devils and men all behave in the same way."!

A more or less similar story is prevalent in Tibet about the death in 1936 of British Political Officer, Mr. Williamson. The Tibetans are convinced that the Political Officer did not die of a heart attack; he died because he had committed a sacrilegious act by photographing the gods in a *gön-kang,* a shrine dedicated to the tutelary deities.[17]

The formation and hierarchy of the 'spirit world' is credited to the great Indian saint, scholar and tantric master Padmasambhava who came to Tibet in the eighth century for the specific purpose of subduing the recalcitrant spirits who

---

16. *Termás* are books, thoughts, works, which the great sages of the past wrote for the benefit of future generations. These lie hidden or buried and come to light only when their time has come.

17. Maraini Fosco: op. cit. pp. 96-97.

were an obstruction to the spread of Buddha-Dharma. He was the founder of Tibetan-Buddhism. In fact, under the name of Lopön Rimpoché he was as highly honoured as the Buddha himself. This was particularly so in the monastery of Samye. It is the oldest monastery in Tibet and was founded by Padmasambhava himself. After he had successfully dealt with all the spirits, one of them came before Padmasambhava in the form of an eight year child-monk wearing a golden hat and holding a crystal rosary. The Great Saint branded the child-monk on the crown of his head with his *dorje* (thunder-bolt), anointed the tip of his tongue with nectar and named him and his brother spirits Pehar Gyalpo, the Five Ferocious Kings. The Pehar Gyalpo was then appointed head of the entire hierarchy of all the Protective Spirits. Thus all opposition to the spread of Dharma by the Spirit-World came to an end. Tibet's hierarchy of guardian spirits assumed the symbolic character of the "Wheel of Protection".

Incarnation of Tagtser in Tengster Village

When the incarnation of Tagtser, a venerated Trülku, died it was indicated that the reincarnation would be found around the same general area. The Abbot of Kumbum in consultation with other monks prepared a list of the boys who were born within a year or two and sent the same to Gyalwa Rinpoché. The name of Thubten Jigme Norbu was not included in that list. The Gyalwa returned the list saying that the right name was not there. Kumbum revised the list and resubmitted, but again without Jigme's name. Perhaps that itself was the test of recognition of Jigme. The Gyalwa again returned the list with the same remark. Finally, Jigme's name was added and the Gyalwa Rinpoché promptly confirmed that Thubten Jigme Norbu was the right incarnation of Tagtser. Obviously, the Gyalwa Rinpoché is endowed with some attribute by virtue of which he can read the past, the present and the future. Jigme was admitted to Shardzong Monastery from where he was upgraded to Kumbum. He was Rapjung meaning a novice monk; after taking the first thirty-six vows he was promoted to

Getsul, meaning a junior monk.[18] It is only after he had taken the rest of the two hundred and fifty three vows that he became Gelong, a full fledged monk. Another seven years of hard studies were required to qualify for appearing in the examination that led to the privilege of entering the assembly of the monks. Indeed, Tibetan Lamas are a highly educated intellectual lot.

All the houses in the village were given a fresh whitewash every year; so it looked like a neat-clean village. A socket fixed in the roof took a flagpole, about ten feet high. There were a number of rooms having well laid out wooden floors; but the greater part of daily life was spent in the kitchen, which was divided into two unequal parts by a stove-oven and a wooden partition with a hatch. The fire-holes were covered by big kettles. It was a lower middle class family having some copper and brass utensils, but milk was always stored in wooden containers. The grain was ground in the village water-mill for a fee of one-tenth of the grain ground. Meat was a common part of daily diet. Buddhism did not come in the way since the killing was done by Muslim[19] butchers. When a sheep was slaughtered, every single part was made use of. Even the intestines were used as casing for blood, sausage, tsampa floor and pieces of fat. Tsampa was the staple. It could be from wheat, peas or maize. Eating-bowls for daily use were made of birchwood while wooden spoons or chop-sticks were used while eating on the table. Bowls used for fermenting liquor were line with brass or silver. Water was fetched from a nearby well that was really a small shallow

---

18. There are three classes of monks: the junior most is called Rapjung, Getsul is next and then Gelong. But all are equally considered as *Trapa*, or monks.

19. Can there be a Tibetan Muslim? Yes! (although a Tibetan, by definition, is a Buddhist). In fact, Muslims were a common feature in major Tibetan cities like Lhasa, Shigatse, and Gyantse. They speak chaste courtly Lhasa dialect; hence a Tibetan saying: "Do not listen to a Muslim's voice; look at what he is eating." — Patrick French: op. cit. p. 162.

pond. *Chhang*[20] (local beer mildly intoxicating) was a common drink for young and old alike. It was brewed at home from barley using home made yeast.[21]

Every one in the village was not a full-time farmer. There were cobblers, tailors, weavers and other handymen for various odd jobs. Thubten's family-house had a big prayer-mast over thirty feet high. Its round base was made of stone-slabs which served as feeding troughs. The prayer-flag in the premises was a long piece of cotton cloth, about one foot wide and covered with prayers imprinted by wood-cut-blocks. It was wrapped around the masts from top to bottom, and renewed periodically. The family also had about seventy white and a couple of black sheep. The sheep were shorn in early summer and the wool preserved. During winter the wool was soaked in big tubs, washed, teased, hung up to dry, and then spun into thick ropes. Dyes extracted from bark of trees and plants were used to colour the woolen ropes. A conical hollow tower, known as *bumkhang*[22] made of clay stood in front of the entrance gate of the house. It was the centre of certain ceremonies and was intended to protect the house and the farm from any harm.[23]

Every village has a protective deity; so did Tengster. A heap of loose stones, known as *labste*, close to the village is dedicated to the Protective Deity of the village. Tengster's labste was surrounded by a wooden fence so as to keep the stones together. A religious ceremony used to be held at the labste, once a year, on the twelfth day of the sixth month, when all the inhabitants of the village would march to the labste in a long procession. Here they used to throw coins, turquoises and corals over the

---

20. Another favourite drink which is more like a dish to eat, is made out of curdled milk, slightly cooked and stirred up in the process. It is a favourite pre-meal dish throughout Tibet and Western Mongolia and is known as *tara* or *tarak*. The Turks call it *yaurt* — *Journey to Lhasa and Central Tibet* by Sarat Chandra Das, London, 1902, p. 36.
21. Grunfeld: op. cit. pp. 25-38.
22. Literally translated: *bumkhang* means 'a hundred thousand houses'.
23 Norbu Jigme: op. cit. p. 50.

heap, burn incense[24] and pray for rain and bountiful crops. Monks from neighbouring monasteries would conduct the ceremonies, beating the gongs and sounding their ceremonial bells. Fresh prayer-flags were erected followed by drinking of *chhang* accompanied by merry-feasting. However, the most important feast, as in the rest of Tibet, is on the New Year's Day.

It should be noted that it was the tip of the tongue, and not the tongue, that was anointed. It is wrongly believed that Tibetans greet with their tongue thrust out of their wide open mouth. The actual process is: While greeting, or presenting a gift, the person opens his mouth wide, draws his breath in deep sigh, showing the tip of his tongue. That is the Tibetan traditional way of expressing loyalty and devotion. By age fourteen, Jigme had acquired a fairly wide knowledge of teachings of Padmasambhava and was therefore a fit candidate for admission in the *Tsogchen*, a great college of more than three thousand highly intellectual monks who devoted themselves to the scholastic life. Tsogchen had various *Tratsangs* or faculties — Menpa Tratsang for medicine; Gyüpa Tratsang for meditation; Dükhor Tratsang for mysticism and Shadpling Tratsang which taught logic and debate. Each Tratsang had its own *Dukhang,* or great hall. Jigme appeared before the Khenpo, the Abbot Superior who tested him for his suitability to enter the Shadpling Tratsang. He had a number of books kept beside him. Picking up one of them at random, he opened a page arbitrarily and loudly read a passage which Jigme had to recite and complete. Jigme did not fail even once. The second part of the first great test was held by the Shengo, the superior magistrate of the Monastery of Kumbum, a sort of Proctor. Jigme prostrated three times before him also, as was the custom. The Shengo tested Jigme from three books only, and declared him 'passed' in all of them after which Jigme could take part in the assembly of his fellow monks as a full fledged monk. He could now onwards carry his traditional hat of yellow wool in his hand and a few years thereafter, on his left shoulder.

---

24. Tibetan incense comes from "incense tree" commonly known as *sal* (In Tibetan, *Po*). Its resin is used as incense.

Monks in Debate

The actual conduct of debate between two aspirants was a spectacle by itself. The Shengo gives advance notice to contestants to prepare themselves adequately. It is a profoundly solemn occasion, totally formal, presided over by the Khenpo sitting on his throne with the Shengo on one side and the Shungleba, the examining inspector, on the other side of the throne. This particular debate, the first one for Jigme, was a *Gelmingel*, which dealt with homonyms, that is, "words and ideas which sound similar but which in fact have different meanings".

Birth Marks

We have already noted that the baby destined to be Gyalwa Rinpoché has at least some of the five distinct marks on his body. Again, this is not merely a coincidence or a superstitious myth. — The Dalai Lama's baby brother died when he was only two years old. It is customary amongst the Tibetans to consult the lamas and astrologers before a funeral. Some times even oracles are also consulted. In the present case his parents were advised that the baby's body should not be buried or cremated; it should be preserved so that he may be reborn in the same house. "As proof, a small mark was to be made on the body with a smear of butter. This was done, and in due course my mother had another baby boy — her last child. And when he was born, the pale mark was seen on the spot of his body where the butter had been smeared. He was the same being, born again in a new body ..." Unbelievable; an enigma indeed! But it must be true, for the simple reason that His Holiness the Dalai Lama himself has vouched for the episode.[25]

Now back to the Princess of Sikkim: She talked of lakes in which if you throw a pebble, a storm would arise. Of a witch died a long time ago and buried near a Lhasa monastery whose head sticks a little out of the ground every day, and there are actual fleas in her hair. Then there are poisons in Tibet. They are living things! They kill without any body noticing them, and the wealth or power of the person so killed accrues to the person who had

25. Dalai Lama: *Autobiography*, op. cit. pp. 52-53.

control over the poison. Or poisoning may be done for more subtle reasons, like inheriting the sanctity of the person so killed, or to obtain a superior position in the cycle of birth and death. In fact, the Princess is said to have claimed that several attempts had been made to poison her uncle for these subtle reasons only. Indeed, poisons are living things. And when they are made ready, they have to be used, used to kill; there is no escape. If you cannot use it against the person for whom you prepared it, you have to give it to someone else, or take it yourself! Tibetan poisons do have a will of their own. Strange and funny indeed. Or are these mere 'cock and bull' stories?[26]

Memories of Previous Life

A Trülku of Kumbum died some years ago but his incarnation had not been discovered for a long time. The person who was managing the estate after the death of the Talk (the Trulku) happened be out on a trading mission when he stayed in a house for rest. As he took out his jade snuff box to take a pinch, a small boy stopped him and asked him why the old man was using his snuff box. True, strictly speaking, the precious little box did not belong to him; it was of the Talk who had died some years back and whose incarnation had not yet been discovered. "Give it back to me at once; it is mine", said the little boy again.

A few days later the boy was taken in a procession to claim his original estate. He corrected the lead-man about the way to the mansion. Then when tea was to be served, he demanded his favourite large decorated china-cup. None in the mansion had seen such a cup. The 'boy-Talk' explained the colour scheme, design of decorations and also where in the store room the servants would find that cup. The cup with all the accessories was eventually found where the 'incarnate-Talk' had mentioned.[27]

Such stories of memories of the past life are galore not only in Tibet but in many parts of world too, particularly India and

26. Maraini Fosco: op. cit. pp. 51-52.

27. David-Neel: op. cit. pp. 126-27.

south-east Asia. But the one about "Rolang: The Corpse who stands up" is in a class by itself.

Before the introduction of Buddhism in Tibet, the ancient Bön religion was prevalent in Tibet. It had originated in the neighbouring country called Shan-Shung. Its followers used to practice a peculiar funeral rite. The sorcerer used to be shut up alone with a corpse in a dark room. He would lie on top of the corpse, mouth to mouth, hold it tight and continue to repeat the magic formula, excluding all other thoughts from his mind. After some time, the corpse would stand up and start moving. But the sorcerer must not let go his hold, or he would die. The dead body would struggle hard to free itself. The struggle goes on and on. Finally, the corpse gets exhausted and the tongue of the dead body protrudes out. This is the critical moment. The sorcerer bites his teeth forcefully into the dead tongue and takes out a piece. It is carefully dried, preserved and it becomes a potent magic weapon. This is the Tibetan version of a corpse coming to life through the medium of another person for some vested interest. Similar stories are galore in India where a person becomes unconscious. His spirit as a man, or as a demi-god or a demon, enters the dead body, acts in the guise of the dead man, and then reverts to his own frame which was lying unconscious during the intervening period.[28]

---

28. David-Neel: op. cit. pp. 134-35, 304.

12

Sonic Power
Magic & Miracles

The phenomenon of levitation by sound has been reported from Tibet. Although a highly respected traveler-researcher like Alexandra David-Neel has vouched for the authenticity of the technique, the circumstantial evidence adduced as proof is not enough to convince the skeptics, more so since her stories are absolutely fantastic. However, that should not detract from the veracity of the narrative. This phenomenon has been observed even in modern times also, as narrated by British biologist-author Dr. Lyall Watson in his book *Supernature*. But why go far to foreign lands. The art of levitation by sound was prevalent in India till recent times; and may be a serious search might reveal its practice and existence even today.

As far Tibet — A complicated combination of varying sized drums and trumpets produced a rhythm of such crescendo that the expert monk controlling the procedure could get a heavy stone block up and above in an arc at the desired level. In this one case thirteen drums of varying size and six trumpets, again in varying sizes, were positioned in a ninety degree arc to move a stone block by sonic power. In another arrangement, an enormous gong made of a golden centre-section ringed with hoops of iron and brass together with a bowl shaped stringed instrument were positioned along with two large screens set to form a triangle. "When the gong was struck, it set up sympathetic vibrations in the strings of the bowl. The screens directed the sound towards a large stone block." The process was repeated a number of times after which the monk was able to lift the heavy stone block with one hand. The monk further claimed that long ago instruments of this type had been used to build defensive stone-walls like the ones described in an earlier chapter. Similar devices were used to produce sound waves that could shatter stone or dissolve matter.

Out of all the musical instruments it is drums that produced rhythm, and certain rhythms have a curious effect on the mind. The Tibetan long horn is a peculiar enormous instrument, about ten to twelve feet in length, made from copper bound with silver. It generates a deep, sonorous, echoing note that travels over long distances.

Acoustic Physics

Professor Gavraud, a French engineer suffered from nausea during his work period in his office. He traced the cause of his illness to constant low frequency sub-sonic hum. Being a professor and an engineer, he decided to build a mechanism that would generate infra-sound. He discovered that the standard issue of police whistle actually generated a whole range of low frequency sounds. Using this as a model, the Professor "built a police-whistle six feet long powered by compressed air". The device was tested by a technician who collapsed on the first blast of the whistle. He was dead! The postmortem 'reported that his internal organs had been turned to jelly'. A precious life was lost; but the incident dramatically vindicates Tibetan theories about sonic or sub-sonic power. A similar experiment was repeated in the open when every window pane was broken within half a mile of the test site. Another similar experiment proved that a building could be demolished at a distance of five miles by directing two sound waves on the target.[1] Thus Tibetan claims of destructive

1. Brennan J.H.: *Magical Techniques of Tibet*, 2002, p. 27

power of sound have been proved beyond any doubt. Temporary reduction of weight of heavy components, floating of grocer's weights in water, and similar stories from Egypt go to prove that there is considerable weight of truth behind Tibetans' claims on 'Sonic Technology'. An English couple, a British army officer and his wife Patricia Slade visited Poona (India). They witnessed a religious ceremony in which eleven white robed priests took part. The priests circled a boulder about forty tons in weight, all the time chanting. On the eleventh circuit they stopped chanting, each priest put a finger tip on the boulder, and they lifted it to shoulder height. They held it up in the air for about half a minute before setting it down gently. The volunteers from amongst the audience then repeated the feat without any problem. Above all else is the sonic-boom experienced when modern military aircraft fly at supersonic speed.

Every surviving temple in Tibet has an orchestra, but not in the western-church sense. Tibetan temple orchestras are required to produce specific combinations of sounds which assist the congregation in meditation and other religious rites and activities. These sounds are exact replica of the sounds naturally produced in the human body, such as heart beat, blood flowing, etc. and are therefore in harmony with the human body system. Another component of the sacred sound system of Tibet is the 'singing bowls', so called because of the musical notes that emanate from them. These are not ordinary bowls as sometimes claimed by the locals; these bowls are specially crafted from special alloys made from metals having planetary associations as follows:

- Gold = Sun
- Silver = Moon
- Mercury = Mercury
- Copper = Venus
- Iron = Mars
- Tin = Jupiter
- Lead = Saturn

The Hindu religion also recognizes the astrological properties of the sound produced by these seven metals, collectively known as "Sapta-Dhatoo". When struck with a beater, the bowls produce a ringing sound. But for religious occasions the Tibetans rub a short wooden baton around the rim of the bowl which then produces a continuous harmonic note. By adding water in the bowls, and varying the quantity of water in each bowl, one can produce a wide variety of musical notes. Similarly, varying the proportions of metals that go into the alloy would vary the nature of the musical note. This is how the Tibetans 'tune' their singing bowls. It is a fairly complicated system which may require years of training and hard practice. It is doubtful if the western scientific brain would be able to comprehend and produce the desired sonar-effects.

Having been in the profession of arms, the Author cannot resist the temptation to point out that some of the above discoveries have immense military potential. Perhaps, the defence-strategists are already on the job. "Acoustic Physics" thus has made its debut in the field of science.

Energy Manipulation

While there is quite a volume of literature on such enigmatic matters as oracles, divination, recognitions, dreams, sacred waters showing visions, et al, there are certain aspects of un-natural phenomena which remain unexplored. For instance: A Princess of Sikkim is reported to have talked about "wind-men" (*lung-pa*). They are monks who after years of 'extreme asceticism' and 'strenuous preparation' succeed in completely freeing themselves from the weight of human frame and then can travel hundreds of miles in a single day. May be, they can complete a circuit of Tibet in a week! While this may sound unbelievable to a skeptic, instances of lamas suspending themselves in mid-air by levitation have been recorded by independent witnesses.

The so called 'magical practices' of Tibet are contingent on energy manipulation of the human system. The *lung-gom-pa* runners are a prime example of the ability of man to detach himself from the body-weight to such an extent that sometimes he may have to be weighed down by heavy chains lest he gets airborne! This rare 'supernatural' state is achieved through years of hard training and practice under expert high lamas. Milarepa was also endowed with *lung-gom* attribute and he ascribed his gift to "clever control" of 'internal air'.[2] David-Neel saw her first lung-gom-pa runner while she was traveling through the vast high altitude uninhabited desert of Chang Thang.[3] The runner was a mere speck in the far distance at the horizon. She tracked him through field glasses, a lone man moving at extraordinary speed. Her fellow travelers cautioned her not to try stopping the runner nor to speak to him lest it breaks his trance, and the deity that possessed him leaves the man completely shaken which might even result in his death. When the runner came closer to the Lady-Lama, she saw his impassioned face, eyes focused on a point in the sky, holding a *phurba*[4] in his right hand. He was not running in the usual sense of the word; it was more like a rubber ball bouncing along, totally unaware of the Lady-Lama and her party. David-Neel had a similar encounter with another lung-gom-pa while she was walking through a forest in western Tibet. In this case the runner was sitting on a rock apparently absorbed in meditation. As soon as he became aware of the traveling party, he moved off at supernormal rapidity.[5] Brennan has summed up this phenomenon: "The fixation of the gaze, the uninteresting environment, and the rhythm of the internalized mantra synchronized with rhythmic breathing and leg movement all combine to become a powerful induction."[6]

---

2. Alexandra David-Neel: op. cit. p. 199.
3. Literally, *Chang Thang* means 'northern plain'.
4. A metal artifact with short ornamental shaft having broad triangular blades. Miniature phurbas carved out of bone are an artistic creation used for some specific religious practices.
5. The Lady-Lama saw her third lung-gom-pa in Kham region of Eastern Tibet. David- Neel: op. cit. p. 210.
6. Brennan: op. cit. p. 57.

Miracles

Tantricism is as old as written history, if not still older. Ancient Northern India was its cradle. It was widely practiced in the seventh century B.C. in the region falling between Kashmir and Afghanistan, known as Urgyen, modern Swat. Although Mahayana school of Buddhism, locally known as Theg Chen, was the dominant creed, but it was inexorably mixed up with tantric practices. Magic, sorcery and miracles were the order of the day. The well known Indian saint, Padmasambhava, Lopon Rinpoché to the Tibetans, was the embodiment of Tantric beliefs and practices. Lord Buddha was destined to be the savior of mankind from the entanglements of Tantric beliefs and practices, but tantric practices got so much intermixed with Buddhism that the two developed into one new entity. This happened about one thousand years after Buddha had preached the Middle Path to attain nirvana. The power behind this revival of Tantric creed was the Indian sage, Padmasambhava who was invited to Tibet by King Trisong Detsan to subdue the demons which were causing lots of problems to the King and people of Tibet.

Lopon Rinpoché (Padmasambhava in India) entered Tibet from Nepal. He had to subdue a number of demons all the way. When he reached the outskirts of Lhasa, he was met by an escort sent by the King to take his entourage to Samye. But the horses were thirsty, so were the members of his party, but there was no water available nearby. Lopon Rinpoché struck a rock with his stick, and water started flowing from the rock. It was a miracle, demonstrating the powers the Rinpoché wielded. "I have seen it myself and water still flows from the solid rock from a point above the level of a man's head. We call it Shongpa Lhachu, or 'Horse's Water of the Gods'.[7]

The King rode out to receive Lopon Rinpoché outside Samye. When the two came close to each other, the King conveyed an impression that he expected the Rinpoché to bow to him. But Lopon Rinpoché said that since he had been invited to Tibet to

7. Norbu Thubten Jigme: op. cit. p. 163.

do good for the people and to rid them of the menace of demons as well as to bring knowledge, it was for the King to bow before him. Saying this, he pointed a finger towards the King. There was thunder and lightening, and the King's royal regalia burst into flames. The King and the whole court promptly bowed before Lopon Rinpoché.

The immediate cause for inviting Lopon Rinpoché was the problem arising from construction work for the first monastery in Tibet at Samye. During the day the workers would put up stone and woodwork but during the night the demons would shake the earth, thereby destroying the day's work. This had gone on for many days; and hence the visit of Lopon Rinpoché who had a great reputation for subduing the demons. Soon after the initial reception outside Samye, Lopon Rinpoché proceeded to exorcize the demons from the work site after which construction work proceeded smoothly. The main temple was dedicated to Chenrezig. Lopon Rinpoché continued his good work in the rest of the country. He took the existing beliefs of the people in demons and miracles and used them to make the people understand the truth. Whether there are really any demons or evil forces or not, is a difficult question to answer. It is what is in your mind that matters. If you think there are demons and ghosts and your mind believes in that, then these evil forces are there. However, if your mind does not believe in demons, well, there may not be any such evil forces like ghosts and demons. "If a mind creates a demon, it exists for that mind .... What often seem to be different deities in fact are really different aspects of the same deity, and all are aspects, ultimately, of one single truth."[8] The real question is the range of your mental capabilities, the wave-lengths of the sounds that you can hear, the range for which the matter is tangible to your sensory perceptions, and so on. It is possible to alter the range of one's perceptions through yogic training and practice. That is the power to materialize and de-materialize matter, substantial or psychic. One may or may not agree with the beliefs and practices of Lopon Rinpoché; but the fact remains that he

8. Ibid; pp. 164-65.

was successful in his mission to Tibet where the first Buddhist monastery was established and the baser practices of Bön religion were outlawed. He successfully established the superiority of Buddhism over Bön.

In Lhasa there used to be a class of magicians known as *Ngak-pas*. They are supposed to be armed with occult powers. Two of them are assigned the job of ensuring that hail is not allowed to fall on the Potala, the Jewel Park or the Great Temple. They are armed with a special horn, red in colour, which has been taken from a bull or bull-yak that has killed another bull in a fight. The horn is filled with seeds of white mustard. The Ngak-pas blows incantations into the horn and in the process the seeds acquire great power. The figures of scorpions engraved on the horn are in turn transformed into thunderbolts when thrown against the hail-storm. This was all very good, but when Sir Charles Bell happened to be in Lhasa and there was a hail-storm, the plantation in all three sites was damaged. The Ngak-pas had failed.

Fake Miracles

Sometimes even ordinary natural phenomena were interpreted as signs of foreboding. For instance: Football caught the fancy of young men. Eleven teams were formed and cup-tie matches organized in Lhasa. During one such match a hailstorm, with hail-stones as big as walnuts, occurred causing extensive damage. It was "interpreted as a sign that the gods disapproved of this frivolous sport, and football was abolished"! Another game that suffered a similar fate was mahjong which was a universal passion resulting in neglect of even official duties. The government finally banned the game and penalties for secret misdemeanors were severe. New Year festivities include horse racing. Tibet had rider-less horses galloping furiously on their own, charting their own course through the crowds. Each horse belongs to a private stable and the name of the owner is marked on a piece of cloth secured to the horse. This used to be followed by mounted race, the riders wearing historic costumes, using their whips liberally to get the best out of the animal. Sometimes the mounted riders put up an excellent competitive performance. They were highly skillful riders and exceedingly accurate sharp-shooters. While the horses were galloping, the riders would stand on the saddle, and shoot a hanging target in the bull's eye. Before they had gone about twenty yards, they would change from musket to bow and arrow, and many of them hit the mark again to joyous applause of the spectators.

In the course of discussion of the football-frivolity, it transpired that Tibet had monks who were specialists in weather-making, not forecasting but actually creating a desired weather condition. When a storm is imminent, they blow on conches and long horns creating vibrations which may mitigate, if not eliminate, the storm-damage. Obviously, it is the effect of vibrations like the church bells rung in mountain villages of Europe when a severe storm is approaching. But to the Tibetans it was pure and simple magic. One such story led to another. The Thirteenth Gyalwa Rinpoché had his Court weather-maker. His special assignment was to protect the God-King's summer garden against storm damage. One day there was a heavy hailstorm which completely ruined the flowers and fruits in the garden. The Dalai Lama was very annoyed. The monk was summoned to the divine presence. Notwithstanding his protestations and prostrations, the trembling magician was ordered to bring about a miracle otherwise he would be punished. In turn he asked for a sieve, just a simple sieve and asked the Thirteenth whether he would be satisfied if the water poured over the sieve held. The Dalai Lama nodded in approval. And lo and behold! Water did not pass through the sieve. The magician's reputation was retrieved and he held his well paid job.

More often than not, even accidents were considered portents of future catastrophic events. In one instance three heavy tree trunks, nearly seventy feet high, were bound together. A huge flag bearing printed prayers was then nailed to the entire length of the huge bamboo pole. But calamity struck the heavy mast which broke into pieces, crushing three persons to death and injuring many others. "The whole of Tibet took this as an evil omen and people prophesied a black future for the country. Catastrophes such as earthquakes and floods were foretold." Others spoke of war and looked with trepidation towards China. One may believe in such omens or not, but the fact of history remains that Tibet did suffer catastrophic tragedies after this accident. However, the saving grace was that the injured were taken, not to a monk-doctor, but to the hospital in British Legation where some beds were reserved for Tibetans.

13

Dreams and Prophecies

Queen Maha Maya had a dream. She saw a wonderful white elephant descending from the stars above in the night sky. It entered her womb. She conceived. That is how Prince Siddhartha was later born around the year 566 B.C in the royal household of Sakya King Suddhodana in Kapilavastu in the Nepal Tarai to the north of Basti district of Uttar Pradesh. A 'Virgin Birth'? How close the Christian concept[1] is to the Buddhist view! When she gave birth to Sakya-Muni, she was picking up an olive branch. Legend has it that the new born baby immediately rose to his feet and walked seven paces towards each point of compass, exclaiming: "This is my last reincarnation". The birth of Siddhartha was also shrouded in a lot of auspicious omens. When her time was near, she happened to be out of the palace, walking in the woods around village Lumbinigrama when a big tree bent its branches to the ground to give her cushiony support. The mother died in child-birth. The new born baby was brought up by his aunt and stepmother Prajapati Gautami. The new-

1. It brings to mind the romantic legend of how Jesus Christ, after quarreling with his parents, ran away to India from where he made his way to Tibet and studied Buddhism in the Hemis Monastery in Ladakh, then part of Tibet. Eventually he returned home to preach his religion, Christianity. Well, legends are legends after all!

born was taken to the Sakya Temple where, as legend has it, even the sacred images prostrated before the Baby who was destined to become Lord Buddha. The temple priest is said to have recognized the Baby as the incarnation of Changchubh Sempa returned to earth from the 'Heavenly Fields' for emancipation of mankind.

The priest prophesied that the new born Prince would stay in the royal household only till the time he had witnessed four things, the "Four Truths" of life: a sick person suffering in pain; an old man bent under the weight of age; a corpse; and a *sanyasi* who had renounced the world. The King made sure that the Prince was so confined to the vast area of the Palace that he would never see the 'four things'. But a prophecy has to come true to life! And it did, notwithstanding even the shackles of married life as the King had tied down the Prince to Bhadda Kachchana Yasodhara. Why did Siddhartha marry Yasodhara when he had no interest in worldly life and pleasures? He is said to have replied that the two had met in a previous life, and the marriage was in fulfillment of that meeting, which in this life led to the birth to a boy, Rahula. However, soon after that Siddhartha saw the 'Four Truths' personified as prophesied. And at the age of twenty-nine he rode out of the Palace complex when the gates opened on their own despite the royal commands to the contrary; Siddhartha had renounced the world — the 'Great Renunciation' as it is known in Indian history — and put on clothes of a beggar 'sanyasi' to move around incognito. Finally, he took a bath in River Niranjana and sat under a *pipal* tree, the 'Bodhi tree', resolved never to move again till he achieved full enlightenment, the final Truth of Life. That came to him in successive stages in due course and he came to be known as the 'Enlightened One', the Buddha, or Sakya-Muni, a sage of the Sakya clan. He taught his followers the four 'Noble Truths', *Arya Satya*:

- Suffering (Truth of Suffering);
- Cause of Suffering;

- Destruction of Suffering; (Truth of Release)
- The way that leads to the destruction of sorrow; (Way to Release).

It was not the way of habitual sensuality, or habitual practice of self-torture. Gautama preached a "Middle Path" called the "Noble Eightfold-Path":

- Right Views — To be free from superstition and delusions;
- Right Thought — High and worthy of human intelligence;
- Right Speech — Kind and truthful;
- Right Conduct — Peaceful, honest and pure actions;
- Right Livelihood — so as not to cause hurt or danger to others;
- Right Effort — in self-training and self-control;
- Right Mindfulness — To have an active and watchful mind;
- Right Contemplation — To concentrate in deep meditation on the realities of life.

This was the path to peace of mind which ultimately led to 'Nirvana' — literally "blowing out" or extinction of craving of the desire for existence. He started preaching at Sarnath, near Benares, setting in motion the 'wheel of law', teaching the Truth of Suffering, the Cause of Suffering, the Truth of Release, and the Way to Release. It will thus be seen that Gautama Buddha was not an exponent of a new religion or sect; he was merely preaching a way of life, pure and 'simple living and high thinking'. He carefully avoided discussion of God, life after death, etc. Thus Buddhism is not a religion in the traditional sense of the word; it is a way of life — good, simple, pure life. Taking this argument a step further — Since there are hundreds and hundreds of gods and goddesses in the Hindu pantheon, and a Hindu would worship any number of them on as required basis, Hinduism too is not one religion; again it is a way of life.

After Altan Khan had conferred the title of Dalai Lama on Sonam Gyatso, the latter prophesied that within eighty years the descendents of the Khan would become the rulers of all Mongolia and China. It would be of interest to note that the Manchu Emperors had not lost sight of the above prophecy during the past few generations — Such was the power of prophetic words of the exalted beings that, between 1649 and 1651, the Shun-chih Emperor of China sent several invitations to the Dalai Lama to visit Peking with a view to persuading him to use his religious influence to forestall a Mongolian invasion of Chinese territory. The Chinese reasoned that since the Fourth Dalai Lama was a Mongol, and two people had close spiritual relations, they were hopeful of averting the looming disaster through the good offices of the Fifth Gyalwa Rinpoché. 'The Great Fifth' (1617-82) was renowned for his spiritual and secular greatness besides his military exploits, which led to secular unification of Tibet. But the Tibetan prophesies are inherently predisposed towards fulfillment. This is precisely what happened in 1903-04. The Tibetans knew all about the centuries old-prophecy regarding the British Military Expedition to Lhasa, and the outcome of the fighting. But they still fought on, getting killed in hundreds.

The Fantastic Tree

The Fifth Gyalwa Rinpoché went on a visit to Peking in 1652 as an 'independent monarch, being at that time neither under China nor under any other nation'. On his way back, he passed through the Kokonor, or Blue Lake, region where he built the monastery of Kumbum on the exact site where Tsongkhapa, the founder of the Gelug-pa sect was borne in 1555. It was prophesied that the new born would have an extraordinary career. His parents were advised to keep the spot clean and tidy where his mother had delivered the baby. Legend has it that in course of time a tree grew over that spot. Soon the leaves had perfect prints of deities miraculously imprinted on them, so were the branches decorated with beautiful neat writings. That is how the name Kumbum, meaning 'hundred thousand images', came into being. A gold-roofed *chörtens* is said to protect the special tree. And that was where the present Dalai Lama was also born. The fame of this extraordinary tree spread far and wide. It aroused skeptical curiosity among the intellectuals, the so-called civilized westerners in particular. The famous Lazarist priest, the Abbe Huc, made it a point to visit Kumbum to see the Tree. Extracts from his account of the pilgrimage to the Tree:

> At the foot of the mountain on which the Lamasery stands, there is a great square enclosure formed by brick walls. We were able to examine at leisure the marvelous tree, some of the branches of which had already manifested themselves above the wall. Our eyes were first directed with earnest curiosity to the leaves, and we were filled with an absolute consternation of astonishment at finding that, in point of fact, there were on each of the leaves well formed Tibetan characters, all of a green colour, some darker, some lighter than the leave itself. Our first impression was a suspicion of fraud on the part of the Lamas; but after a minute examination of every detail, we could not discover the least deception. The characters all appeared to us portions of the leaf itself, equally with its veins and nerves; the position was not the same in all; in one leaf they would be on top of the leaf; in another, in the middle; in a third, at the base, or at the side; the younger leaves represented the characters only in a partial state of formation. The bark of the tree and its branches, which resemble that of the plain tree, are also covered with these characters. When you remove a piece of the old bark, the young bark under it exhibits the indistinct outlines of characters in a germinating state, and that is very singular, these new characters are not infrequently different from those which they replace. We examined everything with the closest attention, in order to detect some trace of trickery, but we could not discern anything of the sort, and the perspiration absolutely trickled down our faces under the influence of the sensations which this most amazing spectacle created ... ... The Tree of the

> Ten Thousand Images seemed to us of great age. Its, trunk, which three men could scarcely embrace with outstretched arms, is not more than eight feet high; the branches, instead of shooting up, spread out in the shape of a plume of feathers, and are extremely bushy; few of them are dead. The leaves are always green, and the wood, which is of a reddish tint, has an exquisite odour, something like that of cinnamon. The Lamas informed us that in summer, towards the eighth month, the tree produces large red flowers of an extremely beautiful character. Such a tree does not exist anywhere else, and all attempts to replicate this tree through various means have been fruitless.[2]

Absolutely fantastic; unbelievable indeed, yet true beyond any doubt whatsoever! This type of unnatural miracles can happen in Tibet only; and that too under pre-ordained environmental conditions. That is why all efforts by botanists to grow a replica failed. This is something like, but far more miraculous than, the waters of Hindu's "Ganga Mai" (River Ganges at Haridwar) whose water, when packed in clean tins, remains fresh; or the waters of various springs (glens) of Scotland that impart that special flavour and distinct taste to Scotch whisky.

Family of Incarnations

The family of the Fourteenth Dalai Lama comes from pure Tibetan stock. His mother gave birth to sixteen children of which nine died when they were very young. This shows that the infant-child mortality rate was much on the higher side, obviously because of lack of proper medical facilities. It has been estimated that child-mortality rate varied between 40 to 75 per cent. The eldest boy was initially called Tashi Tsering, but this name was only temporary, since it was customary that the naming of the child is done in connection with some important occasion like recovery from an illness, or the visit of some high prelate. The

---

2. Huc M. Abbe: *Travels in Tartary, Thibet, and China during the years 1844*-46; Vol. II, pp. 52, 54.

eldest brother of the Fourteenth Gyalwa Rinpoché was thus named Thubten Jigme Norbu when a high lama visited the village and spent a night in the house. Jigme means "Fear Not". However, siblings called him "Jola" which means the "oldest", an honouric form since in Tibet the eldest son enjoys precedence.[3] Jigme soon noticed that he enjoyed certain special privileges over other children not only within the family but amongst the ones outside too. Jigme was a Rinpoché. This was the high titular honour reserved for a reincarnated person, or *Trülku*. Soon after that a group of monks visited the house and announced that they had come to take Jigme away to the monastery for education since he was the reincarnation of Tagtser in Kumbum, a famous monastery. The monks had brought with them large cases containing the clothing that Jigme was to wear hereafter. On the appointed day, Jigme was dressed in new splendid clothing from head to foot; he was to carry nothing with him that had belonged to him in his parental house.

Monastery is not quite the correct word for the Tibetan institutions which have come be known as monasteries in western terminology. But since the usage has become universal, and for want of a better term, monastery continues as the standard term. However, it should be noted that many Tibetan monasteries are more like township, sprawling buildings, streets, odd shops, and eateries too in some cases. When a Tibetan boy joins a monastery, his family ties are not cut off; on the contrary, regular contact is maintained with the family, with family members visiting the boy every now and then. This is all the more necessary since the monastery provides for only the barest needs of the boy-monk who continues to be materially dependent on his ancestral home for daily wherewithal. The same holds good for social stratification within the monastery. Monks from rich families live better, dress better, and are better looked after.

The separation from his parents, brother and sister was indeed a very painful experience for a young boy of merely about four years of age. After his family left for their village, a forty-year old

3. Norbu Thubten Jigme: *Tibet is My Country;* p. 59.

monk named Püntso was to be always with him, as his teacher and servant. And his play-pen? A large *bumkhang* in the woods surrounding the monastery. His duties soon embraced receiving and blessing pilgrims who brought him gifts of butter and flour. All this was preparatory to his move to Kumbum which came about three months since he was taken away from his parents' home.

On the appointed day Jigme was led in procession to Kumbum. His old village of Tengster lay on the way. He was welcomed to his old village, and to his home, in great style. He was pleasantly surprised to notice tremendous improvement and luxurious furnishings in his old home — all this had come about by virtue of Jigme being recognized as one of the highest incarnations, and hence a Rinpoché who took food and drink before even the Abbot and the Steward. His parents, brother and sister were to accompany him from his old home to Kumbum monastery. They too were provided with splendid silken garments from Tagtser Labrang. The ceremonial procession of the Rinpoché arrived at the gates of monastic city of Kumbum on the eighth day of the fifth month of the Iron-Sheep year — an especially auspicious day as calculated by a *Tsipa*, a highly respected astrologer of the Monastery.

The Abbot of Kumbum made his obsequies to the newly installed Rinpoché. He heads the hierarchy of the Monastery followed by *Shengo* who is the highest dispenser of justice and occupies the second place in monastic hierarchy. As a symbol of his office he carries a long four-edged metal sceptre conferring on him a formidable appearance of strict disciplinarian. The Shengo was assisted by a number of *Geyos*, powerful monks with daunting exterior carrying six-foot staves in a threatening manner for vigorous use when necessary. The Geyos had a number of *Chabris* to assist them. It will thus be seen that there was a well organized police set-up to enforce the rule of law in the huge Monastery. The police was in charge of enforcement and were allowed to grow hair while other monks had to shave their heads. They looked fearful, more so since many of them smeared their faces with soot and grease. They carried concealed swords, large keys and iron bars, and hence were often referred to as the "Iron Bars". Since homosexuality was widespread in the monasteries, these "iron bars" often indulged in kidnapping small boys for their nefarious activities, because all said and done, homosexuality was officially considered sinful.[4] The prayers in the assembly hall were led by *Umdze*, or the prayer-leader. Community-breakfast was followed by a sermon by the Abbot after which the Umdze would read out long passages from the holy writings, the *Kangyur* which comprises one hundred and eight volumes having a total of forty-five thousand pages. It may be noted that one hundred and eight is a sacred number amongst the Tibetans so much so that some Tibetan women braid their hair one hundred and eight small plaits. The rosary has one hundred and eight beads. There are 108 signs of Buddhahood, 108 votive lamps, etc. Even the assembly hall had exactly one hundred and eight columns.[5]

The Shengo was followed by about thirty rinpochés who represented the aristocracy of the Monastery. Needless to say that each and every one who came over to pay his respects to Rinpoché presented him with the traditional good-luck scarves, besides some other material gifts. The ceremony went on under the feet of an enormous picture of Buddha guarded by figures of Chenrezi and Jampa on his side. Butter-tea[6] and large quantities of food were continuously served to one and all. A bowl is a very private possession. Every Tibetan owns one in which he alone drinks tea. It may be made of ordinary birch wood, or a costly one made of jade with a golden saucer and a richly carved cover. Good, bad or indifferent, it is never lent

4. Grunfeld: op. cit. pp. 30-31.

5. Norbu Jigme: op. cit. pp.114-118.

6. The Tibetans make butter tea by crumbling a handful of brick-tea into boiling water. It is allowed to stew for about five minutes. A pinch of salt (never sugar) is added. Finally a big dollop of butter is added into a man's tea bowl, and then he stirs the tea with his finger. The Tibetans prefer Chinese brick-tea although it is much poorer in quality than the Darjeeling tea. The brick tea is compressed blocks of coarse twigs caked with refuse tea-dust.

to any one else to drink in. Since Kumbum was a rich monastery, there was no shortage of food or comfort. The lands owned by the Monastery were leased out to farmers who were obliged to deliver a certain portion of the crop to the Monastery. Clocks and watches rather than the sun and cock-crow regulated the various activities to a set pattern of time table. There was hardly any spare time for the monks, or monk-to-be. Prayers and religious exercises were mandatory even after the six o'clock evening meal. Every one said his prayers consciously and painstakingly. First act was to fold the hands and put them to forehead, lips and chest followed by touching the forehead to the ground, again and again, in a kneeling position, continuously repeating the prayer: "*Om mani padme hum*", which roughly translates as: "Oh, thou treasure in the lotus". The practice of touching the forehead to the ground was so common, repeated so very often, that some particularly pious monks used to "develop a permanently horny nodule" on their forehead. But they were not necessarily lamas. The title 'lama' does not apply to every Tibetan monk. Lama is a title; it means "superior". Even a layman who has distinguished himself in the field of religion could be given the title of Lama. In the same vein, it is wrong to refer to Tibetan religion as 'Lamaism'. "If it is to be given a special name of its own at all then it would be much more accurate to call it 'Tibetan Buddhism'."[7] Within Tibet, there is no such religion as 'Lamaism', nor it is called 'Buddhism'; if a person does not belong to one of the religious minorities and is asked what his religion is: he invariably responds he is a "Nangpa", which means "one who belongs". Since Buddhism is an all-pervading, all-embracing religion without any fanaticism, even a non-Buddhist could call himself "Nangpa". However, out side Tibet, a non-Buddhist calls himself as "Chipa", meaning 'one who does not belong', but is therefore taken to mean a "foreigner'; strictly speaking, the correct word for a foreigner is "Chilingpa".[8]

---

7. Norbu Jigme: op. cit. p. 87.
8. Ibid; p. 88.

It was time for Jigme Norbu Rinpoché, the eldest brother of the Fourteenth, to be initiated into the fraternity of monks. On a certain day in the auspicious eighth month, Lama Cheshö Rinpoché along with four other lamas came to Norbu Thubten's *lebrang* to preside over the ceremony, to hear his vows. His head was shaven and all his clothes removed, as if totally wiping out the past from his life. He was then washed[9] with holy water from head to foot symbolically washing out his past as a lay person. While dressed in his new robes of a monk, he was given a new name which was recorded in the monasterial roll. The usual thanksgiving presents, the *kukel,* consisting of a *kata* and some money in an envelope were given for the services rendered. Thus Thubten Norbu became a full fledged monk of the "Order of the Gelugpa sect which had been founded by Tsong Khapa almost six hundred years" earlier. Norbu had thus crossed another milestone to start life as an apprentice in Kumbum Monastery. About a week after this ceremony, Cheshö Rinpoché presented Norbu a beautiful clay statuette of Sangye Chömden De, which was to protect Norbu all his life wherever he went. The statuette was to accompany him all the time.[10]

Pilgrimage by Prostrations

The advent of spring used to be celebrated with great pomp and festivities. On the tenth day of the fourth month — an especially significant period since that day was the anniversary of 'Enlightenment of the Buddha' under the 'Tree of Wisdom' followed by his death anniversary that fell on the fifteenth day of that month. On these holy days every one — novice, monk or lama — had to undertake a circular tour of the Lingkhor which wound in a great circle all around Kumbum. It was an extremely strenuous pilgrimage. The pilgrim had to measure the length of the Lingkhor with his body, repeatedly prostrating all the way.

9. Bathing is rare in Tibet, primarily because of the extreme cold and shortage of water heating of which was another constraint to bathing. Moreover, washing-bathing would irritate the skin by depriving it of natural oils which otherwise are a protection for the skin.

10. Norbu Jigme: op. cit. pp. 88-90.

Since this period was non-meat, people did not have the stamina to complete the pilgrimage in one-go; it was therefore done in parts over a few days. While camping out during festival season, the monks used to erect their round Mongolian tents known as *yurts* held up on poles with an opening at the top.

By now Thubten Jigme Norbu's entire family was in Lhasa. He missed his family so much that his desire to rejoin them intensified to the point of obsession. He hatched a plan to make the journey to Lhasa along with the periodic caravans. And should this not work out the way Norbu planned, the alternative was to travel via Siling to the coast, and from there by ship to India, thence over the Himalayan passes to Lhasa. This circuitous alternative would take more than three times as long as the direct land-route. When the Kumbum Monastery authorities found out his escape plan, they relented and gave him official permission to leave the Monastery and go to Lhasa to complete his studies. Preparation for the move that was to take nearly four months were set in motion. The astrologers had picked the auspicious date for commencing this long, arduous and risky journey — nineteenth day of the fifth month. By the time Norbu's caravan reached the assembly point in Tsaidam, there were about twenty thousand animals in the great caravan.

Kumbum had planned a suitable farewell for Rinpoché Thubten Jigme Norbu. He rode out slowly, followed by a monk carrying a large yellow umbrella[11] behind him as a symbol of his rank. The oboes and the four-sleeved trumpets, making lot of noise rather than music, followed the procession which soon reached the large tent pitched for the farewell ceremony. A cup of tea was offered which he quickly emptied. It was immediately filled but not to be drunk. This second cup was left full, a custom which conveys the hope that he who is leaving will soon return to drink the second cup. The great caravan reached the Ko-Ko-Nor, the

---

11. The type and style of umbrella is a symbol of rank of the person for whom it is carried, more for ceremonial purposes than as a utility item. Tall peacock umbrella is the privilege of Gyalwa Rinpoché; the next in precedence is the gold umbrella for the Regent.

Blue Lake, three days later. This enormous Lake appeared more of an ocean than a lake, and would require three weeks of travel-time to skirt around it. Finishing touches were given to travel equipment and preparations during the few days they stayed on the shores of the Blue Lake. Most of the travelers slept in the open, wrapped up in their coats and blankets. But the Bönpos, the 'Quality', alone slept in tents. On the way through the barren, dry, high plateau, the travelers saw herd of kyangs, or wild asses. They looked wonderfully elegant and graceful. The sight of hundreds of big and beautiful powerful drongs who lived in Tibet's high and barren plateau was equally fascinating. The wild nature at its very best. The wild wolves which attacked the kyangs and drongs were nature's way of balancing the fauna over the barren highlands. However, the rat-hare-bear takes the cake amongst Tibet's fauna. Buried deep in their burrows, rat-hare provide a good source of food for the bears, and at times for the steppe foxes too. However, a Tibetan would never attack the bear, or prowl for rat-hare. Shortage of oxygen in the air is the big problem for the traveler. It leads to shortness of breath and giddiness. Tibet's traditional panacea against this problem is garlic — just chew a clove of garlic to continue the march. Crossing wide turbulent rivers and attacks by Gelogs, a vicious savage tribe of nomadic robbers was another major hurdle for the traveler. However, bands of these robbers and brigands do have a streak of piety and decency about their profession. They pray before they go to rob a caravan. They also donate part of the loot to the monasteries. If they happen to accidentally kill someone, they would go to the monastery and make a confession. After they have done their work, they make sure that they leave enough food and mules for the travelers so that the caravan reaches safely. They may even guide the travelers to the safest and quickest way. To cap it all, these brigands build shrines to their gods and everyone puts colourful prayer flags, the colour of the flag corresponding to the year of his birth. Even robbers and brigands in Tibet follow a code of ethics!

Some of these criminals — that is what they really are — are so religious minded that they undertake a pilgrimage, say all the way from Kumbum area to Lhasa, some thousand or so miles, prostrating all the way, measuring the distance by the length of their bodies. It is called *Kyangchag* in which the man prostrates with arms stretched out, marks the point, and carries through the entire distance in this manner, prostrating all the way. Strange but true, as personally vouched for by Thubten Jigme Norbu himself, the elder brother of Gyalwa Rinpoché, the Dalai Lama. It may be mentioned in passing that Norbu himself too used to do Kyangchag around the Kumbum monastery, say about four miles or so, some time during the fourth month which is considered auspicious for this practice since that is the month in which Gautama Buddha was born.

So far the caravan was in Chinese territory. Gradually, they made their way to the frontier posts manned by the Chinese on one side, and by Tibetan guards on the other. The border-line in this area stretched between the Drichu River and Dang La. The Tibetan frontier guards or *Apohors* belong to the Tibetan nomadic tribe known as Horpas. The strength of the Tibetan post was thirty and they lived in baghurs, dark tents made of coarse yak-hair. These men were regular soldiers armed with modern rifles and their mounts were excellent horses. The detachment was under orders of the government at Lhasa. The commander had received instructions to provide a personal escort for Dalai Lama's eldest brother. After another four days march, the caravan reached the first inhabited settlement they had seen during the past two months. A few more days on the 'road', and Jigme reached the outskirts of Lhasa. While at Penpo D'zong he had already been welcomed by a deputation from Ganden Monastery; now it was the turn of nearby monasteries of Drepung and Sera.

After entering the Tibetan territory, a few days of enforced rest had to be taken to ensure that the Rinpoché entered Lhasa on an auspicious day chosen by the astrologers. Oracles and astrologers were held in high esteem and their dictates were followed without exception. The Rinpoché was struck by the opulence and rich prosperity which had come to the Family by virtue of the Dalai

Lama. Norbu was taken by his father to the inner precincts of Norbulingka, "Garden of Jewels", the summer residence of the Dalai Lama where the six and half years old God-King was doing his lessons under the supervision of three abbots: Simpön Khenpo, the Master of Robes; Söpön Khenpo, the Master of Religious Ceremony; and Chöpön Khenpo, the Master of Tea. Jigme prostrated three times before his little brother as per official protocol, followed by the usual presentation of scarves and gifts. The atmosphere at the meeting of the two brothers was completely formal.[12]

The Mongol Prophecy

Offerings to deities are a common practice in most religious ceremonies. These may be the seasonal fruits, grain, wine, or whatever. Many western 'experts' who observed offering of wine in Tibetan ceremonies have concluded that the practice is derived from Christian custom. A visitor to a western Tibetan town observed a weekly symbolic offering of wine by the local priest. "Father Montserrat of the 'Mogor Mission' thought that this must surely be a Eucharistic rite traceable to Christian influence."[13] Sven Hedin makes a similar reference in his voluminous work, *Trans-Himalaya, Discoveries and Adventures in Tibet,* citing the example of the "Grand Lama in Utsang Province offers small quantities of bread and wine, that he drinks of them himself and distributes the remainder to the other lamas ... wine which he presents to God." A similar, albeit erroneous conclusion is drawn by a Tibet-scholar, W.Y. Evans-Wentz, while dealing with Buddhist beliefs and rituals in a different context. In his view, while Christianity inculcates the belief in forgiveness of sins through repentance or faith in a Saviour, or through some form of atonement, the doctrine of retribution and karma as followed in Buddhism does not depend on any such outside force. He goes on to add: "Some of the rituals of Northern Buddhism may seem to suggest a Christian-like theory of forgiveness or absolution of sins, which, more than any other subsidiary doctrine peculiar to Northern Buddhism, may possibly

12. Norbu Jigme: op. cit. p. 173

13. MacGregor John: op. cit. p. 29.

yet be shown to have been shaped ... by Christianity."[14] Does it not sound presumptuous? Buddhism is so much more ancient than Christianity that, if anything, the reverse would be true. The commonality of rituals of the two Faiths is more a product of cultural evolution of the human race rather than of one copying the other. It is noteworthy that, no doubt, the objective of Christian missionaries undertaking arduous journeys to Central Asia was the spread of Gospel, a subsidiary assignment in that distant past was to find and generally survey overland trade-routes.

Tibet's Book of Lungh-ten, *The Prophecies of Urgyen*, makes a reference to a prophecy believed to have been made in the ninth century A.D. by the Indian Tantric Buddhist scholar, Padmasambhava, (known to Tibetans as Urgyen) that the "Tartars of Lower Tartary would become masters of Tibet". The Prophecy came to be true about eight hundred years later under rather peculiar circumstances.

During the time of Ngawang Lobzang Gyatso, the Fifth Dalai Lama (1617-1682), the Red Hat sect led by his Prime Minister used to cause considerable harassment to the Dalai Lama and his followers of the Yellow Hat sect. Gusri Khan, an Öelot Mongol Chief, from the Kokonor region of Lower Tartary, on Tibet's northern border, had seized the province of Kham in 1638. The Fifth Dalai Lama grabbed that opportune moment. Being the spiritual head of the Mongols like he was of Tibetans and many others, he invited the Khan to march his forces into Tibet. The Khan complied and invaded Tibet in 1641. Thus the Gelugpa sect, the Yellow Hats, attained ascendancy over their rivals, the Red Hats. Gusri Khan assumed the role of secular head of the State while the Dalai Lama continued as the spiritual head. With the power of Mongol arms to back him up, he was supreme in all spiritual matters and crushed all opposition.[15] Although

---

14. Evans-Wentz W.Y.: *The Tibetan Book of the Dead*; Varanasi, 1927, p. 237

15. John Grueber, a Jesuit priest from Austria, — the first white man to enter Lhasa — described him as the devilish God—the Father who puts to death such as those who refuse to adore him." — Bell Charles, Sir: *Portrait of thè Dalai Lama*; London, 1946, p. 34.

theoretically the twin-parts converged in the throne of the Dalai Lama, for all practical purposes Gusri Khan reigned as patron, supreme in secular matters, till his death in 1655.

It may be recalled that while the Tibetan leaders had submitted to superior hordes of Chengis Khan way back in 1207, the day to day administration remained in the hands of the Tibetans — Sakya Pandita, the Abbot of Sakya Monastery was the Viceroy of Tibet on behalf of the Mongols, followed by Sakya Lama, Phagpa, in 1253, and so on and on for nearly five centuries till the Dzungar Mongols invaded Tibet in 1717 and seized Lhasa. In short, the period of Mongol suzerainty over Tibet may be said to have lasted till about the end of the seventeenth century during which period Tibet was autonomous, if not completely independent, particularly after the death of Gusri Khan. It was during the reign of the Fifth Gyalwa Rinpoché that the institution of Panchen Lama came into being when the "Great Fifth" ordained his beloved tutor, Ch'ösgyi Gyaltän, as "Panchen Rimpoché", the High Priest of Tashilhunpo Monastery, second only to the Dalai Lama in the hierarchy of Tibet's Incarnate Lamas. The Panchen was declared as an incarnation of Amitabha, whose spiritual son is Avolokita, the Tibetan God incarnate in the Dalai Lama.[16]

In this context the **Prophecy of North Sham-ba-la** is of interest. Whether it would come true or not is a matter of conjecture — In the distant past Northern India including the whole of Kashmir and surrounding countries followed Buddhism. But at present Islam is the dominant religion in that region. The ancient prophecy says that the Mohammedan power will continue to spread till a Buddhist king arises in a country to the north of Kashmir. That country would be known as North Shambala. And that King would break the Mohammedan power and restore Buddhism. Perhaps, that country would be in the region of 'Mongolia-Russia' is again a matter of conjecture, at least for the present.

---

16. MacGregor: op. cit. pp. 54-55.

The Thirteenth Dalai Lama has further elaborated on the spirit of Cha-na Dorje-je. That spirit is in a mythical country known as Chang Sham-ba-la. It lies to the north of Kashmir. But that spirit will not reincarnate for the next about three hundred years, when Chang Sham-ba-la will become a powerful kingdom. This area is inhabited by cannibals and outside people cannot see it. An old Tibetan prophecy says: "A Muslim ruler will overrun the world, but three hundred years hence the ruler of Chang Sham-ba-la will emerge, defeat him, and restore Buddhism."[17]

Prophecy by the Sixth Gyalwa Rinpoché

Strictly speaking, after the death of the Thirteenth Gyalwa Rinpoché, there was no question of launching a search for the Reincarnation, the Fourteenth Gyalwa Rinpoché. As far back as 1866 it was a popular saying in Lhasa that the Grand Lama will transmigrate only thirteen times. This prophecy was recorded by pandit (survey specialist) Nain Singh[18] who was born ten years after the prophecy was said to have been current. While every prophecy need not come out to be true, this one may not be utterly wrong either, since the first two Dalai Lamas had not, strictly speaking, transmigrated, and even the third, Sonam Gyatso born in 1543, was given the title by Altan Khan in 1578. Therefore, it is well on the cards that there may yet be two or three more trans-migrations. Who knows! Be that as it may, to the religious minded polity of Tibet, the signs were clear indication that the reincarnation of the Thirteenth Gyalwa Rinpoché was to be found in the easterly direction. And the Fourteenth Gyalwa Rinpoché did come from the vicinity of Kumbum. Geographically, Kumbum was in Chinese territory; but for all practical purposes it was in Tibet since the large monastery of Kumbum owed

---

17. Bell Charles, Sir: op. cit. p. 132.
18. Nain Singh was a 'technical spy' on topographical survey mission to Tibet. He was the first British subject to reach Lhasa in the middle of winter — January 10, 1866. He and others of his ilk, used a modified rosary having 100 beads instead of the usual 108, and miniature prayer wheels (*mani chuskor*) specially adapted for recording the readings.

allegiance to the Dalai Lama in Lhasa and not to the Chinese Governor in Siling. To the latter, it owed merely administrative technicalities such as payment of taxes, etc.

The Sixth Dalai Lama loved life — dances, music, poetry, romance and women. However, strictly speaking, as per the Tibetan system and beliefs, he was the same person as the 'Great Fifth'; and no two persons could be less alike than the Fifth and the Sixth. And that holds good for the Seventh too! Be that as it may, Tsang-yang Gyatso (the Sixth Gyalwa Rinpoché: 1683-1706) prophesied about the Seventh Dalai Lama, Kezang Gyatso[19]. He was born in Litang in the Amdo region in1708 at exactly the time and the place as was prophesied by the Sixth Gyalwa Rinpoché before he left Lhasa. The omens were just right. As it was, the people were on the look out for the incarnation of the Sixth Gyalwa Rinpoché, and Kezang Gyatso came on the scene at just the right time. The child told those around him who he was in his previous birth. In fact, he claimed to remember his more than one previous incarnations. The news spread all over the country, so did his fame. However, it so happened that the military commander, Lhazang, supported by the Chinese was busy furthering the chances of another candidate. Fearing for the life of Kezang Gyatso, the promising child was put in Kumbum monastery not merely for his safety but also for his religious education on the right lines. When he was nine years old, Kezang Gyatso was recognized as the rightful reincarnation, taken to Lhasa and enthroned as the Seventh Dalai Lama.

Right from childhood to maturity and beyond, Kezang Gyatso was deep into religious matters and left the political functions to Panchen Rinpoché who took charge along with the two Chinese Ambans stationed in Lhasa. Somehow, the Chinese and other "non-Tibetans have always made the mistake of assuming that the two great leaders of our country must necessarily rival each other for political power. On the contrary, none of the Panchen Rinpoché ...have ever sought to take away from the power and reverence accorded by the Tibetans to the Gyalwa Rinpoché

19. Also spelt as Kalsang Gyatso, (1708-1758).

above all." Some Chinese and pseudo-Tibetologists have even tried to present Gyalwa Rinpoché as spiritually a disciple of Panchen Rinpoché. Again, this is not correct at all. Their relationship is mutually reciprocal. If the Panchen is much senior in age and the Gyalwa is in minority, naturally Panchen performs the role of the teacher. However, as in the case of the Thirteenth Dalai Lama, the Panchen Lama was a minor, the roles were reversed. "For the Tibetans there has never been any doubt that the Gyalwa Rinpoché is our leader, secular and spiritual ..."

Tibetan Prophecy Against Chinese Empire

An old Tibetan prophecy claims: The prosperity of China depends on the happiness of Tibet. "Tibet is the 'root' of China." If Tibet is maltreated, China will suffer. Therefore, when Revolution broke out in China and the Emperor was removed, the Tibetans took this as the natural sequence of the prophecy taking full shape. Now let's hope and pray that the Prophecy continues to develop on its natural curve, eventually leading to an independent Tibet once again. In the same vein, Tibet had religious, and thereby political, connection with Manchu Emperors. They had no connection with the Chinese. Therefore, with the removal of Manchu Emperors from the throne of Peking, that political connection was also automatically cut off; hence Tibet no longer had any political links with China.

More Divine Prophecies

During early 1970's the Nechung Oracle had predicted a period of decline for the Chinese. Another prophecy recorded that the death of Mao Zedong be followed by rapid disintegration of all that he had built over the debris of death and destruction that he had wrought on millions of innocent citizens of his country. As luck would have it, Zhou Enlai died on January 8, 1976. Chu Thé — a close associate of Mao based in Yanan and was instrumental in large scale distribution of the little 'Red Book' — went thereafter; and Mao Zedong himself passed away on 9th September the same year. Thus there occurred a clean sweep of China's triumvirate that had ruled Chinese Communist

Party for nearly four decades, causing all round havoc, particularly on the minorities and the intellectual elite. To cap it all, the Tang Shan earthquake at the end of July took a heavy toll of life and property. The Tibetans were naïve enough to take these tragic events for good omens for their country. They proved right, albeit to a very limited extent only. The truth was hidden in the old Tibetan proverb:

"The clouds of summer float by, but the sky stays where it is for ever."

However, there was an exception. Dr. Tentzin Choedhak[20] having suffered nearly two decades of severe privations in Chinese prisons was released on account of his exceptional ability in Tibetan medical science, and was ultimately allowed to join His Holiness in Dharmsala in India as his personal physician. Dr. Choedrak had received the formula of one of Tibetan medicine's most powerful drugs from Khenrab Norbu, the Master of Mendzekhang, and he was keen to pass on this personal knowledge before it was too late. His Holiness was quite enthusiastic about the project and a staff of eighteen full-time pharmacists was employed for three months to prepare the largest quantity of *tsother* manufactured in the history of Tibet. It was indeed a lucky omen that Dr. Choedhak was one of the four of a group of 176 prisoners who were sent to suffer horrendous brutalities in Chinese prisons managed to survive, so that lineage of *tsother* could also make its mark in the world of modern medicine. Incidentally, penicillin in a disguised form had been known in Tibet for centuries before its invention in the West.

There appears to be a tendency amongst western travelers to, and writers, on Tibet to exaggerate the negative aspects of traditional Tibetan medical practices. Since the sanitary conditions and health care facilities were rather primitive, it was but natural that infectious diseases, small pox, gastro-intestinal, leprosy,

---

20. Dr. Tentzin Choedhak was appointed as personal physician to His Holiness in 1956. He was arrested by the Chinese in 1959, tortured to no end but survived. He was released from prison in 1979, and quite surprisingly, was permitted to leave occupied Tibet the next year.

venereal diseases, et al, would be prevalent on a large scale. Indeed they were. But that does not grant a license to modern medicine to describe the traditional Asian systems in pejorative terms. Tibetan medical system was quite advanced in its own way and their diagnostic techniques proved to be more accurate and to the point without the aid of modern technology and instrumentation. However, this aspect is much beyond the scope of this work; suffice to say that while pills rolled out of excreta of venerable high Incarnations and their urine are merely superstitions and certainly not part of the Tibetan system of medicine, their drugs formulated out of medicinal herbs have proved their worth. After all, what are Aloe Vera and all the rest of products developed and being marketed in the United States and Mexico? Some odd instances of a piece of paper with a prayer written on it being ingested; touch of a monk to cure a headache; wearing blessed rosary made out of human skulls; et al, should not be generalized to represent Tibetan medicinal system. There is no denying that the doctors of Tibet were monks, and most of them were well qualified professionals. They were not surgeons, but in the fields of diagnostics and internal medicine, they were certainly worth their weight in gold — and that too without the benefit of modern instrumentation.

Prophecy regarding British-Indian Invasion of Tibet

This episode in the tumultuous history of Tibet is a classic example of Tibetan enigmaticism carried to the point of total irrationality. Tibetans' trust in their oracles and prophecies is total, irrefutable and unshakable. There is no denying this premise as we understand from the history and religious developments in that country. The question therefore arises why did this suicidal clash of arms take place at all between two totally unequal adversaries — one; a modern well armed, well trained, well organized and disciplined force while the other; a primitive bow-and arrow, swords wielding mass of untrained unorganized mass of humanity offering themselves as fodder for the bullets and explosives of the twentieth century. It is all the more astonishing because the leaders of the then Tibet knew fully well that there was a centuries old prophecy that had given them advance notice — decades if not centuries in advance — that such an event would occur at such and such time with such and such consequences. The Prophecy from Almanac for the Wood-Dragon Year (1904 A.D.] as recorded by Lieutenant Colonel L. Austine Waddell, Chief Medical Officer with the Expedition, in his book, *Lhasa And Its Mysteries*, published by John Murray, London, in 1905 goes as follows:

> "In the Year of the Wood-Dragon (1904 A.D.) the first part of the year protects the young king; (then) there is a great coming forward of robbers, quarrelling and fighting, full many enemies, troublous grief by weapons and such like will arise, the king, father and son will be fighting. At the end of the year a conciliatory speaker will vanquish the war."

The facsimile of the above unique political Prophecy, as personally recorded by Waddell well before the Expedition was even planned, is appended below:

།། དབང་ཐང་བསྟུན་སྐད་གནོཾ་ལོ་ཤིང་ཕོ་འབྲུག

།ལོ་སྟོད་རྒྱལ་པོ་གཞོན་ནུའི་སྐྱོང་།

།ཆོམ་རྐུན་ཐེན་ཆེ་རྩོད་འཁྲུག་འོང་།

།དགྲ་ཀྲུན་ལ་སོགས་འཚེར་བ་མང་།

།མཚོན་གྱི་སྡུག་བསྔལ་སྣ་ཚོགས་འབྱུང་།

།ཆར་བབས་སྐྱེ་རྒྱལ་ཡ་བུ་འཁྲུག

།ལོ་སྨད་གཡུལ་རྒྱལ་སྨན་ངག་མཁན།།

Facsimile of the Prophecy

Colonel Waddell was a Buddhist scholar of repute. He was familiar with Tibetan history, culture and literature for a long time. In his history of the invasion of Tibet by British India, he writes:

> "How the astrologers of Tibet were able to predict this distressful storm which was in store for their country, so long before it happened and to specify that it should occur exactly in this very year is amazing. Certain it is that the prophetic words ... were copied out by myself about a year before our expedition was ever heard of, from a Tibetan manuscript almanac for the ill-starred year of the Wood-Dragon of the fantastic calendar of the Lamas."

The Tibetan leadership was fully aware of the impending disaster, so did their army 'brass'. In spite of the fact that the outcome was certainly going to be what it turned out to be, they still put up a stiff resistance, brave but hopeless, till almost the very end. Very creditable and brave indeed, bravery to the point of foolhardiness; but it also proved beyond any doubt that the Tibetans loved their country and their God-King so very much that they were prepared to sacrifice their very life.

Prophecy by the Thirteenth Dalai Lama

In August 1932 the 13th Dalai Lama wrote his final testament to the people of Tibet, as follows, forecasting a disaster for his country in the near future —

> "It may happen that, here, in the centre of Tibet, religion and government will be attacked both from without and from within. Unless we can guard our own country, it will happen that the Dalai and the Panchen Lamas, the Father and the Son, and all the revered holders of the Faith, will disappear and become nameless. Monks and their monasteries will be destroyed. The rule of law will be weakened. The lands and property of government officials will be seized. They themselves will be forced to serve their enemies or wander the country like beggars. All beings will be sunk in great hardship and overpowering

fear; the days and nights will drag on slowly in suffering."[21]

Thus forecasting a warning to his people, the Thirteenth Gyalwa Rinpoché left for the 'Heavenly Fields' on the thirtieth day of tenth month of the Water-Bird Year, corresponding to December 17, 1933. The official mourning period lasted forty-nine days during which all forms of entertainment were strictly prohibited. All men wore their old clothes only while the womenfolk wore no articles of any jewelery nor any bodily-adornment was permitted. The customary procedures and death-ceremonies followed. His body was embalmed, dressed in gold brocade-robes, placed in the lotus position and seated on a throne in the Norbulingka (it means the 'Jewel Park'), the summer palace, facing south, the direction of long life. The usual official signs of official mourning, like draping the golden roof tops of Potala and Tsuglakhang, or Jokhang, the Central Cathedral, lowering of prayer flags, butter-lamps outside every house, etc. were set in motion. Jokhang and the Ramose are the largest and most famous of all the temples in Lhasa. All monasteries have at least one special temple in which there are no windows and which is kept dark. This is the Temple of the Guardian of the Law. All passages leading to this temple and the temple itself too are richly painted with dark ferocious images. Incidentally, no house in Lhasa was allowed to be more than two storeys high since it was considered blasphemous to compete with the height of the Central Cathedral.

Thubten Gyatso, the Thirteenth Gyalwa Rinpoché made the above prophecy in 1933, the year in which he left for the heavenly fields at the age of fifty-eight years. Unfortunately for Tibet it came true within two decades.

Three days after the death of the Thirteenth, Tsipon Lungshar, an ambitious Finance Minister, so manipulated the unstable situation that the one thousand strong Drong Drak Magar Regiment resorted to rebellion leading to a coup d'état by which the crafty

21. Avedon, John: op. cit. p.3.

Lungshar planned to take full control of the country. However, his detailed plot to overthrow the legitimate government of the country misfired. He was convicted of high treason and awarded the severest punishment — blinding of both eyes. Concurrently, a Chinese delegation led by a Manchu general was allowed entry in the garb of a condolence mission. Thus, the two catastrophic dangers foretold by the Thirteenth came to pass within a few days of his demise: Tibet was under threat both from within and without. The National Assembly therefore immediately nominated a young twenty-three-year lama as the Regent: Reting Rinpoché, a man lacking in political acumen but highly respected for his spiritual attainments. Internal intrigues over the Regency continued leading to imprisonment of Reting Rinpoché in a dungeon in Potala, equivalent of the Tower of London for high Tibetan officials. Reting Rinpoché died soon afterwards. Concurrently, there was a Khampa uprising intended to create a separate independent Khampa State. However, this was put down by the Tibetan army with some help coming in from the Chinese army.

Tibetans are great believers in prophecies. They attach great importance to the prophetic words, proverbs, dreams and sayings of old time. They believe that all these words of wisdom were 'divinely inspired'. Tibetan books of prophecy have warned them against the Islamic nations. "The violence and desecration done tc the Hindu religion by the Mohammedan conquerors of India are remembered by the people of Tibet." Two high lamas quoted the prophecies which foretold that the *Turuka* (Turks) "would do their utmost to destroy the Tibetan religion and would very nearly succeed in destroying it." The Tibetans as a nation, as a race, are fully conscious of the violence and desecration done to Hindu religion, and consequentially to Buddhism, by Mohammedan invaders, but the Europeans would do no harm. That is why Tibetans believe that they can worship in Hindu temples and in Christian churches, but they can have nothing to do with Mohammedan mosques. In fact, the Tibetans go a step still further. They believe that those who kill persons of other religions in cold blood in the vain hope that by doing so they get a passport to paradise do great harm to their faith; thus they find no excuse for the doctrine of Mohammed Ghazi who killed persons of other religions in cold blood to gain merit in the eyes of God. The Prime Minister of Tibet told Sir Charles Bell: "Buddhism, Christianity and Hinduism are all good religions. But Islam is not. It makes the killing of those who belong to other Faiths an act of merit. That is a horrible thing. The true spirit of religion cannot be present, where killing is regarded as an act of merit."[22]

Dreams

Tibetans are strong believers in the veracity and potential of dreams. Unlike most of the rest of the world, they take their dreams seriously, and more often than not, they act on their dreams. They have found their dreams to be useful tools in warding off catastrophes as well as in pursuing positive lines of action leading to control over political, religious and social developments which were otherwise in the boiling pot. Dreams and prophecies go hand in hand. Forewarning of coming events through these psychological mechanisms went a long way in decision-making in personal as well as state matters. To a Tibetan, no dream is random. It is the product of subtle interaction between day-time thoughts and actions with mental and spiritual energies within the body mechanism. These forces acting in tandem inject relevance to the dream world. They bring telepathic messages and, more often than not, they are precognitive in nature in as much as they forewarn the subject. Thus, being precognitive they are essentially prophetic. It is a different matter altogether that advance warnings through the medium of dreams and prophecies were not suitably acted upon in some cases, resulting in unpleasant consequences. All dreams are not pleasant and some dreams may be terrifying. Tibetans are not afraid of or unduly perturbed by unpleasant dreams which are classified as nightmare. While we like to forget the nightmares as early as possible, the Tibetan dream-yogis take these as opportunities to develop fearlessness. After all, pleasant dreams or nightmares are all product of one's mind; so they can do no harm to the

---

22. Bell, Charles, Sir: *Tibet: Past & Present*; Oxford, 1924, p. 260.

subject. An ancient Tibetan 'tantric' text has the following advice to counter nightmarish dreams;

> At the outset, in the process of realizing it to be *Maya*, abandon all feelings of fear; And, if the dream be of fire, transform the fire into water, the antidote of fire. And if the dream be of minute objects, transform them into large objects; .... Or if the dream be of many things, transform them into a single thing: Thereby one comprehendeth the nature of plurality and of unity.[23]

The content of a dream is directly related to Tibetan concept of chakra. The activities of one's waking hours are directly related to a particular chakra, and that chakra produces the karmic trace of the dream. During sleep the mind is therefore drawn into the relevant chakra and manifests itself as the dream. Sometimes dreams bring messages from deceased souls. Such messages are generally in thoughts, rather than in words. And they move pretty fast from one event to the other rather than be bound by time. Dream-events are not marked by time, nor are they bound by time frame, more so since the dream-events move faster than the speed of light. Again, it is a different matter altogether that the subject may not take cognizance of the dream-content, or may not even be aware of it. That is immaterial. The 'nature' has done its duty by providing the subject an opportunity to deal with the karmic trace. And that's all that matters. However, since most subjects remain ignorant of spiritual potential of their dreams, and hence cannot take advantage of the opportunities presented, Tibetan intellectuals developed the concept and practice of 'Dream Yoga', which is a separate subject by itself.

Dreams have played an important role in the religious, political and social life of Tibet. The famous Tibetan saint-poet Milarepa was earlier known by the name of Phopaga and was expert at performing evil acts. But after he was reformed by a saintly spirit, he became a powerful force in doing good deeds and came to be known by his new name, Milarepa. He foresaw the

23. Quoted by W.Y. Evans-Wentz in *Tibetan Yoga and Secret Doctrines.*

death of his mother in a dream. After she died he resolved to attain nirvana, the ultimate spiritual goal of liberation from the cycle of birth, death and rebirth, through karmic action. In the process, he attained a high degree of proficiency in the art of *tumo*[24], a mental discipline that generates great body heat so much so that in the extreme cold of his high mountain cave, he could survive in a light cotton robe called *repa*; hence his new name Milarepa.[25] The modern science has also come to accept the veracity of dreams forewarning of events yet to come, and such other strange phenomenon.

The formation and hierarchy of the 'spirit world' is credited to the great Indian saint, scholar and tantric master, Padmasambhava who came to Tibet in the eighth century for the specific purpose of subduing the recalcitrant spirits who were an obstruction to the spread of Buddha Dharma. He was the founder of Tibetan-Buddhism. In fact, under the name of Lopön Rimpoché he was as highly honoured as the Buddha himself. This was particularly so in the monastery of Samye. It is the oldest monastery in Tibet and was founded by Padmasambhava himself. After he had successfully dealt with all the spirits, one of them came before Padmasambhava in the form of an eight year child-monk wearing a golden hat and holding a crystal rosary. The Great Saint branded the child-monk on the crown of his head with his *dorje* (thunder-bolt), anointed the tip of his tongue with nectar and named him and his brother spirits Pehar Gyalpo, the Five Ferocious Kings. The Pehar Gyalpo was then appointed head of the entire hierarchy of all the Protective Spirits. Thus all opposition to the spread of Dharma by the Spirit-World came to an end. Tibet's hierarchy of guardian spirits assumed the symbolic character of the "Wheel of Protection".

24. *Tumo* is actually 'psychic heat', but it is not ordinary heat or warmth. It is of three types; it is the esoteric version that keeps the body physically warm. It is a subtle fire which warms the generative fluid and runs all over the body along tiny channels of vein, artery or nerve. Two other types are exoteric *tumo* and mystic *tumo* — David-Neel; op. cit. pp. 216-17.

25. Milarepa preached: "My religion is to live — and die — without regret".

Fourteenth Dalai Lama's Dream

Lhasa was in turmoil. The uprisings spread to other regions of the country. The *kachem* and subsequent prophecies were following their predestined course. Demand for *Rangzen* (Independence) was the talk of the town. The Gyalwa Rinpoché was extremely perturbed. The events could take a catastrophic turn any moment. The ensuing clash would be totally disastrous. The unarmed Tibetans were no match against the highly trained and heavily armed PLA who could reduce Lhasa to smithereens in a matter of minutes. "The likelihood of such a calamity had long been clear to Tenzin Gyatso." In fact, His Holiness had dreamt a year earlier of Norbulingka becoming a "killing ground", but he had refrained from mentioning this to any one at all. He also dreamt about his exile to India. It may be recalled that the Nechung Oracle had already made a mention of this impending event. The ongoing crisis now confirmed these forebodings, howsoever unpleasant they might have been. In any case there is no doubt about the veracity of most, if not all, of the prophetic divinations through human mediums, or dreams for that matter. It was now well on the cards that the PLA would unleash a reign of terror on the hapless populace of Tibet, more so after the female population of the City had taken out a procession shouting. The Lhasa women had made a number of anti-Chinese posters which they carried in procession, shouting slogans: "From now on Tibet is Independent". "The Chinese must go; leave Tibet to Tibetans". And so on. Gyalwa Rinpoché could hear what the people were shouting.

A Prophecy Fulfilled

Yet another political prophecy made in 1922 by a Doctor of Divinity in Chumbi Valley came out to be true a few years after it was given out. It said: "This is the time for the Lower Horpas (Japan) to rise to the position of a Great Power." There were already rumours in Tibet that Japan was making preparations to attack some foreign country. Around this time European colonialism was already on the decline. During the 1920's the Dutch were facing problems in Java and Sumatra. In 1928 the Japanese tried to prevent Nationalist Chinese (KMT) soldiers from operating against local warlords in the north. At that time the Japanese forces were in effective control of Manchuria. In 1931 they concocted an incident near Mukden[26] and used it as an excuse for taking over the entire province. Concurrently, the French were facing a revolt in Vietnam by the 1930's, proving that the Doctor of Divinity from Chumbi was correct in his forecast of the political events yet to come. The accuracy of such prophecies was indeed an enigma to a rational mind.

---

26. Mukden (Sheng-king) is an important place in the history of relations between Tibet and the Manchu dynasty. A letter, together with precious gifts, was sent by the Dalai lama to the Emperor of China. The mission arrived at Mukden in the winter of 1643 (10th Moon, 7th year Ch'ung-té) after "several years" of journey through hostile regions. The Emperor went out of the town gate to receive them, and in the reception hall he rose and advanced forward to receive the letter — W.W. Rockhill: *The Dalai Lamas of Lhasa and their relations with The Manchu Emperors of China; 1644-1908*, p. 8.

14

Death Horoscope

The Tibetan Doctrine of Death asserts that death is not an event but a process. Several minutes after the heart has stopped functioning, the brain continues to be alive. Electro-encephalograms have recorded brain-activity in that state of the body. Although the Tibetans did not know about such devices, but they were certainly aware that electrical-activity in the brain continues for four minutes or more after the heart has stopped functioning. The Tibetan Doctrine of Death has been proved beyond doubt since doctors found that a 'dead' man's pupils contract violently in reaction to pilocarpine drops in the same manner as if the person was alive. Certain symptoms precede death. Certain sounds which are 'the psychic resultants of the disintegrating process called death' are heard before and up to about fifteen hours after death. These sounds are the signs of approaching death, indicating to the near and dear ones of the dying-person to be prepared for death-rituals, particularly recitation of religious mantras. As the patient is just about to cease breathing, being at the threshold of life and death, pressure is applied to his arteries so as to keep the dying person conscious with a consciousness rightly directed. That is the primary function of recitation of sacred words and religious texts so that the dying person's consciousness imbibes the right attributes while in the process of transformation.[1] This ensures that the out-going essence of life, the *Prana*,[2] shall take the right path so that the next life of the departing person is fully taken care of. Here it may be of interest to point out that one of the reasons, or the primary reason even without knowing it to be such, for the devout Hindus to maintain a crest-lock, *Shikhâ*, on the top of the cranium is to provide the most suitable exit point for the outgoing *Prana* — *Brâhmarandhra*, the fissure at the top of the cranium being one of the nine apertures in the human body, the top of the cranium being the cleanest one. The Tibetans hold an identical view.

Death, or near death experiences have been recorded by parapsychologists while treating psychic patients under hypnotic regression. One of them narrated her experience of death in one of her past lives. At the moment of death she floated up to the ceiling. "She could see her body in the bed ... she was just floating waiting for some one to come and help her. She became aware of a light, feeling herself drawn toward it. The light was becoming brighter and more luminous...." It is of interest to note that, since she remembered many lives, she had experience of many deaths too. Nonetheless, her experiences of death were uniform and consistent every time. "A conscious part of her would leave the body around the moment of death", and float above to seek the bright light.[3]

Attributes of *Prana*

One two-line shlokas in *Bhagvad Gita* has condensed a volume of literature on the qualitative attributes of 'breath of life', the *Atma*:

---

1. It may be recalled that when M.K. Gandhi was shot, his immediate response was the sacred words "Ram.....Ram....". That is the name of Indian Hindu God. Tibetan's first reaction to such noble personalities as Gandhi, Einstein, Tolstoy, Abraham Lincoln, St. Francis, Mother Teresa, et al, is that they were *bodhisattvas*.
2. In Buddhism the breath of life, *Prana* in Sanskrit, is the "vehicle of the mind" since it is the *Prana* that makes our mind move. So if you control your breath, you may correspondigly control your mind also. It is *Ruah* in Judaism, *Ruh* in Islam and soul or 'life-breath' in Christianity.
3. Weiss Brian: op.cit. pp. 52-53.

Weapons cleave him not, nor fire burneth him;
Nor waters wet him, nor wind drieth him away

The unbounded philosophy of Bhagvad Gita has a similar message for the embodied beings:

He is not born, nor he dies;
Nor having been ceaseth he any more to be;
Unborn, perpetual, eternal and ancient;
He is not slain when the body is slaughtered.[4]

It might sound strange that, notwithstanding the above ethereal attributes of the *Atma*, the souls of the dead continue to hold on to their original beliefs of Hinduism or Christianity as the case may be. The Hindu rites for the dead, the annual *Shraddha* ceremonies are a case in point. In fact, it is the *Preta Shraddhas* that really prove the point at issue. There are numerous stories of hauntings by ghosts for whom the requisite religious rites were performed to allay their dreadful activities. Since such instances have not been fully investigated and scientifically proved beyond doubt, it is better to leave the subject here. Nonetheless, Tibetans strongly believe that the after-death *Bardo*[5] experience for a Hindu, or a Muslim, or a Christian would be appropriately different, since such experiences are contingent on the mental make up of the deceased-consciousness. In this respect the *Bardo* experience may be considered to be akin to the dream-state. A person's dreams are based on his or her mental make up; so is the case with *Bardo* or after death-state of that individual. However, after scientifically hypnotizing some subject(s), parapsychologists have come to a conclusion that reincarnates need not necessarily adhere

4. The English translations are by Annie Besant (1847-1933) who made India as her spiritual motherland.

5. *Bardo* is a Tibetan word meaning 'transition';, a gap between completion of one phase and commencement of the next. Bar='in between and 'do'= 'suspended.' The word *Bardo* has become well known because of popularity of the *Tibetan Book of the Dead* since its first translation into English language in 1927. Sogyal Rinponché: op.cit. p. 106.

to their earlier-life religious beliefs, or even belong to the same old racial group should the rebirth take place in human frame.

It is necessary that the spirit of the dead man be drawn out of his body and directed on the right lines for its journey in the next world. This is done by the lamas, generally two, who officiate at the death-rituals. One of them cries '*Hik*' in a 'peculiar abnormal shrill note'. The other follows suit after a few minutes. *Hik* is followed by '*phat*'. This process goes on with long intervals of silence during which the lamas remain motionless, in meditation posture. The shriek 'Hik' requires considerable physical effort and comes out of from deep inside their entrails. One of them then puts his hands on his throat, turns his face aside, and spits out a stream of blood. The combination of *hik* and *phat*, uttered in the right note in the prescribed manner, 'invariably leads to the separation of the body and spirit'. Since Consciousness finally leaves the body after about 3½ days of death. It is therefore customary in Tibet to ensure that the body is not touched or disturbed in any way during that period. Complete silence is observed and peaceful atmosphere is maintained around the body.

Funeral Services

The funeral services may last for a whole week. It all depends upon the financial capability of the dead man's family. Extermination of the devils is essential to ensure prosperity of the family. This is done by the *Gomchen* who comes on the scene with all the trappings of a magician — 'a five sided crown, a rosary-necklace made of one hundred and eight round discs, cut out of human skulls, an apron of human bones bored and carved, and in his belt the ritualistic dagger (phurba). Thus attired, he stands in the open near a flaming fire and makes stabbing-gestures in the air while reciting incantations in a low voice.[6]

The 'realm' into which rebirth shall take place is contingent on one's karmic trace in the present life. That is the basic principle

6. David-Neal: op.cit. pp. 13-14, 52.

of karma. One cannot escape one's karma; however, it is one's 'predominant karmic trace' — the 'karmic pattern' conditioned by one's 'karmic perceptions' — that dictates the next birth, which need not necessarily be in the human form. There are six possible realms:

- The Hell Realm in which anger is the root emotion.
- The Hungry Ghost Realm is rooted in greed.
- The Animal Realm where ignorance predominates.
- The Human Realm.
- The Demi-God Realm in which 'pride' has the place of honour:
- The God Realm is almost like nirvana.

Environment is a significant factor in determining the evolution of local customs, rituals and practices. Since the ground is very hard, burial is virtually impossible except for the children and persons suffering from contagious diseases.[7] Since wood is extremely scarce, cremation is also out of question, except of course for the high incarnates. So the bodies of poor people were just thrown into the river. However, bodies of Dalai Lama and the top incarnations are embalmed. Leaving aside all these variations, the most common practice in Tibet used to be cutting up of the bodies into small pieces, grinding the bones and mixing the powder with some grain, and then leaving the remains on some hilltops for the vultures to do the rest. A most grisly nauseating process indeed, particularly for the near and dear ones. However, "There is not a trace of evidence to support" the Chinese hypothesis that human sacrifice was prevalent in Tibet in order to obtain skulls and thigh bones for ritual purposes.[8] Indeed, the question of human-sacrifice amongst Tibetans has remained a moot point, Sir Charles Bell, a Tibetologist of considerable standing has placed on record:

---

7. Michael Peissel has described a practice prevalent in Mustang of burying the bodies within the walls of houses.

8. Grunfeld: op.cit. p. 27.

"High above all the villages, on the crest of the mountain range that separates the Chumbi Valley from Bhutan, is the Pang-kar Bi-tsi chö-ten, a strong square building, made of stones laid on top of one and another without mortar or mud. It is fifty feet in length and breadth, forty feet in height, and roofed with flat, slate-like stones .... Inside is a chö-ten or stupa, and inside this is a copper urn .... blood was poured into this urn, and inside of this were placed the corpses of a boy and a girl, each eight years old, who had been slain for the purpose. The bodies were placed head downwards, the feet pointing towards the roof. It is a boundary mark between Bhutan and Tromo ...."[9]

While it is difficult to unequivocally deny the existence of practice of human sacrifice in Tibet, may be, it was restricted to Chumbi Valley alone where the Tibetan population is of a somewhat different stock from the Tibetan plateau.

From the foregoing it would be seen that the Tibetans had five ways of dealing with the dead:

- Give the flesh to the birds after chopping the body into pieces; same for the bones except that these were first crushed and mixed with some tsampa.
- Throw the body in a stream.
- Cremation, if the family could afford the expenses on firewood.
- Burial, if ground conditions permitted.
- Embalm, if the dead person was of a very high standing.

Whatever method is adopted, the family of the dead person has to make sure that bones, particularly the skull and the thigh bone, do not fall into the hands of *tantrics* and other undesirable persons. For this reason, some persons have to keep vigil on the dead body till it is fully consummated.

---

9. Bell, Charles, Sir: *Tibet: Past and Present;* p. 80.

The Tibetan Book of the Dead[10]

Death is inevitable. Every being that is born must die, sooner or later. Death is end of a life-form. What is life? When and how life is extinguished? Life is a state of consciousness commencing with 'Birth Consciousness'; how does that consciousness come to an end, if at all? The 'Death Consciousness'. Or can a state of consciousness be terminated as a natural process? In the human realm: how to accept death, and how to die? Every being that dies must be re-born, not necessarily in human form. That is essentially the oriental view. What is the time-period that elapses between death and rebirth? What happens to that 'being' in that intervening period which the Tibetans call as *Bardo* or the Intermediate state? Tibetan Doctrine of Death is no longer an enigma, more so since Tibetan philosophy is derived from ancient Hindu scriptures and concepts. However, while elaborating on the Hindu concepts Tibetan sages and thinkers have evolved their own specific versions some of which are at considerable variance to the Hindu thought. For instance, in the Tibetan view, death is not a natural process, although it does come naturally to all beings. Tibetan philosophy has gone to great lengths in dealing with the phenomenon of death, activities immediately before and after death, and the rebirth in whatever form. — This is a vast complex subject. In this work, the Author can only very briefly scrape the Tibetan iceberg and leave the reader to fend for himself to whatever depth he desires.

It is universally believed that in the body of flesh and blood there is something ethereal, a subtle and death surviving element, that the Hindus call *Atma*, Muslims as *Ruh*, Christians as Soul, and for the Buddhists a 'complex of activities in continual change' (*Skandha*), a continuous transformation of life-like activities. In other words, none of the Faiths, at least the major ones, accept that

10. This title was coined by the compiler and editor, Americanm scholar W.Y. Evans-Wentz, of this singularly remarkable Book in imitation of the *Egyptian Book of the Dead.* The actual Tibetan title of the Book is: *Bardo Todrol Chenmo,* meaning "Great Liberation through Hearing in the Bardo"—Sogyal Rinpoché: op.cit. p. 106.

death is the absolute end of life's functions. In the words of Dr. Evans-Wentz: "Death disincarnates the 'soul complex' as Birth incarnates it." Therefore, 'death' is just the beginning of life in another form, whatever that be. Since the new life does not, or cannot start at once after death, what happens to the dying-consciousness till it embraces birth-consciousness? That is where the intermediate state, the Tibetan concept of *Bardo* comes in. The dying consciousness continues to be held into a short-life consciousness called *Gandharva* which lasts for seven days, or seven times seven 'forty-nine days of the *Bardo*'. — The number Seven is considered sacred amongst most religions. After that temporary abode, does the 'human soul' transmigrate to another human life, or does it regress into sub-human body? Can a human soul survive in a sub-human body on a permanent basis? These questions, though relevant and interesting, are much beyond the scope of this work. However, the number seven is directly connected with *Bardo* even though the idea of 'seven' being a sacred number did not originate with the Tibetans; it has been a sacred number since time immemorial amongst the Aryan and other races of the world, the Hindu or Aryan philosophy having developed the concept to the extent that *Bardo Thödol* is now deemed to have a scientific basis. It is "The Great Doctrine of Liberation by Hearing and by Seeing".

What happens to the *Atma* before it takes permanent abode in a new body? The Tibetans believe that while the departed consciousness is in the *Bardo*, for the first four days four elements — Fire, Air, Water and Earth — manifest themselves to the deceased. The fifth, the Earth does not do so because the 'Wisdom (*Boudhic*) faculty of consciousness of the deceased has not been perfectly developed'. After the fifth day the natural divinity of the *Bardo* visions starts reducing gradually until the deceased consciousness sinks deeper and deeper into self-hallucinations and delusions.

Death Horoscope

We are aware of the normal horoscope of a person's life forecasting the various possible events in his life time from birth till death; horoscope for the marriage, for profession or business, for political career at the individual or collective level, and such other mundane activities in a person's life. But never heard of anything like a 'Death Horoscope'!

Soon after the pre-death symptoms have completed their course, the face and the corpse are covered with white cloth. No one may touch the dead body after that so that the process of separation of the *Bardo*-body from its earth-plane counterpart is not interfered with in any way. Tibetans believe that this process may take anything from 3½ to four days. They further believe that the deceased-consciousness becomes aware of having been separated from the human body only after that much time has elapsed. On the instructions of the priest deputed to ensure extraction of the spirit from the body, all doors and windows of the death-chamber are closed to ensure complete silence. The process of extraction of the consciousness principle is assisted through a ceremony conducted by the priest known as *hpho-bo*. Meanwhile, the astrologer-lama (*tsi-pa*) is busy casting the 'death horoscope' based upon the exact time of death and the planetary configuration at that point of time. This horoscope determines as to who all may approach the corpse, method of disposal of the corpse, funeral ceremonies, rites to be performed, et al. The corpse is then tied up in a sitting position and placed in a corner of the death chamber. During this entire period monks continue to chant mantras, by relays, day and night, to assist the deceased-consciousness to reach paradise. The mourning friends and relatives are feasted for a couple of days till the end of the funeral service. Same food and drink is placed regularly before the corpse also. After the corpse has been removed, an effigy of the dead person is placed in the corner of the death-chamber earlier occupied by the corpse. The effigy is prepared by dressing a block of wood or some such suitable material dressed in the clothes of the deceased. In the place where the face should come, a printed paper depicting a special person is inserted. Food and drinks continue to be offered to the effigy for the forty-nine days period of *Bardo*. At the termination of funeral rites, the face paper is burnt over a butter lamp, and the spirit of the deceased person is given a final farewell. A feast is generally hosted one year after the death. The widow of the deceased is now free to remarry.

The after-death state is very much like the dream-state. Finally, the deceased consciousness faces Judgment before the impartial "Religious King of the Dead", the Dharma-Raja, the Hindu god of the dead. The Tibetans call him *Shinje-chho-gyal.* He holds a mirror in which the naked soul is reflected, while his servant Shinje weighs out on scales the good deeds represented by white pebbles as opposed to the bad deeds represented by black pebbles. The nature and domain of rebirth form part of the Judgment.

The Rebirth Doctrine could be literally interpreted as based on scriptural authority, or on 'symbolical or esoteric interpretation' based on knowledge. It is not at all obligatory for the Creator to order re-embodiment of a human-consciousness into another human body; on the contrary the reverse is generally the case. The Tibetans irrespective of Buddhist-sect affiliations accept that a human life-flux often takes re-embodiment in sub-human form. The Hindus too hold a similar view. How low the form of re-embodiment should be? That would depend on the Karmic trace of the entity concerned. If we were to accept this version of Karma, how could the seed of life-flux of human give rise to life form of an animal, or a worm or any other form of life lower than human? Looking at it from another angle: The human life form has evolved from lower forms of life over a period of eons; therefore, if a monkey could evolve into a man, why could a man not degenerate, or atrophy, into a monkey? A further discussion of this line of thought is obviously beyond the purview of this work.

Bibliography

Ahmed, Zahiruddin: *China and Tibet, 1708-1959*; Oxford, 1960.

Andrugstsang, Gompo Tashi; *Four-Rivers-Six Ranges: A True Account of Khompa Resistance to Chinese in Tibet*; Information Office of His Holiness the Dalai Lama, Dharamsala, India, 1973.

Ashcroft Nowicki, Dolores and J.H. Brennan: *Magical Use of Thought Forms*; Llewellyn Publications, Minn., 2001.

Avedon, John F.: *An Interview with the Dalai Lama*; Littlebird Publications, New York, 1980.

______: *In Exile from the Land of Snows*; Michael Joseph, London, 1984.

Barber Noel: *The Flight of the Dalai Lama*; Hodder & Stoughton, London, 1960.

_______: *From the Land of Lost Content*; Houghton Mifflin & Co., Boston, 1970

Bell, Sir Charles: *Tibet: Past & Present*; Oxford University Press, London, 1924.

______: *The People of Tibet*; Oxford University Press, London, 1928.

______: *The Religion of Tibet*; Oxford University Press, London, 1931.

______: *Portrait of the Dalai Lama*; Collins, London, 1946.

Bishop Peter: *Dreams of Power*; Athlone Press, London, 1993.

Bonavia Davis & Magnus Bartlett: *Tibet*; The Vendome Press, New York, 1981.

Brennan J.H.: *Magical Techniques of Tibet*; New Age Books, USA, 2002.

————: *Discover Reincarnation*; Aquarian Press, London, 1992.

———: *Secret History of Ancient Egypt*; Piatkus, 2000.

Burman, Bina Roy: *Religion & Politics in Tibet*; Vikas Publications, New Delhi, 1979.

Chandola Khemchand: *Across the Himalayas Through the Ages*; Patriot Publishers, New Delhi.

Chogyam Trungpa: *Born in Tibet*; Allen and Unwin, London, 1966.

Collins Andrews: *Gods of Eden*; Headline, 1998.

Come G.A.: *Tibetan on Tibet*; Ratna, Kathmandu, 1975.

David-Neel Alexandra: *Magic and Mystery in Tibet*; Southern Press, London, 1967.

———: *Bandits, Priests and Demons*; The Hague, 1988.

———: *Initiations and Initiates in Tibet*; Rider, London, 1970.

Dalai Lama the Fourteenth: *My Land & My People*; MacGraw-Hill, New York, 1962.

_______: *The Buddhism of Tibet and the Key to the Middle Way*; Harper & Row, New York, 1962.

_______: *The Opening of the Wisdom Eye*; The Theosophical Publishing House, Wheaton, Ill. 1972.

_______: *An Introduction to Buddhism*; Dharmsala, India, 1965.

_______: *Short Essays on Buddhist Thought and Practice*; Dharamsala, India

Enders B. Gordon: Nowhere Else in the World; Farrar & Rinehart, New York.

Evans-Wentz W.Y.: *Tibetan Yoga and Secret Doctrines*; Oxford University Press, London, 1969.

______: *The Tibetan Book of the Dead*; Pilgrims Publications, Varanasi, 1927.

Fisher, James F.: *The Indo-Tibetan Interface; (Tibetan Oracles in Himalayan Anthropology)* Mouton Publishers, The Hague, 1978.

Fisher, Margaret, Leo Rose and Robert Huttenback: *Himalayan Battleground*; New York, 1963.

Francke A.H.: *Antiques of Indian Tibet*; Calcutta, 1926.

Goodman Harris Michael: *The Last Dalai Lama*; Sidgwick & Jackson, London, 1986.

Gould B.J.: *The Jewel in the Lotus*; Chatto and Windus, London, 1957.

Govinda Lama Anagarika: *Foundations of Tibetan Mysticism*; Samuel Weiser, Maine, 1969.

Grunfeld Tom A.: *The Making of Modern Tibet*; Oxford University Press, Delhi, 1987.

Gulati M.N.: *Tibetan Wars through Sikkim, Bhutan & Nepal*; Manas, New Delhi, 2003.

Gyatrul Rinpoché: *Ancient Wisdom*; New York, 1993.

Harrer Heinrich: *Seven Years in Tibet*; E.P. Dutton, New York, 1954.

Hoffman Helmut: *The Religions of Tibet*; New York, 1961.

Holditch, Sir Thomas: *Tibet, The Mysterious*; New York, 1906.

Holmes Peter: *Mountains and a Monastery*; Bles, London, 1958.

Illion, Theodor; *In Secret Tibet*; Stelle, Ill., 1991

Jain, Girilal: *Panchsheela and After*; Asia Publishing House, 1960.

Jansen Eva Rudy: *Singing Bowls*; Holland, 1997.

Knight GEO: *Intimate Glimpses of Mysterious Tibet and Neighboring Countries*; The Golden Visa Press, London, 1930.

Kawaguchi Ekai *Three Years in Tibet*; London 1909. Kewley Vanya: *Tibet Behind the Iron Curtain*; London, 1990.

Lang-Sims, Lois: *The Presence of Tibet*; Cresset Press, London, 1963.

Landon Perceival: *The Opening of Tibet*; Doubleday Page & Co., New York 1906.

Lati Rimboche and Jeffrey Hopkins: *Death, Intermediate State and Rebirth in Tibetan Buddhism*; Rider, London, 1979.

Levenson B. Claude: Oxford University Press, Bombay, 1989.

Li Tie-tseng: *Tibet, Today and Yesterday*; New York, 1960.

Macdonald David: *Tibet*; Oxford University Press, London, 1945.

————: *The Land of the Lama*; London, 1929.

————: *Twenty Years in Tibet*; London, 1932.

Lowell Thomas: *Dalai Lama*; Ballentine Books, New York, 1961.

MacGregor John: *Tibet: A Chronicle of Exploration*; Routledge & Kegan Paul, London, 1970.

Maraini Fosco: *Secret Tibet*; Hutchinson, London, 1952.

Markham, Clements R.: *Narratives of the Missions of George Boggle and of the Journey of Thomas Manning to Lhasa e to Tibet*; London, 1879.

Martin, Desmond: *The Rise of Chingis Khan and His Conquest of North China*; Baltimore, 1950.

Mele Pietro Francesco: *Tibet*; Oxford and IBH Publishing Co., Calcutta.

Migot Andre: *Tibetan Marches*; Rupert Hart-Davis, London, 1955.

Mitter, J.P.: *Betrayal of Tibet*; Allied Publishing, Bombay, 1964.

Moraes, Frank: *The Revolt in Tibet*; Sterling Publishers, New Delhi, 1960.

Mullik, M.N.: *My Years with Nehru*; Allied Publishers, Bombay. 1976.

———— *The Chinese Betrayal*; Allied Publishers, Bombay, 1976

Murphy, Dervla: *Tibetan Foothold*; John Murray, London, 1966.

Ngawang Nagpo Jigme: *Tibet*; Fredrick, London, 1981.

Norbu Dawa: *Red Star Over Tibet*; Collins, London, 1974.

Norbu Jamyang: *Horsemen in the Snow*; Information Office of His Holiness The Dalai Lama, Dharmsala, India, 1979.

Norbu Namkai: *The Necklace of Gzi*; Information Office of His Holiness the Dalai Lama, Dharmsala, India, 1981.

Norbu Thubten Jigme and Heinrich Harrer: *Tibet is my Country*; E.P. Dutton, New York, 1961.

Norbu Thubten Jigme and Collin M. Turnbull: *Tibet: Its History, Religion and People*; Penguin, New York, 1969.

Palijor Kunsang: Tibet: *The Undying Flame*; Information Office of His Holiness the Dalai Lama, Dharamsala, India, 1977.

**Patterson George N.: *Tragic Destiny*; Faber & Faber, London, 1959.

______________________: *Peking versus Delhi*; Faber, London, 1963.

____________________: *Tibet in Revolt*; Faber & Faber, London, 1960.

Peissel Michel: *Cavaliers of Kham*; Heinemann, London, 1972.

_______: *Mustang: A Lost Tibetan Kingdom*; Futura Publications, London, 1968.

————————: *Mustang: The Forbidden Kingdom: Exploring a Lost Himalayan Land*; EP Dutton & Co, New York, 1967.

———: *The Secret War in Tibet*; Little Brown & Co. Boston, 1972.

Petech L.: *China and Tibet in the Early 18th Century*; Leiden, E.J. Brill, 1950.

Rao, S.K. Ramchan: *Tibetan Tantric Tradition*; Arnold Heinemann, London, 1967.

Rato Khyongla Ngawang Losang: *My Life and Lives*; E.P. Dutton, New York, 1977.

Rau, A.V.: *Dalai Lama and India*; The Institute of Asian Affairs, New Delhi, 1959.

Richardson H.E.: *Tibet and Its History*; Oxford University Press, London, 1962.

Rockhill William Woodville: *The Dalai Lamas of Lhasa and Their Relations with the Manchu Emperors*; Leyden, 1910.

Roerich George N: *Trails to Inmost Asia*; New Haven, 1931.

Sandberg Graham: *The Exploration of Tibet*; Calcutta, 1904.

Seaver George: Francis Younghusband: *Explorer and Mystic*; John Murray, London.

Scientific Buddhist Association, Dharmsala: *Tibetan Facts*.

Shakabpa Tsepon W.D.: *Tibet: A Political History*; Yale University Press, New Haven, 1967.

Shaumian Tatiana: *Tibet*; Oxford, 2000.

Shelton Albert L.: *Pioneering in Tibet*; Fleming H. Revell Co., New York, 1921.

Shen TsungiLien and Shen-chi Liu: *Tibet and Tibetans*; Stanford University Press, Stanford, California, 1953.

Snellgrove David and Hugh Richardson: *A Cultural History of Tibet*; Prajna Press, Colo. 1968.

Sogyal Rinpoché: *The Tibetan Book of Living and Dying*; Rider, London, 2002.

Stein R.A.: *Tibetan Civilization*; Stanford University Press, Stanford, Cali. 1962.

Stron Anna Louise: *When Serfs Stood Up in Tibet*; Red Sun Publishers, San Francisco, 1959.

Sünner Paul: *The Brain and the Mind*; George Allen & Unwin, London, 1926.

Tada Token: *The Thirteenth Dalai Lama*; The Centre for East Asian Cultural Studies, Tokyo, 1965.

Taring Rinchen Dolma: *Daughter of Tibet*; John Murray, London, 1970.

Teichman Eric: *Travels of a Consular Officer in Eastern Tibet*; Cambridge, 1922.

Thomas Lowell Jr.: *Out of This World*; Greystone Press, New York, 1950.

French Patrick: *Tibet Tibet*; India Today, New Delhi, 2003.

Tieh-Tseng Li: *The Historical Status of Tibet*; King's Crown Press, New York, 1956.

Topping Audrey: *The Splendors of Tibet*; Sino Publishing Co., New York, 1980

Tsongkhapa Je: *Compassion in Tibetan Buddhism*; New York, 1980.

Tucci Giuseppe: *The Religions of Tibet*; Routledge and Kegan Paul, London, 1980.

Tung Rosemary Jones: *A Portrait of Lost Tibet*; Thames and Hudson, London, 1980.

Waddell Austine L.: *Tibetan Buddhism*; Dover Publications, New York, 1895.

Wangdu Sonam: *The Discovery of the Fourteenth Dalai Lama*; Khett Thai Publications, Bangkok, 1975.

Wangyal Rinpoché Tenzin: *The Tibetan Yogas of Dream and Sleep*; New York, 1998.

Williams E.T.: *Tibet and Her Neighbors*; Berkeley, 1937.

Younghusband, Francis: *India and Tibet*; John Murray, London, 1910.

Index